Demystifying the School Psychology Internship

If you are a doctoral or non-doctoral student about to begin your internship in school psychology, you may have several questions about the process and what it will involve, and you may even be facing some anxiety about it. If you are a site or university supervisor preparing for the beginning of the internship year, you may be looking for ways to improve the internship experience for your students or for yourself and your fellow supervisors. Newman has used his many years of experience working with interns and field supervisors to create this guide to the school psychology internship process to address these common concerns. He provides a comprehensive overview of the school psychology internship process from start to finish, describing actions that can be taken to promote a high quality, dynamic internship experience. Emphasis is placed on the idea that the internship year is a dynamic and formative experience, not a static event, and that interns and supervisors both must be active planners, coordinators, and shapers of the experience. Each part of the book explores a different phase of the internship, from the first days through job applications and interviews. Helpful and pragmatic tools are included throughout, such as evaluation tools, best practice guidelines, and sample forms.

Online resources are also available to complement the book and include reproducible material from the book, videos students can use to practice their interviewing skills, and links to helpful resources. These can be accessed at www.routledge.com/9780415897327.

Daniel S. Newman, PhD, NCSP, is an assistant professor in the school psychology program at National Louis University in Illinois. He currently teaches and supervises courses in school consultation, clinical supervision, and a school psychology internship seminar, and is co-chair of the NASP Early Career Workgroup.

Demystifying the School Psychology Internship

A Dynamic Guide for Interns and Supervisors

Daniel S. Newman

Routledge
Taylor & Francis Group

NEW YORK AND LONDON

Please visit the eResources website at www.routledge.com/9780415897327

First published 2013
by Routledge
711 Third Avenue, New York, NY 10017

Simultaneously published in the UK
by Routledge
27 Church Road, Hove, East Sussex BN3 2FA

Routledge is an imprint of the Taylor & Francis Group, an informa business

Library of Congress Cataloging in Publication Data
Newman, Daniel S.
  Demystifying the school psychology internship: a dynamic guide for interns and
  supervisors/Daniel S. Newman.
  p. cm.
  Includes bibliographical references and index.
  1. School psychologists – In-service training – Handbooks, manuals, etc.
  2. School psychology – Study and teaching.   I. Title.
  LB3013.6.N439 2012
  370.15023 – dc23
  2012025713

ISBN: 978-0-415-65709-9 (hbk)
ISBN: 978-0-415-89732-7 (pbk)
ISBN: 978-0-203-80421-6 (ebk)

Typeset in Perpetua and Bell Gothic
by Florence Production Ltd, Stoodleigh, Devon

Printed and bound in the United States of America
by Edwards Brothers, Inc.

*To the supervisors, supervisees, and collaborating field supervisors
I have worked with over the years: You have inspired me both
personally and professionally.*

Contents

The Capstone Internship Experience

Shaping a Career as a School Psychologist

Mark E. Swerdlik, Ph.D., ASPPB

Illinois State University

Recently I visited with my former supervisor, Jim Mooney. In 1976, he served as Director of Diagnostic Services during the first year of my tenure as a school psychologist. We were collaborating on an article about the history of school psychology in Illinois, to be published in our state school psychology association newsletter. Being retired for many years, my former supervisor reflected on his career as a school psychologist spanning four decades. He noted that he had written a letter in 1954 to the then Illinois Director of Special Education, applying for what was described as "at least a year of supervised clinical practice in the individual examination of children of school age". Jim was accepted as the second trainee to what would in the next decade be referred to as a "school psychology internship". Thus his career in school psychology was launched. Jim also commented on the enormous impact the supervision he received on his internship had on his development as a school psychologist. If you are a current or prospective intern supervisor, perhaps you have similar sentiments about your internship. As I reflect on both my master's- and doctoral-level school psychology internships, both school-based, I recognize the significant impact my supervisors had on shaping me as a professional school psychologist. If you are a current or prospective intern reading this book, my hope is that your internship experience will be as rewarding to you as it was for the many of us in our field who have practiced before you.

In addition to the potential for significant impact the capstone internship experience can have on one's professional knowledge and skills, the reality is that completion of an internship is required for certification and/or licensure as a school psychologist in all 50 states. APA and NASP have developed internship standards, which have been adopted by state boards of education and professional psychology licensing boards that must be met to satisfy certification and/or licensing requirements. The *NASP Blueprint for Training and Practice* series has also had a significant impact on school psychology training and practice. The authors of *NASP Blueprint III*, as compared to *Blueprint I and II*, recognize that competence in school psychology knowledge and skills is a developmental process. They conceptualize trainees as demonstrating novice levels of competence prior to beginning their internship. The internship is viewed as a formative process of skill development, with the expectation that after the capstone internship the trainee will be competent for entry-level practice as a school psychologist. Being an expert in any of the eight practice domains is not expected until after 5–10 years of professional practice. Further, expert status is only expected in a limited number of domains. The *Blueprint III* also stresses the need to develop "rich" internship sites, both in terms of breadth and depth that offer opportunities to build expanded competencies in all of the eight domains of practice. However, despite the requirements and guidelines offered by these documents, no two internships will provide the same experience. Individual internships will require interns, field supervisors, and university supervisors to collaborate to build the most diverse and enriching experience possible.

Since my former supervisor completed his internship in the 1950s, there has existed only a limited research base related to best practices in the administration of, and supervision during, the school psychology internship and the roles and responsibilities of all of the "players" including the intern, field supervisors, and university supervisors. *Demystifying the School Psychology Internship: A Dynamic Guide for Interns and Supervisors* (hereafter, the *Guide*) represents a significant contribution in applying the relevant literature from clinical, counseling, and organizational psychology to the school psychology internship to identify best practices during a school psychology internship. Dr. Newman views school psychology as a field experiencing perpetual change and the internship as part of the ecology of the system that serves as the setting for the specialist or doctoral-level internship.

For many decades, surveys on job satisfaction of school psychologists have suggested that the quality of the supervision school psychologists receive in their professional lives, including their internship, is one of the most important correlates of career satisfaction or dissatisfaction. Further, these surveys relate that in practice most field supervisors, and many university supervisors, have not received any formal training in supervision. The *Guide*'s "keystone" chapter focuses on supervision during the internship and includes an up-to-date review of supervision models, frameworks, and techniques of effective supervision to help field and university intern supervisors structure supervision during all phases of the internship.

Dr. Newman brings to this *Guide* his years of experience working with interns and field supervisors in his role as his university's internship supervisor and instructor of their required internship seminar. The *Guide* is organized around "big ideas" and provides a thorough review of the relevant literature, integrating numerous examples presented through illustrative vignettes to reinforce effective practices.

The internship is addressed through all of its stages and phases with implications for both interns and their supervisors, using a developmental perspective. The *Guide* begins early in the internship experience, focusing on the topic of developing and using an internship plan, both to guide the internship and for formative and summative evaluation. Additional topics addressed are entry into the internship setting/system, changes that occur in the intern and the supervisory relationship as the internship progresses through the year, and termination issues to consider with clients, colleagues, and supervisors. The development of the school psychology intern's professional skills is considered from the perspective of an integrated process rather than a series of isolated skills.

Newman recognizes that a successful internship experience is based on several critical "building blocks". These "blocks" include developing a positive supervisory experience to reduce anxiety on the part of both supervisor and intern; engaging in ongoing communication and collaboration with all parties to the internship; and facilitating interns to be actively involved in advocating for a productive internship experience. As there are limited opportunities to receive clinical supervision beyond the internship in many work settings, a major goal of any internship should include the development of the intern's ability to self-supervise. The promotion of self-evaluation throughout the internship is a critical component of self-supervision. The *Guide* stresses that interns should be self-advocates including serving as active planners, coordinators, and shapers of their internship experience.

The *Guide* also addresses a number of the often-neglected topics in the school psychology literature. Such topics include differentiating a doctoral- from a specialist-level school-based internship and the often ambiguous relationship between the university and the field site, including how they both impact each other. Newman expands on the idea that specialist and doctoral internships should have similar breadth but doctoral internships have the potential for greater depth because of the more extensive on-campus coursework and varied practical experiences the intern brings to the internship. Practical strategies are also provided for building mutually beneficial relationships between university preparation programs and internship sites. Throughout the *Guide* the importance of collaboration is stressed. Practical strategies to promote collaboration among interns and their supervisors, interns and their work colleagues and fellow interns, university and field supervisors and within university preparation programs are discussed.

Newman also addresses in the *Guide* the important topic of the frequently occurring divergence between training and practice such as the expanded role advocated by training programs versus a more limited role encountered in some internship settings. Related to the common school-based setting for school psychology internships, the *Guide* explores the complexities of school systems and draws on organizational psychology and communication sciences literature to highlight "best practices" on how to effectively integrate the intern into a school-based placement. Dr. Newman also discusses the issue of burnout, particularly among young professionals, and practices that can be learned on the internship to prevent it from occurring in the future. The critical role of modeling, by both the field and university supervisor, is emphasized throughout the *Guide* from the perspective of promoting not only professional skills related to direct and indirect service roles but also restorative/self-care to prevent burnout.

Particularly for interns, the *Guide* includes a discussion of the next steps in their career path including transitioning to the first year of professional practice with practical strategies for the job search, application, and interview processes. For university internship supervisors, Newman provides a useful guide to structure their internship seminar, which is a component of many university preparation programs. University supervisors will also find the *Guide* helpful in providing topics to discuss with field supervisors during site visits, and helpful points to consider when reviewing proposals and approving internship sites, supervisors, and plans.

As I read the *Guide*, I was impressed with how Newman actively engages his reader through critical thinking questions and case examples. Through engaging in novel perspective taking, Dr. Newman challenges experienced intern supervisors to offer a dynamic versus static internship experience based on the needs of each individual intern.

No matter what your role – intern, field supervisor, or university supervisor – reading the *Guide* will assist you in the process of learning ways to ensure a successful capstone professional training experience. You will gain knowledge and strategies to ensure you have as professionally satisfying an experience as my former supervisor Jim and I had as interns over four decades ago and during our careers as internship supervisors. I assure you the rewards in completing such an internship will last a lifetime.

Preface

If you are reading this book, then the chances are you play a role in the school psychology internship year. Regardless of your role or your prior experiences, you are probably wondering how exactly the year will turn out. I do not presume to have a crystal ball containing the answer to this question. However, I do believe the internship year has an increased likelihood of being successful when interns, field supervisors, and university supervisors (a) *purposefully* prepare for the year, and (b) engage in ongoing communication and collaboration. The necessity of these actions is more evident than the processes by which they are accomplished. Therefore, one purpose of this text is to provide interns and supervisors with things they can do (i.e., actions) to promote a high quality internship experience.

In addition to clarifying important actions for interns and supervisors, the second purpose of this book is to demystify what tends to be a mysterious and often anxiety-provoking process for school psychology students. As described by Boylan and Scott (2009), anxiety is a typical experience for interns. In my opinion, and based upon my own personal experiences as an intern and a university internship supervisor, anxiety is often the product of unclear expectations. Clarifying the expectations of supervisors and interns can increase feelings of preparedness for all, and significantly decrease this anxiety. By reading this text, I hope that prospective interns, current interns, and those supervisors who work with interns achieve increased clarity regarding (a) what to do during the internship year, (b) how to do it, and (c) expectations from the earliest days of the internship through the end of the year.

Big Ideas

Several big ideas are incorporated in this text and woven throughout each section and chapter, much like the themes of a symphony.

- The school psychology internship year is a dynamic and formative experience, not a static event.
- The development of an intern's professional skills should be treated as an integrated process, not a series of isolated activities.
- Supervision is a critical component of the internship year, but supervision processes need increased clarity for interns, site supervisors, and university supervisors to be maximally effective.
- Interns should be active planners, coordinators, and shapers of the internship experience.

If these big ideas are used to inform the actions of interns and supervisors, the internship year will be a meaningful experience for all those involved.

Structure of the Text

The book consists of 10 chapters divided into three parts: (a) getting oriented, (b) clarifying roles, developing relationships, and (c) moving beyond the internship. Each part focuses on different facets of the internship year and contains chapters that integrate the big ideas of the section and overall book. The appendices supplement the text's content with professional guidelines and a variety of tools to support interns and supervisors.

Part One: Getting Oriented

The first section of the book (Chapters 1 to 3) addresses issues important to consider during the first few weeks of the internship experience. The section is intended to orient interns, and their supervisors, as they begin the internship year. Concepts and terminology vital to internship success are defined. A key component in this section is establishing a dynamic internship plan, which provides a formative roadmap to structure the internship year. The section concludes with strategies to help interns successfully enter the internship site.

Part Two: Clarifying Roles, Developing Relationships

The second section of this book (Chapters 4 to 8) moves beyond introductory concepts, vocabulary, and entering the internship site to describe the role of the school psychology intern and the critical relationships that are developed over the course of the internship year. One goal of this section is to empower interns and supervisors to clarify the expectations of the intern, a key to successful navigation of the internship. Related to this, a second goal is to clarify the expectations for interns and supervisors within the internship supervision process. A third goal is to describe how to build relationships through effective communication and collaboration; relationship-building is a critical skill as interns are interactive professionals who work with teachers, administrators, children, parents, and supervisors.

Part Three: Moving Beyond the Internship

The third section of the text (Chapters 9 and 10) focuses on concluding the internship year and transitioning into the first year of professional practice as a school psychologist. The job search, application, and interview processes are described to help interns be competitive candidates for open positions. Concluding the year is considered from professional (e.g., concluding cases, transitioning case information), personal (e.g., saying goodbye to students, staff, and supervisors), and administrative (e.g., completing university-based requirements) perspectives.

How to Use this Book

The text is intended to be useful for several audiences including prospective and current interns at the non-doctoral and doctoral levels, internship field supervisors, other individuals from the school district contributing to internship supervision, and university supervisors.

Non-doctoral and Doctoral Internships

School psychology is unique among psychology disciplines because, in most states, school psychologists can practice at the non-doctoral level (e.g., with degrees such as Master's of Education, Education Specialist, and others) as well as the doctoral level. The structures of most non-doctoral school psychology programs are based on a specialist level of training as recognized by the National Association of School Psychologists (NASP, 2010c) including 60 hours of graduate training (Miller, DeOrnellas, & Maricle, 2010). Approximately two-thirds of school psychologists in the United States are trained at the specialist level, and only one third at the doctoral level (Crespi, 2010). This book aims to provide information that is applicable and useful for school psychology interns at both levels of training.

Although the big ideas of the text are universally relevant, distinctions between interns at different levels of training are recognized when implications are salient. Some distinctions between non-doctoral and doctoral interns include:

■ number of years of coursework and practicum prior to the internship (e.g., in general, non-doctoral interns are in their third year of their school psychology program and doctoral interns are in their fifth);

- length of internship (e.g., the length of the internship is 1,200-plus hours for non-doctoral interns versus 1,500-plus hours for doctoral);
- internship selection options (e.g., internships are typically obtained by applying directly to schools or districts, but doctoral-level interns have the option to pursue internships through the Association of Psychology Postdoctoral and Internship Centers [APPIC], approved by the American Psychological Association [APA]);
- exposure to research prior to and during the internship (e.g., doctoral programs often require more intensive research experiences than non-doctoral programs; some doctoral interns may work on a doctoral dissertation while on the internship);
- post-internship options (e.g., doctoral interns may have a wider selection of options such as post-doctoral or faculty positions).

Prospective Interns

For school psychology students who are not yet on the internship this book offers a sneak preview of what is to come; future interns can develop a clear picture of the internship year. In addition, prospective interns may apply ideas from this text to practicum or other field-based experiences that take place prior to the internship. For example, topics such as developing goals and a plan (Chapter 2), site entry (Chapter 3), proaction (Chapter 5), supervision (Chapter 6), and self-care (Chapter 8) are broadly applicable.

Interns

Current school psychology interns are the main audience for this book. To get the most out of this text, interns should first preview the chapters before reading the book in depth from beginning to end. Although the book starts at the beginning of the internship year and moves towards the end, particular topic areas may be relevant early in the year but are not detailed until later in the book. For example, internship supervision is covered in depth in Chapter 6 though it is immediately relevant during the internship year, and the job process is explored in Chapter 9 although interns should begin searching for jobs in the middle of the year. Second, if possible, supervisors should utilize this book concurrently with interns. Even if supervisors do not purchase the text, interns are encouraged to share with their supervisors any ideas they find striking, or believe would promote a high quality internship experience. Proposing and discussing ideas and actions with one's supervisor is part of being a proactive intern (Chapter 5). A third suggestion is for interns to take the time to work through the various critical thinking questions and case examples integrated within the chapters; these activities are designed to enhance the learning experience.

Site Supervisors

This text serves several pragmatic purposes for site supervisors – the school psychologist(s) responsible for the daily functioning of the intern at the internship site. Included in the book are guidelines on how to create an internship plan (Chapter 2), actions to help successfully integrate interns into the internship site (Chapters 3 and 4), and best practices in internship supervision (Chapter 6). The text also provides an opportunity for site supervisors to engage in novel perspective taking. In other words, supervisors may develop new ways to think about the school psychology internship year. For example, the internship year is illustrated as a dynamic whole, rather than a single isolated event or a series of isolated activities to be accomplished. In a *dynamic internship*, supervisors collaborate with each other as well as with the intern to formatively adapt supervision processes and training activities to be responsive to the intern's developing goals, skills, and needs. In contrast, in a *static internship*, training and supervision are provided as they always have been regardless of the intern's goals, strengths, needs, or formative development of professional skills.

Thinking critically about whether the internship being offered is dynamic may be a new consideration for many supervisors. Engaging in novel perspective-taking challenges supervisors to check their assumptions, beliefs, and actions. While reading this text, supervisors are also encouraged to revisit their own internship experiences, reflect on what experiences were most helpful, and consider how they might apply these lessons learned to the interns they are supervising.

Other Field Supervisors

Site supervisors are not the only supervisors that work with the school psychology intern. Other field supervisors such as heads of psychological service units, resource psychologists, and administrative supervisors are also contributors to the internship year. The text can help field supervisors to work with each other, and with the intern, to achieve shared perspectives, vocabulary, and expectations regarding the internship year. For example, the text may spark ideas and discussion about big ideas underlying the internship, how to develop a dynamic and formative internship plan, and how to best coordinate a structure for internship supervision.

University Supervisors

Many school psychology training programs provide an internship seminar led by a university supervisor – a designated faculty member who works with the program's interns. The structure of internship seminars likely differs from program to program, but may include exposure to professional content knowledge as well as opportunities for supervision (from the university supervisor *and* from peers). University internship supervisors may find this text to be a useful guidebook for internship seminars. For instance, even though internship seminars are frequently shaped by supervision of students' content knowledge needs (e.g., What is the best research-based intervention to deal with this particular problem?), the book provides an overview of *processes* that in many ways anchor the internship year (e.g., see aforementioned big ideas). In addition, the book offers a means for university supervisors to collaborate with field supervisors by discussing various topics when conducting site visits, reviewing the internship contract, developing the internship plan, and considering the structure of internship supervision. University supervisors will also benefit from various resources in the text's appendix.

Acknowledgments

First and foremost, I would like to thank my wife Yael for her support, patience, wisdom, and especially for her confidence in me throughout the writing process.

I owe a huge debt of gratitude to Allison Nebbergall and Nancy Scott for their editorial feedback on all chapters of the book. I am also grateful to those who provided early feedback during the book's conceptualization, especially Robert Phillips, Mark Shinn, and William Strein. Thank you to Linda Brodie, Jenni Cole, Lauren Dawes, Laura Jaffe, Monica Muciaccia, Sarah Palys, Anna Peña, Kate Savett, and Samantha Valsamis for providing feedback, resources, and case examples. I would also like to thank Kim Adamle, Elise Pas, Sylvia Rosenfield, Diane Salmon, Mary Frances Schneider, Arlene Silva, and Mark Swerdlik who engaged in meaningful discussion with me during the writing journey; their input and feedback is reflected in the final product.

Thank you as well to Dana Bliss (Senior Editor) and Christopher Tominich (Senior Editorial Assistant) at Routledge who have been responsive and supportive, and have provided invaluable guidance along the way.

I am indebted to all of the supervisors who supported me during my own school psychology internship and helped me understand what makes for an optimal internship experience: Ivan Croft, Nancy Enders, Mary Levinsohn-Klyap, Clyde Robinette, and Cynthia Schulmeyer. Finally, I would like to acknowledge the interns that I have supervised over the past few years, as well as the supervisors I have worked with in the field. My own professional development and learning has hinged on our work together.

Acronyms and Abbreviations

ABD   All but the Dissertation
ABPP   American Board of Professional Psychology
ACCA   APA Advisory Committee on Colleague Assistance
APA   American Psychological Association
APPIC   Association of Psychology Postdoctoral and Internship Centers
APPLE   *A*cknowledge opportunities; *P*repare; be *P*ersonable; *L*eap/take risks; and *E*ngage in follow-up
ASD   Autism Spectrum Disorder
ASPPB   Association of State and Provincial Psychology Boards
CASEL   Collaborative Academic, Social, and Emotional Learning
CBM   Curriculum Based Measurement
CBT   Cognitive Behavioral Therapy
CDSPP   Council of Directors of School Psychology Programs
CI   critical incident
CIT   consultant in training
CSB   career-sustaining behavior
ELL   English Language Learning
EPPP   Examination for Professional Practice in Psychology
ETS   Educational Testing Service
FBA   Functional Behavior Assessment
IDM   Integrated Developmental Model
IEP   Individual Education Plan
IRB   Institutional Review Board
LEA   Local Education Agency
NASP   National Association of School Psychologists
NCSP   Nationally Certified School Psychologist
NLU   National Louis University
NSPCS   National School Psychology Certification System
PBIS   Positive Behavior Interventions and Supports
PPC   problems of professional competence
RTI   Response to Intervention
SASP   Student Affiliates of School Psychology
SPCC   School Psychology Coordinating Committee

Part One

Getting Oriented

Chapter 1

Introduction

The internship year marks the culmination of school psychology training. It has been described as a "capstone experience" (Hebert & Patterson, 2010, p. 55), "a rite of passage" (Hoff, 2006), and "the most important single experience in school psychology training programs" (Alessi, Lascurettes-Alessi, & Leys, 1981, p. 468). Surprisingly, few resources exist to support interns or their supervisors through a year considered so vital to school psychology training. This book is intended to offer increased clarity on the school psychology internship process from start to finish, and to provide interns and supervisors with things they can do to promote a high quality internship experience.

The chapter begins by defining the school psychology internship, with consideration given to documents that guide training such as the National Association of School Psychologists' *Standards for Graduate Preparation of School Psychologists* (NASP, 2010c), *Best Practice Guidelines for School Psychology Internships* (Prus, 2009), and *School Psychology: A Blueprint for Training and Practice III* (Ysseldyke et al., 2006). Next, other key concepts and terminology central to the internship are introduced and described. Once clearly defined, the internship is considered within the context of the evolving field of school psychology. The chapter concludes with critical thinking questions for interns, field supervisors, and university supervisors to consider as the internship year begins.

Defining the School Psychology Internship

Since the turn of the 19th century, student completion of field-based experiences has been considered an essential component of school psychology training (Fagan, 2010). Historically, the terms *practicum* and *internship* were not distinguished in definition or in practice; however, contemporary school psychology training programs do discern between practicum and internship experiences (Fagan).

How Do Practica and Internships Differ?

In most school psychology training programs, distinctions between practicum and internship are informed by the NASP (2010c) *Standards for Graduate Preparation of School Psychologists*. According to the NASP Standards, practica are defined as:

> Activities . . . completed as part of separate courses focusing on distinct skills or as part of a more extensive practicum field experience that covers a range of skills. Candidate skill and competency development, rather than delivery of professional services, is a primary purpose of practica.
>
> (p. 7)

The document also specifies that practica "are distinct from, precede, and prepare candidates for the school psychology internship" (p. 7).

The subsequent internship in school psychology is defined as "a supervised, culminating, comprehensive field experience that is completed prior to the awarding of the degree or other institutional documentation of completion of the specialist or doctoral level program" (NASP, 2010c, p. 7). The internship is intended to provide interns with the "opportunity to integrate and apply professional knowledge and skills acquired in program coursework and practica, as well as to acquire enhanced competencies consistent with the school psychology program's goals and objectives" (NASP, 2010c, p. 7). In short, at the end of practicum experiences, it is expected that students will be prepared to embark on their internship year; following completion of the internship, they are expected to have attained the skills to practice professionally as entry-level school psychologists.

Internship Standards and Guidelines

In addition to distinguishing between and defining practicum and internship experiences in school psychology, the NASP (2010c) *Standards for Graduate Preparation of School Psychologists* specify five broad standards that should be included as part of the school psychology internship. The NASP Standards that are specific to the internship are listed in Table 1.1, including a truncated summary of the elemental components composing each. NASP's *Best Practice Guidelines for School Psychology Internships* (Prus, 2009) reiterate the standards, and add a few guidelines consistent with expectations for the profession: these guidelines can be found in Appendix A. Foundational components of the internship include a contract between the intern and his or her internship site, sufficient depth and breadth of experiences, collaboration among contributors to the internship year, and supervision with formative and summative evaluation. These documents offer helpful starting points for interns and supervisors to structure the internship year, and provide universal expectations for school psychology interns across the country.

School Psychology: A Blueprint for Training and Practice III

In addition to NASP standards and guidelines, a series of documents called the NASP *Blueprints for Training and Practice* (Ysseldyke et al., 2006; Ysseldyke et al., 1997; Ysseldyke, Reynolds, & Weinberg, 1984) have largely influenced training and practice in the field of school psychology. In fact, the *Blueprints* have shaped the composition of standards, shifting the focus from specific course content towards domains of practice around which content is organized (Fagan, 2010; Ysseldyke, Burns, & Rosenfield, 2009). Lest we forget that interns are in fact school psychologists in training and not yet full-time practitioners, *School Psychology: A Blueprint for Training and Practice III* (Ysseldyke et al., 2006) treats internship as a formative process of skill development, and is a reminder of the competencies we expect interns to build during the internship year.

The Model

The model from the *Blueprint III* (Ysseldyke et al., 2006) is depicted in Figure 1.1. As described by the authors, training and practice in school psychology is informed by eight integrated domains of competence – four foundational and four functional. These competencies are built upon knowledge bases in psychology and education, and the application of the scientific method to school psychology service delivery. As illustrated in Figure 1.1, school psychologists' services are delivered using a three-tiered model (multitiered models of service delivery are defined later in this chapter) with the intention of building the capacity of systems and improving the competencies of all students. The *Blueprint III* model is intended to inform the training students receive prior to the internship as well as the paradigm of practice they will encounter and contribute to as interns, and eventually practitioners. The reader is referred to the *Blueprint III* document (Ysseldyke et al., 2006) for a full description of each domain and a more in-depth overview of the model.

Levels of Development

Unlike previous *Blueprint* documents, *Blueprint III* (Ysseldyke et al., 2006) recognizes that competence in school psychology knowledge and practice emerges over time. The developmental frame of *Blueprint III* has several implications for interns and internship sites. As explained by Ysseldyke et al. (2006):

As training programs prepare their students for expanded roles, appropriate internships must be available to support novice practitioners. Given the anticipated capacity of training programs to build skills relevant to the new domains at the "novice" level during the coursework phase, internship sites will need to provide enriched experiences to assist trainees to develop these competencies by the conclusion of their internships. Developing standards for internships and supporting schools with innovative service delivery systems to become rich internship sites that meet those standards are critical goals.

(p. 21)

Table 1.1 *NASP Standards for Graduate Preparation of School Psychologists Describing Internship*

Standard wording	Abridged details
3.2 The school psychology program requires a comprehensive, supervised, and carefully evaluated internship in school psychology	Completed for academic credit Includes breadth, quality, attainment of competencies, and integration/application of school psychology domains Results in direct, measurable, and positive impact on children, families, schools, and others Includes formative and summative evaluations completed by program faculty and field-based supervisors to ensure attainment of professional competencies
3.3 The school psychology program requires that the internship be completed for a sufficient time period and in appropriate settings to achieve program objectives	Minimum of 1,200 (specialist) or 1,500 (doctoral) clock hours Minimum of 600 hours in a school setting Minimum of one academic year (full-time) or over two consecutive years (half-time) Settings are relevant to training program objectives for candidate competencies, and allow direct oversight by the training program
3.4 The school psychology program requires that each intern receive appropriate and regularly scheduled field-based supervision	Field supervision provided by a school psychologist with appropriate state school psychologist credential Average of at least two hours of field-based supervision per week Field-based supervision provided on at least a weekly, individual, face-to-face basis, focused on attainment of competencies
3.5 The school psychology internship represents a collaboration between the school psychology program and internship placement agency consistent with program goals and assures attainment of competencies by interns	Completion of a written plan specifying collaborative responsibilities of the training program and internship site Formative and summative performance-based evaluation of intern by program faculty and field-based supervisors Appropriate support for the internship by the placement agency, including (a) internship as a learning experience for a school psychology trainee; (b) a written, detailed agreement; (c) expense reimbursement, a safe and secure work environment, adequate office space, and support services for the intern consistent with that afforded agency school psychologists; and (d) ongoing professional development
3.6 The school psychology program employs a systematic, valid process in which program faculty ensure that interns, during their culminating internship experience, demonstrate competencies to begin effective practice as school psychologists	Integration of domains of knowledge and application of professional skills for delivering a comprehensive range of services Effective service delivery evidenced by direct, measurable, positive impact on children, families, schools, and others

Note: Adapted from *Standards for the Graduate Preparation of School Psychologists* (pp. 7–9) by the National Association of School Psychologists, 2010c, Bethesda, MD: Author.

Figure 1.1 *School Psychology: A Blueprint for Training and Practice III model for training and practice in school psychology. Copyright by the National Association of School Psychologists, Bethesda, MD. Reprinted with permission of the publisher. www.nasponline.org*

The concepts of developmentally appropriate training and supervision, including defining terms such as novice and expert, are revisited in greater depth at the end of the chapter.

Every Internship is Different

NASP training standards (2010c), best practice guidelines (Prus, 2009), and *Blueprint III* (Ysseldyke et al., 2006) jointly provide a map of several necessary components of the internship year. However, each internship experience will have differentiated aspects influenced by a multitude of factors. First, interns differ from one another in the breadth and depth of training they received in the various areas of school psychology prior to internship. Therefore, it is vital for interns and supervisors to carefully consider the intern's unique strengths and needs prior to beginning the internship year (Hebert & Patterson, 2010).

Second, district and school sites differ from one another on applied opportunities that may be available to interns. For example, while one intern may spend some of the internship working in a school with students with severe and profound special needs, another intern may not have this opportunity, but be exposed to a different unique experience such as the rolling out of a system-wide initiative, such as a Positive Behavioral Interventions and Supports (PBIS) program.

Third, given the variety of school psychologist roles, site supervisors may prioritize different areas of their practice. Even though interns ideally participate in a breadth of activities, it would be expected for each intern to be exposed to one or more areas of practice in more depth than others, in part based on supervisor interests and functions. Related to this, a supervisor's priorities may be informed by state-, district-, or school-wide initiatives. For instance, a district may be beginning to use a multitiered service delivery system and implementing scientifically based instruction and interventions prior to making special education eligibility decisions. In such a scenario, the intern would learn about the school psychologist's shifting role with respect to special education decision making and also the process of system-level change.

To summarize, there are innumerable dynamics that compose one intern's internship experience. Therefore, despite the delineation of standards and guidelines from NASP, it is unlikely that any two internships are exactly the same. Given the array of possibilities, it is important for interns and their supervisors to work collaboratively to consider internship expectations and flexibly structure a successful internship year. As you read this text, it is hoped that you begin to view the internship as an organic and dynamic process to be collaboratively shaped rather than a list of static guidelines or isolated standards.

Frameworks of Development

For school psychology interns, the internship year is a learning process that is developmental in nature. In this book, two stage-based models – a model of adult learning principles utilized in the field of education (Joyce & Showers, 1980, 2002) and a developmental approach to supervision (Harvey & Struzziero, 2008; Stoltenberg, 2005; Stoltenberg & Delworth, 1987; Stoltenberg, McNeill, & Delworth, 1998) – provide frameworks that encapsulate interns' learning processes during the internship year. These two models, plus the role of supervision across the stages, are summarized in Table 1.2. The discussion of frameworks of development that follows is theoretically based, but the concepts are included in the book for pragmatic purposes. To explain, the development of clinical skills can be seen as a nebulous process resulting in many questions regarding internship training and supervision. For example, how do we know an intern made developmental progress in a given area of clinical skills? Which activities are most appropriate for the intern to be involved in at a given point in the year? How does the role of the supervisor change as the intern's skills develop?

With a developmental framework in mind, an intern's skill growth can be more clearly monitored by the intern and intern supervisors, and interns can better advocate for their own needs. Further, supervisors can respond to intern needs with developmentally appropriate supervision techniques such as increasing or decreasing the scaffolding provided to the intern during various activities and supervision sessions. For example, an intern with limited knowledge and applied experience in the area of group counseling may begin the year observing the internship supervisor facilitating a group, take a more active co-facilitator role in the middle of the year, and take responsibility for being the primary group leader by year's end. Related to this, the supervisor may encourage the intern to take a more autonomous role in identifying his or her own needs for supervision as the intern's skills develop. In the sections that follow, theoretical foundations of frameworks of development are summarized. A case vignette is provided to illustrate the importance of taking developmental level into consideration during internship training.

Adult Learning Outcomes

Joyce and Showers (1980, 2002) described professional development learning outcomes for adult learners such as teachers and other education professionals. According to the authors, a first outcome is the learner's development of initial knowledge or awareness of theories, practices, or other content. Next, adult learners establish a greater understanding of their own attitudes towards themselves, those they work with, and the content they are learning; accordingly, content knowledge is better organized than their initial levels of awareness. Once understanding of self and others as well as organization of knowledge increase, adult learners acquire skills and begin to apply them in action. The final developmental outcome for adult learners is the "transfer of training and 'executive control'" (Joyce & Showers, 2002, p. 71). In other words, skills are internalized by the learner in such a way that they can be applied appropriately, consistently, and with increasing automaticity in real-life situations.

Table 1.2 *Convergence of Stage-Based Models of Learning, Development and Supervision*

Adult learning outcomes (Joyce & Showers, 1980, 2002)	Developmental levels of supervision (Harvey & Struzziero, 2008; Stoltenberg, 2005)	Supervision statuses (Knoff, 1986)
Awareness: Realize the importance of particular content and hone in to learn more.	Novice or beginner: No prior training or experience in the field. Focus on own behaviors, high levels of mixed emotions, and high levels of motivation. Need high levels of supervisory support.	Practicum: Supervision provided primarily by university faculty; may be supplemented in field.
Conceptual/organized knowledge: Organize chunked information into larger concepts.	Advanced beginner: Shift focus from self toward the client. Practice with more independence and less anxiety than novices. Have limited conceptual understanding, so need continued support in supervision, but with less structure and more autonomy.	Internship: Supervision provided primarily from external (i.e., field-based) peer and administrative supervisors; may be supplemented by university faculty/staff.
Principles and skills: Become aware of content and use skills in real or simulated situations.	Competent: Focus on the client and self are both enhanced. Increased levels of reflection and confidence, and autonomous practice. May be the final stage of development for some practitioners. Can structure supervision sessions themselves based on needs.	Entry: Same as internship, without supervision from university faculty/staff.
Application/problem solving: Integrate concepts, principles, and skills into practice during their work.	Proficient: Both reflection and integration of skills are at higher levels. Recognize nuances and patterns of situations, and think about long-term consequences. Supervision helps maintain subjectivity, reduce resistance, and upgrade skills.	Independence: One may simultaneously supervise and be supervised. Peer supervision is commonplace.
	Expert: Ability to handle complex and changing situations. No longer reliant on rules or guidelines. Practice with intuitive automaticity. Supervision with same purposes as in proficiency, but may act as metasupervisor.	Metasupervision: One supervises a supervisor.

Levels of Development

As also demonstrated in Table 1.2, learning outcomes described by Joyce and Showers (1980, 2002) converge with Harvey and Struzziero's (2008) developmental model of supervision for school psychologists. The Harvey and Struzziero model is largely informed by the prominent Integrated Developmental Model (IDM) of supervision (Stoltenberg, 2005; Stoltenberg & Delworth, 1987; Stoltenberg et al., 1998) and an additional developmental model by Benner (1984). With integration of skills, knowledge, and qualitative changes in thinking over time, school psychology supervisees move through the levels of novice or beginner, advanced beginner, competent, proficient, and expert (Harvey & Struzziero, 2008). At each stage, supervisees should be met with developmentally appropriate supervision. Hallmarks of the developmental stages are summarized in Table 1.2. It should be noted that the definitions of each stage are consistent with the use of the terms "novice", "competent", and "expert" in the NASP *Blueprint III* (Ysseldyke et al., 2006).

In the third column of Table 1.2, various supervision statuses have been adapted from the work of Knoff (1986) including practicum, internship, entry, independence, and metasupervision. This demonstrates the relevance of supervision at every stage of school psychologists' careers, irrespective of developmental level of clinical skills (Harvey & Struzziero, 2008; Knoff, 1986). In this book, supervision processes are emphasized as central to the school psychology internship experience.

Developmental Trajectory Prior to and During the Internship

General developmental expectations for non-doctoral school psychology students from the first year in their program through the internship year are delineated in Table 1.3. Developmental levels are aligned with learning outcomes (Joyce & Showers, 1980, 2002), as well as with developmental benchmarks building towards the capstone internship experience. Table 1.3 is constructed based on the assertion that interns will develop competence over the course of the internship year (Ysseldyke et al., 2006).

Table 1.3 *Three Years in the Making: Developmental Steps Towards a Successful Non-Doctoral School Psychology Internship*

Year in program	Developmental level	Learning outcomes	Internship-related developmental benchmarks
1	Beginner	Awareness to organized knowledge	Awareness of field of school psychology including assessment, consultation, and counseling Early practicum experiences Supervision primarily from university, but coordinated with site(s)
2	Beginner to advanced beginner	Organized knowledge to skill acquisition	Develop applied skills in assessment, consultation, and counseling More extensive practicum experiences Supervision primarily from university, more involvement from site than Year 1 Self-reflection regarding specific areas of interest and need is used to inform internship decisions
3	Advanced beginner to early competence	Skill acquisition to skill application	Self-reflection regarding goals for the internship year based on areas of interest and need Begin internship Develop initial internship plan and goals for the year Plan and goals are formatively shaped based on development of skills Supervision primarily from site, but coordinated with university

Working inductively, it can be assumed that most students begin their first training year with beginner skills in most clinical areas (e.g., foundational and functional competencies designated by *Blueprint III*, or NASP domains designated in the NASP Standards). Theoretically by their second year, students move from beginner to advanced beginner developmental levels in many clinical areas of practice, acquiring skills to be applied during field-based experiences. By the end of the internship year, trainees should move from advanced beginner levels to achieve early levels of competence, and be ready to successfully enter the field as a first-year school psychologist.

The reader is encouraged to think of developmental levels as domain specific rather than an overall collection of clinical skills. As noted by Harvey and Struzziero (2008), "All school psychologists are beginners when they enter situations in which they have no previous experience, either in terms of the population with which they are working or with regard to the procedures and/or tools used" (p. 41). For example, an intern who is applying Cognitive Behavioral Therapy (CBT) for the first time is developmentally a beginner in that area despite being in the third year of training. Further, some school psychology students may enter the program with more advanced skills in some domains. For instance, an incoming student who worked as a teacher for several years may have prior knowledge and competence in several relevant clinical skill areas. It is also possible that there are developmental differences between non-doctoral- and doctoral-level trainees during the internship year and beyond, especially given differences between hours of coursework and amount of time spent in the field. However, no research yet exists to confirm developmental differences between non-doctoral and doctoral trainees at commencement or conclusion of the school psychology internship (Miller, DeOrnellas, & Maricle, 2010).

Supervision

A consideration of skill development during training is inexorably linked to processes of supervision. Supervision is a critical component of the school psychology internship for many reasons, perhaps the most striking being that the internship is the last opportunity for students to learn and apply skills with a safety net before entering the field (Sullivan & Conoley, 2008).

VIGNETTE 1.1 **DAVID, REBA, AND DEVELOPMENTAL LEVEL**

A contrast between David and Reba, two specialist-level interns in the same school psychology program, demonstrates the applicability of frameworks of development to the internship year. David and Reba both briefly learned about the NASP school crisis prevention and intervention model called PREPaRE (see Brock et al., 2009) during a second-year course on mental health interventions. As part of Reba's practicum experience at a high school she participated on her school's crisis team, including taking part in three days of PREPaRE training. Later in the year, a venerated teacher at the high school died unexpectedly, greatly affecting the school community. Reba participated in the crisis response, including attending the crisis team's planning and debriefing meetings, observing her supervisor during the crisis, and doing direct triage counseling for a few students.

While David developed awareness of crisis response through coursework, he has not yet developed a deep level of understanding regarding the process of crisis prevention and response, acquired skills, or applied them in a real-life circumstance. He would fall in the novice or beginner level with regard to crisis skills. On the other hand, Reba has learned about crisis prevention and intervention in some depth, and is on the verge of independent application of skills. Reba can be considered to be at an advanced beginner level of skills in this clinical domain on entering the internship, and can move into competence with some more opportunities for applied practice. Given distinctions in their skills at the start of the internship year, training and supervision regarding crisis management should be different for David and Reba. For example, David would benefit from gaining additional content knowledge, and engaging in simulated practice of skills such as crisis counseling prior to engaging in an actual crisis response.

Defining Supervision

In a position statement by NASP (2011c), supervision is defined as "an ongoing, positive, systematic, collaborative process between the school psychologist and the school psychology supervisor [that] focuses on promoting effective growth and exemplary professional practice leading to improved performance by . . . the school psychologist, supervisor, students, and the entire school community" (p. 1). A broader definition by McIntosh and Phelps (2000) describes supervision of psychological services in schools as "an interpersonal interaction between two or more individuals for the purpose of sharing knowledge, assessing professional competencies, and providing objective feedback with the terminal goals of developing new competencies, facilitating effective delivery of psychological services, and maintaining professional competencies" (pp. 33–34).

The McIntosh and Phelps (2000) definition is inclusive of supervision structures other than hierarchical supervisor–supervisee dyads (e.g., group supervision, peer supervision) and settings other than schools (e.g., university-based settings). Further, the authors highlighted the inherent complexity of supervision given the variety of potential settings (e.g., university; field; post-doctoral), the assortment of contexts for supervision within each setting (e.g., amount of formality; level of depth; subject matter discussed; amount of teaching involved), and the number of individuals who may act in the role of supervisor (e.g., faculty member; practitioner; advanced graduate student; classroom peer). The complexity of supervision is likely confusing to interns, and at worst may be experienced as overwhelming. Therefore, it is essential that supervisors achieve clarity on their approaches to supervision and how responsibilities are divided among the various internship supervisors, and that they are able to communicate these expectations to interns.

Models of Supervision

The supervisor's theoretical orientation and model of supervision contribute to the construction of supervision. There are numerous supervision models represented in the psychology supervision literature including (a) those rooted in psychotherapy; (b) developmental models, some of which are stage based (e.g., the IDM) and others that are process oriented; and (c) social role models (Bernard & Goodyear, 2009). Although much has been written about theoretical models of supervision, research does not yet point to one model as superior to others (Kaufman, 2010a). Consistent with contemporary approaches, developmental models are the primary supervision models applied throughout this text and will be explored in greater depth in Chapter 6.

Types of Supervisors

School psychology interns are often supported by several supervisors at the same time including a Local Education Agency (LEA) or administrative supervisor, the primary site or professional supervisor, the internship supervisor or coordinator, the university supervisor, and peer supervisors (Hebert & Patterson, 2010). The LEA supervisor is often responsible for supervising several professionals at once, and plays a role in helping the intern successfully enter into the district or school and to learn policies and procedures (Hebert & Patterson). An example of an LEA supervisor may be the head of the psychological services unit of the district. A second type of supervisor, the professional or site supervisor (sometimes also called the field supervisor), "monitors best practice and ethics", "is responsible for the [intern's] day-to-day functioning . . . and has ultimate responsibility for clients under the intern's care" (Hebert & Patterson, p. 59). Many interns have more than one professional supervisor, but one is often designated by the LEA supervisor as the primary supervisor.

Some school psychology internships are organized by a third type of supervisor, an internship coordinator, who is accountable for managing and coordinating the internship curriculum, coordinating the supervision provided to interns, and troubleshooting through any difficulties that arise. For APPIC internships – highly sought-after internships accredited by the APA that facilitate licensure eligibility in most states – the internship coordinator may also be responsible to make sure the internship experiences are consistent with APA expectations (Hebert & Patterson, 2010). A fourth type of supervisor during the internship year is the university supervisor, a designated faculty member from the student's training program who monitors the internship experience to make sure it is consistent with training program goals. The university supervisor evaluates the intern's skill development as commensurate to enter the profession, conducts site visits (in person, via videoconference, or other means), and provides ongoing feedback to students (Hebert & Patterson). Some university supervisors facilitate ongoing university-based seminars to support interns' continuing professional development and to provide in-person supervision to those interns completing the internship locally.

In addition to the aforementioned supervision processes, interns may also be engaged in peer supervision. Peer supervision can take place at internship (e.g., all of the interns at one district) and/or university (e.g., all of the interns from one training program) settings, and can be in a small or large group format. Peer supervision differs from the types of supervision provided by other supervisors because it is non-hierarchical. However, Hebert and Patterson (2010) stressed that supervisors from the internship site and/or university should (a) provide clear expectations and guidelines for peer supervision time; (b) ask interns to develop ground rules, establish a peer supervision schedule, and document how the supervision time was spent; and (c) utilize a specific process for problem solving through concerns. It is important for supervisors to encourage interns to engage in a peer supervision process that is formal, strategic, and purposeful because their process is modeling the primary type of supervision the interns will likely engage in once they enter the field (Hebert & Patterson).

Timelines, Roles, and Responsibilities

With so many individuals simultaneously contributing to the internship year, it is helpful to delineate roles and responsibilities. The internship year is divided chronologically in Table 1.4 with the roles and responsibilities of prospective interns, current interns, primary site supervisors, and university supervisors designated. Prospective interns are engaged in coursework and practicum experiences throughout the year, and should begin considering potential internship sites as early as the fall. The internship search, application, and interview process is in full gear by the winter, commencing with a decision in the early spring.

For current interns, the summer prior to the internship provides an opportunity to consider one's own skills, and to decipher goals for the year to come. Early in the year, interns should collaborate with their field and university supervisors to develop an internship plan related to strengths and needs. Consistent with developmental frameworks and the consideration of the internship as dynamic and formative, interns' goals and the internship plan should be periodically revisited with supervisors to inform activities. Also in the fall, or perhaps even earlier depending on state requirements, interns should take any exams required for certification. Some states require interns to pass a state certification exam, and others accept a passing score on the National Examination for School Psychologists, which leads to the Nationally Certified School Psychologist (NCSP) credential. Interns should begin the job search process during the winter, ideally securing a position during the spring.

The responsibilities of the primary site supervisor and the university supervisor are consistent with earlier descriptions regarding types of internship supervisors. University internship supervisors may consider providing a professional development conference for supervisors and interns prior to or at the beginning of the internship year, and if possible, at other times throughout the year. For example, school psychology educators in Massachusetts implement an annual supervision institute for practicum and internship supervisors evaluated by participants as highly beneficial (Harvey et al., 2010).

The interrelated nature of responsibilities in Table 1.4 intentionally underscores the importance of collaboration between field and university supervisors, and supervisors and the intern. For example, attendance at local and national conferences is included to highlight the value of ongoing professional development and networking for interns, practitioners, and university educators. Further, all parties are involved in ongoing evaluation processes and the development of a dynamic internship plan. The

Table 1.4 Roles and Responsibilities of Prospective Interns, Current Interns, and Supervisors throughout the Internship Year

Timing	Prospective intern	Intern	Primary site supervisor	University supervisors
Summer prior to Internship		Self-reflection regarding strengths and needs* Broad-based goal setting for year to come	Consider opportunities available to incoming intern(s) Introduce intern(s) to school staff, and include intern(s) in new staff orientation, if possible	Encourage interns' self-reflection and goal setting* Professional development conference for interns and intern supervisors*
August to November	Attend fall state association conference, if possible Consideration of potential internship sites Continue to develop content knowledge in coursework* Practicum and other field-based experiences*	Site entry (see Chapter 3) Identify unique opportunities at site Collaborate with supervisors to develop dynamic internship plan that addresses strengths and needs (see Chapter 2) Use evaluation and discussion to inform activities* Attend fall state association conference, if possible Completion of state certification exam (if applicable) (see Chapter 10) Completion of the National School Psychology Examination to attain the NCSP (see Chapter 10)	Facilitate site entry (see Chapter 3) Discuss dynamic internship plan with intern, and university supervisor (see Chapter 2) Formative evaluation: discuss intern's developmental points of entry including strengths and needs (see Chapter 6) Use evaluation and discussion to inform activities* Attend fall state association conference, if possible	Initial site visit: discuss internship contract and dynamic plan; clarify expectations from intern and supervisors Attend fall state association conference, if possible
December to March	Attend NASP conference, if possible Internship search, application, and interview process	Attend NASP conference, if possible Job search, application, and interview process (see Chapter 9)* Complete graduation audit	Attend NASP conference, if possible Formative evaluation: discuss intern's developmental points of entry including strengths and needs	Attend NASP conference, if possible Distribute/collect/analyze formative, midyear evaluations Second site visit: discuss formative evaluation and intern growth
April to June	Attend spring state association conference, if possible Finalize internship decision	Attend spring state association conference, if possible Finalize job decision Attain signatures on state and national certification documents from site and university supervisors (see Chapter 10)	Attend spring state association conference, if possible Complete summative evaluations	Attend spring state association conference, if possible Distribute/collect/analyze summative evaluations Final site visits: discuss closure, transitions into professional practice and continued needs/options for support Assure completion of internship and graduation requirements Sign state and national certification documents

Note: *Indicates a year-long, ongoing process.

intention of Table 1.4 is to provide an overview timeline of benchmarks for various parties to consider before the year begins rather than to provide a comprehensive list of every role and responsibility. Of course, given the wide differentiation in structure between internships, there may be facets that are more or less relevant to an individual's experience.

Critical Thinking

A final key concept to be explored in this chapter is critical thinking. The phrase "critical thinking" frequently appears in both popular and academic education literature, but its definition is not always clarified. In this text, critical thinking refers to "a unique kind of purposeful thinking . . . [that] involves the careful examination and evaluation of beliefs and actions in order to arrive at well-reasoned decisions" (Gambrill, 2012, p. 11). Characteristics of critical thinking include: (a) identifying and questioning our beliefs and assumptions; (b) attending "to the process of reasoning (how we think), not just the product"; (c) considering "questions from different points of view"; and (d) taking into account "the possible consequences of different beliefs or actions" (Gambrill, p. 11).

In a field that increasingly requires the application of a problem-solving model, data-based decision making, and evidence-based practice, the need for school psychology practitioners to engage in critical thinking is greater than ever before. As described by Gambrill (2012):

> Critical thinking, evidence-based practice, and scientific reasoning are closely related. All use reasoning for a purpose (i.e., to solve a problem), relying on standards such as clarity, relevance, and accuracy. All regard criticism (self-correction) as essential to forward understanding; all encourage us to challenge our assumptions, consider well-argued opposing views, and check our reasoning for errors.
>
> (p. 12)

Critical thinking skills can be learned. The internship year provides an excellent opportunity for interns to learn, develop, and practice the critical thinking skills they will later employ as practitioners. Interns learn critical thinking by making mistakes and planning for better decision making in the future. For example, early in my internship year a first-grade teacher asked me to work with three boys she said were disruptive in her class. I knew the students from having spent time in the classroom, really enjoyed my interactions with them, and eagerly began meeting with them once a week to work on "social skills". After meeting with my site supervisor, I realized there was a lack of clarity on the nature of the problem(s) that necessitated the group (e.g., what was meant by "social skills"?). Further, the teacher was in her first year and had challenges with classroom management that may have inadvertently created some of the behavioral problems. I used my mistake as an opportunity to formally consult with the teacher. We discussed the use of classroom management strategies, which she increasingly employed as the year went on. The group, which the students greatly enjoyed, was used as a behavioral incentive, and its curriculum tied directly to classroom expectations. The students' behavior improved, as did the teacher's classroom management skills.

Trial and error is not the only way to learn critical thinking skills. For interns that have supervisors that apply critical thinking in their clinical practice (hopefully the majority!), observing supervisor decision making can be an excellent learning tool. In supervision sessions, the supervisory dyad can discuss how and why certain decisions (either the supervisor's or the intern's) were made, what the intern might do similarly or differently in the future, and how decisions are linked to evidence-based practices (Bernard & Goodyear, 2009).

At the end of each chapter of this book, critical thinking questions are presented to interns, site supervisors, and university supervisors. Consistent with the aforementioned definition of critical thinking, these questions are intended to encourage readers to question their own assumptions and beliefs, attend to the process of decision making, engage in perspective taking, and consider the consequences of their beliefs and actions.

Internship in an Evolving Field

The school psychology internship is embedded within the context of a changing field. For most practitioners the traditional "refer-test-place" role is no longer the preferred method of practice. School psychologists increasingly favor alternative and expanded roles and functions (Fagan & Wise, 2007; Reschly, 2008). Broader roles for school psychologists include moving away from a medical model paradigm towards an ecological framework of service delivery (Sheridan & Gutkin, 2000); applying an experimental/problem-solving model of practice rather than a correlational model (Merrell, Ervin, & Gimpel, 2006; Reschly, 2008); and utilizing a multitiered service delivery system of early intervening services as a preventative tool (Walker & Shinn, 2010; Ysseldyke et al., 2006). Examples of alternative practices include data-based decision making at the individual student *and* system levels (Ysseldyke et al., 2006), implementation of direct interventions (e.g., counseling), indirect interventions (e.g., consultation), and conducting of research (Hosp & Reschly, 2002; Reschly, 2008).

Multitiered Models and RTI

Consistent with the ongoing paradigm shift in the field of school psychology, schools are increasingly incorporating multitiered models of service delivery that include scientifically based interventions of varying intensity at each tier. Interventions are matched according to student needs as indicated by universal screening and progress monitoring data (Walker & Shinn, 2010). A multitiered service delivery system is often considered synonymous with what has become known as Response to Intervention (RTI). However, as described by Walker and Shinn, "RTI has become a ubiquitous term that seems to have taken on a life of its own . . . it means different things to different people" (p. 7). Although many educators view RTI as a means to special education entitlement, Walker and Shinn defined RTI as:

> a means of building a more comprehensive, coordinated, and effective service delivery system that is based on the proactive foundational practices of (a) prevention, (b) evidence-based interventions across tiers, (c) data-based decision making, and (d) early intervention that uses universal screening rather than referral.
>
> (Walker & Shinn, 2010, p. 8)

A three-tier model of service delivery consistent with the above definition illustrated by Walker and Shinn (2010) is featured in Figure 1.2. The Figure is similar to earlier illustrations of multitiered models (e.g., Sugai, Horner, & Gresham, 2002) but is flipped to emphasize prevention and promotion of positive outcomes for all students, and to deemphasize the interpretation of RTI as a special education eligibility process (Walker & Shinn, 2010). Readers are referred to Shinn and Walker (2010) for a more in-depth consideration of multitiered service delivery, RTI, and evidence-based interventions.

Interns May Encounter Discord between Training and Practice

Because multitiered service delivery systems for early intervening services are documented to be successful (e.g., see Gresham, Reschly, & Shinn, 2010) and are increasingly prevalent in schools, chances are interns will encounter and perhaps contribute to the implementation of such a model during the internship year. However, the reality remains that for a variety of reasons, many school psychologists still tend to devote the majority of their time to traditional "refer-test-place" services (Reschly, 2008). Practice trends contrast with training programs structured to be consistent with NASP training standards (2010c) and the *Blueprint III* (Ysseldyke et al., 2006), which aim to prepare students for practice in expanded roles. As a result, differences may exist between emphases of interns' training programs and what is happening within schools or districts. For example, an intern may have taken coursework that stressed the importance of Curriculum Based Measurement (CBM) as a preventative progress monitoring tool, and even collected and analyzed CBM data on practicum, but be based at an internship site which does not utilize CBM data to monitor student progress. As a result of gaps between training and practice,

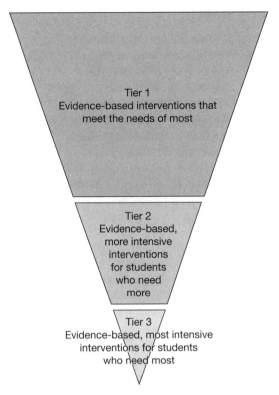

Figure 1.2 *Three-tier model as conceptualized by Walker and Shinn (2010). Copyright by the National Association of School Psychologists, Bethesda, MD. Reprinted with permission of the publisher. www.nasponline.org*

interns may experience feelings of surprise or dissonance as they observe their supervisors in action (Fagan & Wise, 2007).

On the other hand, site supervisors may perceive interns as naïve, sheltered from the realities of school-based practice. To be extreme, interns might as well forget what they learned in the classroom because to begin the internship is to enroll in the proverbial "school of hard knocks". In actuality, most interns *will* encounter experiences that will make them think, "Wow – this is certainly different than what I learned in class!" Such realizations are consistent with moving from early levels of awareness and conceptual understanding to acquisition and application of skills in practice.

Internship as a Bridge

Although divergences between training and practice are inevitable, what makes the internship year so special is the opportunity to bridge those divides. Interns are students that have not yet graduated, and are still embedded within their training program – especially those interns enrolled in an ongoing, university-based internship seminar. Simultaneously, interns work full time in the school psychologist role and thus are entrenched in the field. Given their hybrid identity, interns are well suited to "articulate how university and field-based trainers can work together to create congruent change" (Hughes, Kaufman, & Hoover, 2010, p. 314), thereby bridging gaps between two worlds.

Bridging Training and Practice

It is increasingly challenging for training programs to prepare students for the evolving nature of school psychology practice; building symbiotic relationships between universities and the field is central to creating and sustaining positive change (Hughes, Kaufman, & Hoover, 2010). Opportunities for collaboration between universities and the field abound. For example, Hughes, Kaufman, and Hoover pointed to several potential university–field partnerships such as sharing of resources; co-documenting the implementation of interventions; co-conducting action-based research that can be presented in courses or at conferences; providing training (e.g., inservice presentations at a school by faculty or students, or practitioners presenting in the graduate classroom); and offering professional development opportunities (e.g., discounted graduate courses for practitioners, or faculty or student access to district or school workshops). Interns can act as liaisons between training programs and the field, and encourage such collaborations.

Interns as Learners and Leaders

The hybrid identity of interns is further reflected in the fact that they can be both learners and leaders during the internship year. From the perspective of interns as learners, even individuals that begin the internship year with highly developed clinical skills should still be considered students engaged in a learning experience. In fact, internship guidelines for doctoral-level internships from the Council of Directors of School Psychology Programs (CDSPP, 1998), NASP *Best Practice Guidelines for School Psychology Internships* (Prus, 2009), and APA (2009) accreditation guidelines all direct internship programs to use a title such as "intern" or "resident" to make it clear that the intern is of student status. Further, intern access to ongoing professional development and supervision from their internship sites as well as training programs is considered a vital component of the internship year (Hughes, Kaufman, Crespi, Riccio, & García-Vázquez, 2010; NASP, 2010c; Prus, 2009).

What is sometimes forgotten is that interns can also take on leadership roles during the internship year, especially as the year progresses. For example, interns with a strong consultation background may be able to take on more advanced consultation work (e.g., a system-level consultation case involving multiple students, or more than one consultee) than novice consultants-in-training (e.g., see Newman, Cocol, & Coffin, 2010). To provide another example, at National Louis University (NLU) in Illinois, under the direction of Dr. Mark Shinn, students engage in extensive training regarding the implementation of a multitiered service delivery model of early intervention services, including RTI. With the recent requirement in Illinois law to use an RTI framework in special education eligibility and entitlement decisions (Illinois State Board of Education, 2007) students from NLU are often asked to contribute their knowledge and skills towards the successful implementation of these processes at their practicum and internship sites.

As demonstrated by these examples, interns often have state-of-the-art training, including access to the most current research, and have the potential to link their training programs with the front lines of practice in a constantly evolving field. It is important to stress that taking on leadership roles does not nullify the fact that interns are students. The internship supervision process should provide interns with a safety net of supervisory support during all activities. Additionally, although an intern might have highly developed skills in one or more areas, some skill areas likely need further development. As stated by Hebert and Patterson (2010), "in order to create an internship experience that supports integration of skills, internship trainers need to appreciate the range of roles typical for the school psychologist and address each" (p. 66). The internship should be treated as a dynamic experience structured to best fit the needs of individual interns; doing so calls for internship activities and supervision to be differentiated to fit with each intern's training needs.

A Bidirectional Bridge

As asserted in the NASP *Blueprint III* (Ysseldyke et al., 2006), "there is a growing need to build bridges between academic generated research and applications by practitioners" (p. 22); this includes the dissemination of evidence-based practices facilitated by research, informed by issues pertinent to the field and relevant to practitioner needs. Just as the research of students and faculty can influence school psychology practice, so too should practice inform the content and process of training programs. When university educators communicate with field-based practitioners, training goals become more relevant to contemporary practice, and students are better prepared to enter the field (Kaufman, 2010b). In short, the nature of internship training demands a collaborative process in which interns, university educators, and practitioners work together to shape the culminating experience.

From Internship into Practice

Today's interns are tomorrow's practitioners. The practice of early career school psychologists is determined by a combination of content knowledge developed during coursework and professional development opportunities, applied experiences including practicum and internship, and ongoing supervision from university- and field-based supervisors throughout training. Consequently, the individuals who educate and supervise interns have a wealth of influence over the future directions of the field of school psychology. When interns and their field- and university-based supervisors treat internship training as a collaborative opportunity, the potential to build the capacity of systems and to promote positive outcomes for students is maximized.

Summary

The school psychology internship is the culminating experience of school psychology training, a chance for students to integrate classroom training with real-world experiences. During the internship, students are supposed to attain the necessary competencies to be ready to enter the field as entry-level school psychologists. Several documents including the NASP Standards (NASP, 2010c), best practice guidelines (Prus, 2009), and *Blueprint III* (Ysseldyke et al., 2006) outline recommended features of school psychology internships. However, internships each have some unique features due to differences in interns' entry-level skills, opportunities available at internship sites, site supervisors' preferred practice roles, and school- or district-level initiatives.

The school psychology internship is embedded within a field of change. Increasingly, the school psychologist role is informed by an ecological perspective that incorporates problem solving, prevention, and a multitiered model of service delivery to promote positive outcomes for children and systems. Accordingly, practitioners' employment of critical thinking skills is vital to effective clinical practice. Although interns may be trained for expanded roles, some internship sites have not yet caught up. In many ways, the internship can contribute to bridging gaps between training and practice. For instance, field and university supervisors can collaboratively plan the internship training program. The importance of collaboration is further demonstrated by the complex developmental processes interns experience during the internship year. Collaborative dialogue between interns and their supervisors promotes training and supervision processes that are formative, dynamic, developmentally appropriate, and individualized to support the intern's goals and needs.

Critical Thinking Questions and Activities

The following are critical thinking questions for interns, site supervisors, and university supervisors to ponder immediately prior to the beginning of the internship year.

For Interns:

- What areas of school psychology practice are your areas of strength? What areas are most challenging for you?
- How will the internship year help you build upon your strengths and improve upon areas of need?
- List three broad-based goals for the internship year.

For Field Supervisors:

■ What unique opportunities are available for interns at your internship site (think about both school and district levels)?

■ How do available opportunities match with the intern's reported needs?

■ How will you assess the intern's entry-level content knowledge and applied skills in various areas of school psychology practice?

For University Supervisors:

■ How can you assist interns in thinking critically about their strengths and needs, and setting broad-based goals for the coming year?

■ Do the interns' goals match the training program's goals for interns?

■ In what ways can collaboration between interns, internship sites, and training programs be improved?

Chapter 2

The Internship Plan

As the university supervisor for our school psychology program, I work with interns and field supervisors to develop and implement a plan to organize the internship year. We use a highly structured format required by the state of Illinois that includes the designation of prescribed activities as well as formative and summative evaluation of professional growth. The plan aligns with state (and accordingly NASP) standards. In my experience, I have noticed a phenomenon which I refer to as *internship plan hibernation*:

1. At the very beginning of their internship, the intern spends a significant amount of time developing a plan for the year. The result often is a comprehensive list of every activity a school psychologist may encounter in his or her role rather than a specific plan. The intern also evaluates his or her entry-level skills across domains.
2. The field supervisor(s) and intern collaboratively review the plan as well as the evaluation, and perhaps make a few minor changes.
3. I conduct a site visit at the beginning of the year (in person, by phone, or by videoconference) and discuss the plan and evaluation with the field supervisor(s) and the intern.
4. The plan gets filed away.
5. A few months later I conduct a midyear site visit and we briefly discuss the plan, which may or may not peek out from the file cabinet. In most cases, we talk about what the intern is doing at the site without specific reference to the plan.
6. At the end of the year, the field supervisor completes a summative evaluation of the intern, and I conduct a final site visit where we revisit the plan and evaluation together. With rare exception, interns and supervisors report that they have not looked at the plan since the beginning of the year.

When an internship plan is used to structure the internship year (as is required by a few states, some training programs, and some internship sites), I imagine that internship plan hibernation is not uncommon. For others, an internship plan is not developed at all. A plan that is hidden away during the year or no plan at all are unsurprising considering the fast-paced and overscheduled realities of daily school psychology practice. Interns and supervisors are busy engaging in experiences, including discussing how to address real challenges during supervision, rather than deliberating about whether or not the intern has completed activities in various domains of practice.

This is not to say that an internship plan is not an important feature of the school psychology internship. On the contrary, if developed in a pragmatic way that is meaningful to interns and supervisors, the internship plan can be a critical facet of a successful internship. In this chapter, the concept of an internship plan is defined and features of an effective internship plan are described. The development and implementation of an internship plan is illustrated by a diagram and by various case examples throughout the chapter. The chapter concludes with critical thinking activities and questions for interns and supervisors.

Internship Agreement versus Internship Plan

Before delving into a consideration of internship plan development and implementation, it is important to first distinguish an *internship plan* from what is called an *internship agreement*. An internship agreement is a written contract signed by the intern, internship site, and training program that specifies administrative and logistical details of the internship. Such a contract is required by some school psychology training programs as well as some state boards of education, and is recommended in NASP Standards (2010c) and best practice guidelines (Prus, 2009). Several items may be included in an internship agreement including but not limited to beginning and end dates of the internship; total hours of service required; details regarding supervision (e.g., supervisor information, number of supervision hours required); information about the school and/or district sites; release time and/or reimbursement for attending professional development activities; access to office space; and monetary compensation and other benefits. An example of an internship agreement, adapted from the state of Illinois (2006), is provided in Appendix B of this book.

Like the internship agreement, the internship plan is also a formal written document, and in some ways is a type of contract between the intern and his or her supervisors. However, the purpose of an internship plan is to map out the year with reference to the intern's knowledge and performance skills in various domains matched with various opportunities available at the internship site. The internship plan is formative, and individualized changes are made during the year to fit with the intern's developing needs. Let us look more closely at what ingredients go into creating an effective internship plan.

Features of an Effective Internship Plan: The Big Ideas

As indicated in Chapter 1, every school psychology internship experience is in some ways different. Variations relate to (a) the intern's prior training, including coursework, fieldwork, supervision, and interests; (b) unique opportunities available at the school or district site; (c) field supervisor areas of expertise and preferences for school psychology practice; and (d) school or district initiatives that inform school psychology practice. Although an internship plan should be designed to match with available opportunities and individualized needs, there are several common underlying features, or big ideas, that can guide interns and supervisors in the successful development of an internship plan. An effective internship plan:

- Includes the intern as an active contributor to plan development by incorporating the intern's self-identified needs, strengths, and goals.
- Includes formative evaluation so that the internship experience is adaptive to the intern's developing needs.
- Includes summative evaluation to determine the intern's readiness to enter the field at the end of the year.
- Covers a breadth of training experiences in an integrated and practical manner.
- Incorporates at least one area of professional focus or interest (i.e., depth of training) as determined by the intern.
- Promotes accountability with regard to (a) the intern's developing competencies, (b) the support provided by supervisors to promote skill development, and (c) professional standards.
- Is useful for all parties involved in supporting the internship year including interns, field supervisors, and university supervisors.

It is not coincidental that the big ideas behind effective internship plans tie back to the big ideas that are weaved throughout the book (see Preface). In the sections that follow, the central features of internship plans are explored in depth.

Interns Should Actively Contribute to the Internship Plan

Optimally, interns are engaged as active planners, coordinators, and shapers of their own internship experience. The development of an internship plan presents an opportunity for interns to meaningfully influence what they are doing from early on in the year. Using data to assess one's own needs and strengths and setting goals are two logical starting points for interns to contribute to the plan.

Assessment of Skills

From its initial creation, an internship plan should be informed by the intern's needs and strengths as determined through various forms of assessment. A first type of assessment is self-assessment, the appraisal of one's own skills as a school psychologist in various domains of knowledge and practice. Self-assessment is a learned process, and ideally occurs throughout one's professional career (Boylan & Scott, 2009). Therefore, learning to apply self-assessment skills should be supported by supervisors during the internship year. For example, at the beginning of the internship year, I require our program's interns to (a) read an annotated description of the NASP domains of graduate education and practice (NASP, 2010c, pp. 11–16), (b) consider their perceived competence in each domain, and (c) use this information to prioritize three broad goals for the internship year. This process promotes self-reflection regarding deficiencies and strengths, and allows interns to see the year as an integrated whole instead of multitudes of isolated activities. Self-assessment provides "evolutionary information" – data that may change interns' self-perceptions, perceptions of the world around them, and thoughts and actions (Levitov & Fall, 2009, p. 54). In other words, self-assessment is directly related to interns becoming increasingly critical thinkers.

However, self-assessments are limited due to their inherent subjectivity and the fact that many interns simply are not aware of what they do not know as they embark on their internship journey. Therefore, it is beneficial to simultaneously consider data from other sources. First, interns may consider data they receive from field and university supervisors. For example, Stephanie, a second-year practicum student, received summative feedback (verbally, and using a university-created tool) from her field supervisor regarding concerns with her presentation style in front of parents and teachers (e.g., a lack of eye contact, excessive use of jargon, not being collaborative). The concerns were also communicated between the practicum supervisor and university supervisor with Stephanie's knowledge. The feedback was critical to Stephanie self-prioritizing work in the NASP domain of Consultation and Collaboration at the beginning of her internship year. Her skills in this area will be supported through ongoing supervised practice.

Another type of assessment comes from peers who can provide helpful insight into one's own entry-level skills through informal and formal discussions (Levitov & Fall, 2009; Oberman, 2010). For instance, training cohorts often have an e-mail listserv through which students ask for and offer each other support; this process provides a gauge for each intern's skills as compared to his or her peers.

Yet another type of assessment comes from individuals who are impacted by the intern's services. At a school site this can include students, parents, teachers, and administrators. For example, a survey can be given to a counseling intervention group to understand how the participants felt about or experienced the group (Oberman, 2010), or a teacher may rate the intern's skills as a consultant (Klose, Plotts, & Lasser, 2010). Of course, as with self-assessment, other types of assessment are also subject to limitations such as reporter bias. Therefore, it is helpful to triangulate various forms of assessment data in consideration of entry-level skills and skill development over time.

To summarize, there are many ways for interns to assess their skills upon beginning the internship as well as throughout the year including self-assessments, field and university supervisor assessments, peer assessments, and client assessments. Assessments provide critical information for initially creating an internship plan, and can be used throughout the year (i.e., formatively) to adapt the plan to fit with the intern's developing needs.

Setting Goals

The assessment of skills should be directly linked to goals that are identified by the intern. Goals may include (a) skills that are absent or deficient and need to be gained for the intern to be ready to enter the field, and (b) professional strengths that the intern wants to enhance. Self-identifying and setting goals, and formatively evaluating whether goals have been met, helps interns determine their ongoing effectiveness in the work they are completing (Oberman, 2010).

There is no hard and fast rule for how many goals should be created, and different interns will likely approach the goal-setting process in different ways. As an internship supervisor, I have found that interns benefit from setting at least three broad goals for their year after reflecting on and assessing their skills across the 10 domains of the NASP Standards. Obviously, having three goal areas does not mean that these are the only areas that the intern will work on during the year. Once interns have determined three priorities they can make the goals more specific to the work they are doing at their internship sites, as well as consider their needs in other domains.

Interns know themselves best (especially at the beginning of the year prior to developing a relationship with field supervisors) and should take the lead in developing their own goals. However, supervisors are likely more familiar with various components of the internship context (e.g., specifics about the site, training program expectations, available opportunities) and may have their own perspectives on goals that would be beneficial for the intern. Further, interns are not always aware of what they do not know and accordingly might not realize that they need work in a particular area. Therefore, once the intern develops goals, a collaborative discussion that includes the field supervisor(s), university supervisor, and the intern is beneficial for all parties.

Goals should be considered formative. They are expected to develop and change throughout the year. There are a variety of reasons goals may change, such as the intern determining that opportunities to meet the goal are not available, postponing a goal until later in the year, making developmental progress with regard to a particular skill or set of skills, or meeting the goal. The number of times goals should be discussed in supervision over the course of the year varies; *at least* three (beginning, middle, and end of the year) is a reasonable expectation. However, given the formative nature of goal setting, interns and supervisors likely benefit from discussing goals at other times during the year as well.

Using the Plan to Evaluate Intern Progress

The collection of assessment data and discussions about goals are not finished when the internship plan is created. The plan is a living document that should be modified during the year according to the intern's development of skills. As defined by Harvey and Struzziero (2008), "evaluations that occur at the end of a specified time period and emphasize conclusions and gatekeeping are *summative* [italics added], while those that occur on an ongoing basis and emphasize corrective feedback are *formative* [italics added]" (p. 410).

Formative Evaluation

Interns should be evaluated continuously, and evaluation data should be used to tweak the internship plan as needed (Harvey & Struzziero, 2008). This process has been described as a "continuous loop in which evaluation information guides decision making, development of serviceable alternatives, implementation of treatments, and assessment of effectiveness" (Levitov & Fall, 2009, p. 45). Formative evaluation helps interns and supervisors to identify deficiencies and strengths and to note specific means for improvement through discussions in supervision.

Summative Evaluation

As defined earlier, summative evaluations are used to draw conclusions at the end of a period of time. At the end of the internship, a summative evaluation may be used to determine the intern's readiness to enter the field. Since summative evaluations may be used for high-stakes decision making, formative evaluations should be linked to summative evaluations. Likewise, goals should be linked to outcomes, and the internship plan should be explicitly clear on what support is needed for the intern to achieve goals (Levitov & Fall, 2009). For example, an intern who feels she is lacking knowledge about special education law may request from her supervisor recommendations for supplementary readings on the subject, additional time to observe Individual Education Plan (IEP) meetings, or to discuss in detail how a special education eligibility decision was made. When it is time for summative evaluation, the intern will have already collaborated with supervisors on an internship plan and goals, documented progress towards goals, and determined actions to address any concerns that arose along the way.

Breadth of Training

In addition to promoting goal setting and providing direction for meaningful evaluation, effective internship plans cover a breadth of experiences in an integrated manner without being impractical. The consensus from school psychology educators is that internship experiences should provide sufficient exposure to "the full spectrum of services" so that "graduates feel effective across all domains" (Harvey & Struzziero, 2008, p. 19). The impetus for interns to have multiple experiences is understandable considering (a) the multifaceted nature of the school psychologist role, and that (b) specialist-level trainees (the majority of school psychology interns) will have had only two years of coursework and a nine-month-long internship before entering the field as full-time practitioners.

There are two major barriers to the incorporation of breadth of experiences in the internship plan. The first problem is that sometimes attainment of breadth is emphasized without sufficient consideration given to the intern's overarching goals. In such instances, the plan is devoid of context, and it risks becoming nothing more than an exhaustive list of isolated activities. Such a plan is likely not meaningful for interns. The second problem is that the role of a school psychologist is ever-expanding and complex; it is not realistic that an intern will engage in every activity that a school psychologist may encounter in every domain of practice.

Despite these barriers, it is essential for interns and supervisors to incorporate a variety of activities and roles into the internship year. A narrow internship experience may create a practitioner with a narrow perspective on practice. Take for example an intern who spends the internship year engaged primarily in special education "refer-test-place" practices. It would not be far-fetched to predict that the intern's practices upon entering the field would emphasize special education assessment and placement, and thereby neglect other school psychologist roles (Curtis, Hunley, & Grier, 2002). To paraphrase Abraham Maslow, if the only tool you have is a hammer, you tend to treat everything as if it were a nail. To incorporate breadth into the internship plan, interns and supervisors should treat activities as integrated and cutting across domains. Discussion and planning should move beyond *what* activities are occurring to a consideration of *why* and *how*. Similarly, breadth of activities should be informed by broad-based goals, and should be accomplishable. The concept of breadth of experience will be revisited in Chapter 7.

Depth of Training

Even though having a wide range of experiences during the internship year is important, it is also essential for interns to pursue one or more areas in greater depth. Haworth and Brantley (1981) defined depth of training as the "progression of training in a given area, from beginning to advanced coursework, and to the application of methodologies and skills with differing populations and at different service levels" (p. 283). According to this definition, achieving training depth in a given domain first requires trainees to develop content knowledge through continuing coursework or other forms of professional development. Introductory coursework in a given area is likely not enough to facilitate depth of training. Second, trainees at each level of training (e.g., practicum and internship) need to apply their clinical skills to individuals from a variety of backgrounds. Without sufficient content knowledge *and* multiple and differential opportunities for practice, a given trainee may only have developed surface-level knowledge or skills in a given domain (i.e., an awareness level of understanding [Joyce & Showers, 1980, 2002], as described in Chapter 1). Developing internship goals and an internship plan provide an ideal opportunity for interns to determine a specialized area of interest to pursue in greater depth than other areas.

Accrual of Hours: A Misleading Number

It is critical to note that "the passage of time, in and of itself, does not produce professional competence" (McCutcheon, 2009, p. S51), nor does it indicate one's depth of experience. Take for example an intern named Marcella who engaged in consultation with teachers and parents for approximately 400 of her 1,200 internship hours. On the surface, it may appear that Marcella achieved depth of training in consultation during the internship year, and perhaps developed competence in the NASP domain of Consultation and Collaboration. However, by taking a closer look at her experiences we can see that the number of hours is deceiving. First of all, Marcella only took one quarter (10 weeks) of consultation coursework at the pre-service level with a brief period of applied consultation experience and no individual supervision. Second, she did not receive any additional professional development on the topic of consultation during the internship year. Third, Marcella did not discuss processes of consultation (e.g., purposeful use of communication skills) during internship supervision. Lastly, Marcella did not learn a specific consultation model in her coursework, or apply a model in practice. Although Marcella engaged in consultation for a greater number of hours than other activities, it can be argued that she is not yet a competent consultant nor has she achieved sufficient depth of experience in this area (see Rosenfield, Levinsohn-Klyap, and Cramer, 2010 for further description of consultation training).

To summarize, supervisors should be aware that looking at the number of hours to assess an intern's depth or competence can be misleading. As described by McCutcheon (2009):

> Competence is achieved by engaged participation in structured educational activities and closely supervised experiences that, in fact, do occur over time. That is, competence is a product of both intentional educational interventions and a sufficient passage of time to allow for development. Both are necessary; each alone is insufficient.
>
> (p. S51)

This point is ironic given the emphasis on completing a specified number of internship hours to fulfill graduation and certification (state and/or national) requirements. Instead of focusing solely on number of hours completed, an internship plan can be used to make explicit goals regarding depth and spell out clearly how depth will be achieved.

Doctoral-Level Interns

Doctoral-level school psychology interns are distinguished from those at the specialist level, given their unique positioning to achieve depth of training. First of all, doctoral trainees take more coursework than specialist-level trainees; this presents opportunities for doctoral-level trainees to achieve greater depth of content knowledge in particular clinical areas. Second, doctoral trainees likely spend more time engaged in fieldwork prior to the internship and therefore have a greater number and diversity of experiences within specific domains. Third, doctoral trainees are required to engage in research, the focus of which ideally connects to one's primary interests. Achieving depth in one or more areas can be particularly important for doctoral-level school psychology trainees who may wish to pursue non-school-based positions following their training. For example, an individual who wants to take on a research or academic position following the internship may seek out opportunities to be involved in activities such as action research, program evaluation, and data analysis during the internship year. An individual who is more clinically oriented may seek out experiences in alternative settings such as a community mental health clinic or a children's hospital to supplement his or her work in schools (e.g., see Wasik, Song, & Knotek, 2009).

VIGNETTE 2.1 **RODNEY'S INTERNSHIP DEPTH**

School psychology student Rodney's interests in social-emotional assessment and intervention were sparked during his graduate training while taking two counseling courses (one required, one elective), and co-facilitating a counseling group on issues of bereavement with his practicum supervisor. In addition, in conjunction with his university's counseling center, Rodney conducted intake evaluations under supervision from a faculty member in the school psychology program; he also engaged in peer group supervision with students from the university's Counseling Psychology and School Counseling programs.

When beginning the internship, Rodney sought out counseling experiences to help him gain additional depth in this area. He co-facilitated with his internship field supervisor a group to support boys with Asperger's syndrome at a middle school (including goal setting, progress monitoring, and evaluation of effectiveness), attended a full-day workshop on using Cognitive Behavioral Therapy (CBT) in schools at the NASP convention, and applied what he learned in providing therapy to two individual high school students while receiving ongoing supervision. Additionally, Rodney worked with a faculty member in researching school climate and its impact on the social-emotional health of students, and completed a presentation on this topic during his training program's end-of-year research symposium.

Notably, Rodney's training focus in the area of social-emotional assessment and intervention did not preclude his involvement in a breadth of school psychology experiences at the elementary, middle, and high school levels over the course of his training, including the internship. What is more, Rodney's highly developed skills in counseling were looked on quite favorably by the internship sites to which he applied. His specialization will also make Rodney distinguishable from other interns when he begins the job application process later in the year (see Chapter 9).

Accountability

An internship plan should promote accountability for interns, field supervisors, and university supervisors. The plan documents what the intern has done during the year, and how supervisors have formatively responded to the intern's needs. The notion of accountability integrates several components already addressed in this chapter, including regular documentation of intern activities, and formative and summative evaluation of the intern's developmental progress. Clear documentation of the internship year is beneficial to the professional development of interns, and demonstrates the impact of internship sites and training programs on the intern's skill development. Further, in instances where there are any internship concerns such as problems of professional competence (PPC), an ineffective internship training program, or insufficient university support, the intern or supervisors can respond pragmatically using informational evidence from the internship plan.

Useful for Interns and Supervisors

The final big idea to keep in mind when developing an internship plan is that a useful plan provides a roadmap for *all* internship navigators, not only the intern. The plan should be a catalyst for dialogue between the intern and his or her supervisors during supervision sessions, site visits, university internship seminar discussions, and other points during the year. The plan can be used by all parties to consider the intern's development, and whether or not opportunities provided are meeting the intern's needs. If not, site supervisors and university supervisors should work with the intern to adapt the internship experience. In order for a plan to be useful to all parties, it must be accessible. Accessibility requires a succinct plan rather than a laundry list of activities, and a plan that is readily available to pull out for discussion. One way to make the plan easily accessible is to use technological innovations that promote collaboration. Using such programs, the document can be easily shared and collaboratively adjusted.

In short, a useful internship plan is an organic and dynamic document rather than an archived document to be autopsied at year's end.

Putting it All Together: Internship Plan Development and Implementation

The process of internship plan development is illustrated in Figure 2.1. The curved arrows on the outside of the figure demonstrate an intern's ongoing professional development (i.e., content knowledge, professional dispositions, applied skills) over the course of time. The intern's developmental progress influences four interrelated processes, each of which also influences the internship plan: (a) formative and summative assessment; (b) goal setting; (c) activity selection/completion; and (d) supervision. As previously described, assessment can come from a variety of sources (e.g., self, supervisors, peers, clients) and helps determine the intern's needs and strengths. Assessment is directly tied to what goals the intern and supervisors set to be accomplished during the internship. Both assessment and goal setting influence what activities are taken on by the intern during the internship year. Lastly, assessment, goal setting, and activities are all important topics determined and discussed during ongoing supervision interactions. All four processes formatively inform and are informed by the internship plan. In short, assessment, goal setting, activities, and supervision are naturally linked together and with the internship plan; changes made to any one process result in changes to all.

Now that the theoretical process of internship plan development and implementation has been illustrated and explained, the chapter will conclude with an overview of one intern's internship planning process.

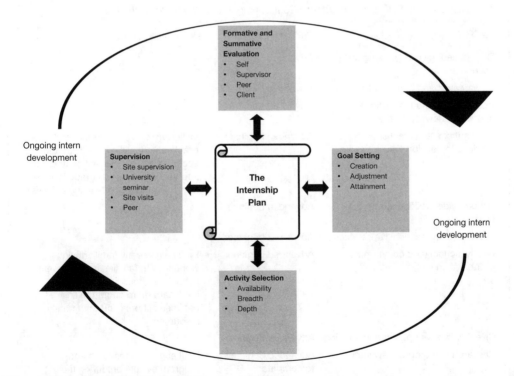

Figure 2.1 *Developing an internship plan*

VIGNETTE 2.2 **LAURA'S INTERNSHIP PLAN**

Internship Site Selection and Entry

Laura was a specialist-level school psychology graduate student who was successful both academically and in her fieldwork in her first two years in her school psychology program. She was offered and accepted an internship at Riverton School District, a medium-sized district (8,000 students) in the suburbs of a large city. Laura selected Riverton because it was conveniently located (a 10-minute drive from her home), but more importantly because she determined during the application and interview process that the opportunities that would be available to her overlapped greatly with her interests. In other words, before the internship even began, Laura already reflected on her interests, skills, and professional development, which helped inform her internship decision.

Initial Assessment, Goal Setting, and Drafting the Plan

In the first university-based internship seminar, interns were asked by the university internship supervisor to review the 10 annotated NASP Standards and to consider their own needs, strengths, and goals. Students rated themselves as either beginners, advanced beginners, or competent in each of 10 domain areas. Laura prioritized the domains of (a) Interventions and Mental Health Services to Develop Social and Life Skills; (b) Home–School (and Community) Collaboration; (c) Research and Program Evaluation; and (d) Legal, Ethical, and Professional Practice as key areas to focus on during the year. Next, using the four domains as a starting point, Laura developed broad-based goals for her year. The results of Laura's initial assessment process including self-assessment and self-identified goals are shown in Table 2.1. Although the self-assessment listed

Table 2.1 *Laura's Self-Assessment and Goal Setting at the Beginning of the Internship*

NASP domain	Self-rating	Self-identified goals
Data-based decision making and accountability	Advanced beginner	
Consultation and collaboration	Advanced beginner	
Interventions and instructional support to develop academic skills	Advanced beginner	
Interventions and mental health services to develop social and life skills	Advanced beginner	• I will learn and support the best practices offered by the district for social-emotional prevention and intervention across all grade levels and with students of varying abilities
School-wide practices to promote learning	Advanced beginner	
Preventive and responsive services	Advanced beginner	
Family–school (and community) collaboration	Advanced beginner	• I will increase my familiarity in working with families from different cultures and family systems • I will learn more about the link between schools and community resources
Diversity in development and learning	Advanced beginner	
Research and program evaluation	Advanced beginner to competent	• I will engage in research and program evaluation during the internship year
Legal, ethical, and professional practice	Beginner to advanced beginner	• I will increase my knowledge of special education law

in this table reveals the overall self-rating for each domain area, note that Laura rated herself on sub-domains as well and then determined an aggregate rating for each broader domain.

The Formative Process

After completing a self-assessment and developing goals, Laura discussed prospective activities with her site supervisor, and then with the site supervisor and university supervisor during a site visit. Together, Laura and her supervisors determined that all of the activities seemed feasible to accomplish during the year and matched well with her goals. The activities that were identified to achieve Laura's goal in the domain of Interventions and Mental Health Services to Develop Social and Life Skills are listed in Table 2.2. Formative changes to goals and activities are also illustrated.

Table 2.2 *Example of Formative Internship Planning*

Goal	Examples of activities initially identified	Formative adjustments/ additional activities completed
I will learn and support the best practices offered by the district for social-emotional prevention and intervention across all grade levels and with students of varying abilities	• Attend a professional development presentation on social-emotional prevention and intervention • Review social-emotional curriculum used at district level • Complete a site-based needs assessment regarding social-emotional supports in place for students[2] • Review crisis plans at school and district level • Participate in NASP PREPaRE crisis training • Facilitate counseling groups at middle school and high school[2] • Conduct individual counseling at middle school and high school	• Laura determined she wanted to see how the district's social-emotional programming linked with best practices, so she researched national and state social-emotional learning standards through Collaborative Academic, Social, and Emotional Learning (CASEL). • Although Laura was initially set to co-lead a group with her internship supervisor, she instead collaborated with the school social worker to support social skill development for students with Asperger's syndrome. • Laura was able to conduct two individual counseling cases at the high school level, but none at her middle school site. • A student from a district middle school was killed in a car crash. Although it was not Laura's primary site, since she was part of the district's crisis planning process and was trained in NASP PREPaRE, she participated in the crisis response.
I will learn best practices of working with gifted and talented students[1]	• Observe in multi-needs, general education, and gifted programs at the middle school and high school	• After observing in a gifted and talented class at the middle school, Laura decided she wanted more experience working with this population. She observed some pullout classes in an elementary school as well as advanced placement classes in the high school, interviewed teachers of gifted and talented students, learned more about the gifted and talented eligibility process, and completed a research project for an end-of-year university-based symposium regarding best practices in working with gifted and talented students in schools.

1 Indicates a goal that was added during the year.
2 Indicates an initial activity that was not fully completed by the end of the year.

For the purpose of keeping this vignette parsimonious, the remainder of the narrative focuses only on the goals and activities within this domain area. However, note that Laura identified activities related to goals in each of her prioritized domain areas in a manner similar to that shown in Table 2.2. Further, Laura planned to, and did in fact, engage in activities across *all* domain areas, thereby completing a breadth of activities during her internship experience.

Looking at Table 2.2, formative changes made to Laura's plan from the beginning to end of the year are evident. For instance, immediately prior to the winter break, Laura realized that she had not yet completed a school-based needs assessment regarding social-emotional concerns. However, Laura had started consulting with the assistant principal at the middle school to learn about perceptions of bullying in the school, and worked with him and her supervisor to design and implement a school-wide bullying prevention program. She and her site supervisor decided that this experience met and exceeded the experiential intentions of the needs assessment initially described on Laura's plan. By midyear, Laura and her site supervisor determined that Laura had been making progress in all goal areas, based on their own perceptions, a university-based intern assessment, and the progress of several students and groups of students with whom Laura had been working.

As winter turned to spring, Laura had completed several activities that were not part of her initial plan, including being part of a crisis response within the district. In addition, after observing in a gifted and talented classroom, Laura realized this was a specific area of interest. Laura discussed this interest with her supervisors, and she created a new goal on her internship plan. Collaboratively, they determined additional ways for Laura to gain knowledge and experience on this topic, including completing additional classroom observations across age levels, interviewing teachers of gifted and talented students, learning more about the gifted and talented eligibility process, and completing a research project for a university-based research symposium. By the end of the year, Laura and her supervisors felt that Laura had gained a specialized depth of knowledge and skills in working with this population of students.

Summative Use of the Plan

At the end of the school year, Laura and all of her supervisors met to discuss Laura's progress over the course of the year, and her readiness to enter the field. Since Laura and her supervisors had all been in constant contact throughout the year, no one was surprised that Laura had met all of her internship goals, completed a breadth of activities during the year, and achieved competence in her prioritized domain areas. The domain which has been described in this vignette became Laura's primary area of interest. Laura gained specialized experiences in crisis prevention and intervention, and working with gifted and talented students. Before terminating her internship, Laura and her supervisors looked back at the formatively developed plan, and used it as a starting point to discuss appropriate goals and activities for Laura as she prepared to enter her first year of practice.

Summary

An internship plan provides a guide to navigate the internship from beginning to end. Like a driver traveling in a new city without a map or GPS, interns and supervisors who do not plan for the internship year risk driving along aimlessly and getting lost along the way. Although internship plans should be differentiated to create individualized internship experiences, there are some features that make an internship plan optimally effective.

The intern should be an active contributor to the plan from the very beginning of the year, including processes of assessment (e.g., self, supervisors, peers, and clients) and goal setting. Both formative (i.e., used to make adaptive decisions throughout the year) and summative (i.e., used at the end of the year) evaluation are tied to the internship plan. The plan should include a breadth of experiences in an integrated and pragmatic fashion (i.e., not be a laundry list), but also allow the intern to prioritize one or more areas to learn and practice in greater depth. An internship plan should promote accountability for interns and supervisors by leaving a trail of evidence of progress. Lastly, the plan should be useful for the intern and supervisors by being sufficiently accessible and by promoting productive dialogues in supervision between interns and supervisors.

Critical Thinking Questions and Activities

The following are critical thinking questions for interns, site supervisors, and university supervisors to ponder immediately prior to the beginning of the internship year.

For Interns:

- What experiences during the internship year are non-negotiable for you? Are these reflected in your plan?
- How will you ensure your goals are met over the course of the year?
- What skill area(s) would you like to focus on in greater depth than other areas?

For Field Supervisors:

- Specify the process you will use in supporting the development of an internship plan. How often and in what ways will the plan be revisited during the internship year?
- How do/does the intern(s) you are supervising this year vary from previous interns you have supervised? How is this reflected in the internship plan?
- If the intern's goals do not match with your skills or the opportunities available at your site, what steps will you take?
- What experiences during the internship year do you feel are non-negotiable for interns?

For University Supervisors:

- How can the internship plan be used to help structure meetings (e.g., site visits) with the intern and field supervisor(s)?
- How will you ensure interns' goals are being addressed over the course of the year?
- How might interns' internship plans inform university-based supervision and/or internship seminar content?

Chapter 3

Entering the Internship Site

Entry is the process by which interns become a part of their internship sites, generally during the first few weeks of the school year. As explained by Marks (1995), "it is hard to have an effective impact on teachers, administrators, and programs (and thereby students) without first being accepted into the school and its social system" (p. 22). Although this idea was expressed with reference to external school consultants, the same logic holds true for school psychology interns. That is, upon entering the internship, interns are challenged to become part of a system that already has an established identity and way of functioning. Therefore, an intern's potential to make an impact during the internship year is facilitated by successful entry into the internship site.

The chapter begins with a consideration of school culture and its role in internship entry. Various characteristics of school culture are considered with an emphasis on collaboration, and examples of potential collaboration between school psychology interns and school staff are provided. Next, actions that both interns and supervisors can take to promote a successful entry process are illustrated. The chapter concludes with critical thinking questions and activities for interns and supervisors.

School Culture

The level of ease or difficulty with which the intern enters into the internship is related to school culture. School culture consists of:

> unwritten rules and traditions, norms, and expectations. The unofficial pattern seems to permeate everything: the way people act, how they dress, what they talk about or consider taboo, whether they seek out colleagues or isolate themselves, and how teachers feel about their work and their students.
>
> (Deal & Peterson, 2009, p. 8)

Further, as explained by Sarason (1969/2003), "school culture refers to those aspects of the setting that are viewed by school personnel as 'givens' or essential features, which they would strenuously defend against elimination or marked change, and which to them reflect psychological concepts and value judgments" (Sarason, 2003, p. 81). Like the air we breathe, school culture is often taken for granted and overlooked (Deal & Peterson, 2009).

Sarason (1996) referred to the most important norms in school culture as regularities, and suggested that regularities have *intended* outcomes, which are not always the *actual* outcomes achieved. Sarason (1996) offered examples of programmatic regularities such as the school schedule of Monday through Friday with weekends off, and behavioral regularities such as educators' tendencies to ask lots of questions of students without students themselves having sufficient opportunity to ask questions.

To further demonstrate school culture, consider the divergent experiences of two interns: One intern entered a school where the school psychologist was viewed as a collaborative problem solver who was welcome in teachers' classrooms and was constantly sought out by teachers for consultation. In contrast, a second intern entered a school where seeking support from colleagues was viewed as a weakness, and teachers were wary of being evaluated or deemed as incompetent if they asked others for assistance. Variations in school culture have implications for the way interns are perceived by others in the school, which actions are seen as acceptable for the intern to take, and how communication interactions and relationship building are approached. For interns, understanding norms, regularities, and intended outcomes is critical for understanding school and district culture, and understanding school and district culture is essential for navigating entry into the internship.

Sarason's (1996) point was not that we should always be critical of existing regularities, but rather that in order to understand school culture we need to identify regularities, think about the rationales behind them, and consider the universe of alternatives. In so doing, we better understand intended outcomes, and are perhaps in a better position to effect positive change. The work of Sarason (1996) is of primary interest to reformers interested in introducing change in schools; it is also extremely relevant to individuals who may have a limited opportunity to introduce change, such as school psychology interns. That is, even though interns have limited opportunity to be change agents during (especially at the beginning of) the internship year, their navigation of the year is in part contingent on understanding the school culture in which they are embedded.

Thinking Critically about "Blinders"

A common theme in writings about school entry and school culture (e.g., Caplan, 1970; Marks, 1995; Sarason, 1996) is that one's own culture (including values, beliefs, and prior experiences) influences one's perspective on the school and interpretation of school culture. Prior assumptions and beliefs have been called "distortions" (Caplan, 1970, p. 59) or "blinders" (Sarason, 1996, p. 136), and inevitably influence one's perspective when entering a school setting. For example, those entering schools tend to view experiences through the lens of their own prior experiences as students, parents, or educators (Caplan, 1970; Sarason, 1996). School psychology interns should think critically about (a) the assumptions, values, and beliefs they hold about the world, (b) their prior experiences in schools and resulting perceptions about school culture, and (c) how these perspectives influence their work in the schools. Being aware of one's own cultural values is a fundamental component of being a psychologist (APA, 2003) and school psychologist (NASP, 2010a), and is a vital to school entry.

School Culture and Collaboration

Fullan and Hargreaves (1996) distinguished between *individualistic* and *collaborative* school cultures. Individualistic cultures are consumed by isolation. Teachers work alone, do not frequently (if at all) receive feedback from their colleagues, and may experience increased feelings of professional stagnation and uncertainty. As opined by Fullan and Hargreaves, isolation and individualism act as armor for staff members against scrutiny, intrusion, and evaluation from the outside, and are limiting to professional growth.

In contrast, in schools with collaborative cultures, teachers engage in joint work, are interdependent, and are open to giving and receiving support (Fullan & Hargreaves, 1996). In collaborative schools, ongoing professional development and professional improvement are prioritized, and teachers experience enhanced professional growth. The most effective collaborative cultures create and sustain more satisfying work environments for teachers. What is more, collaboration and professional development for teachers have been shown to result in positive academic outcomes for students (Wei, Darling-Hammond, Andree, Richardson, & Orphanos, 2009; Goddard, Goddard, & Tschannen-Moran, 2007; Pritchard, Morrow, & Marshall, 2005).

According to Fullan and Hargreaves (1996), there are varying levels of collaboration in schools – some that are more ambitious and fruitful than others. Interns will enter sites with varying levels of collaboration permeating the school culture. While some interns may enter highly collaborative schools, others may enter balkanized schools where groups of teachers function collaboratively in cliques, but there is not much building-wide collaboration. Other interns may enter schools with norms of comfortable collaboration, where teachers celebrate each other's birthdays and other milestones, but collaboration does not seem to relate to professional work. And yet other interns may be in buildings or districts where collaboration is contrived from the top down, and not valued by staff. Interns are advised to pay attention to the nature of collaboration in their schools and districts, and to use this information as a starting point for actions taken during the entry process.

Interdisciplinary Collaboration

Although I have emphasized the value of collaboration in the preceding sections, the majority of courses that students take during their school psychology training tend to be isolated from other disciplines, in terms of both subject matter and composition of students. This is ironic considering that collaboration is placed at the core of NASP Standards and the NASP *Blueprint III* (Ysseldyke et al., 2006). It seems that many school psychology programs inadvertently model a culture of individualism or isolation. However, when trainees enter a practicum, the internship, or early career practice, they are expected to successfully collaborate with others in the school despite not having prior modeling or practice. Therefore, the internship (and prior fieldwork) can provide ideal opportunities for trainees to learn about and engage in interdisciplinary collaboration.

In Table 3.1, some of the individuals school psychologists will work with in schools are identified, and examples of collaborations are described. Although Table 3.1 provides some ideas for interns and supervisors about collaborating with others in schools, it should be remembered that collaboration is not prescriptive, and if too contrived may be less successful (Fullan & Hargreaves, 1996). On the other hand, when supervisors encourage interdisciplinary collaboration during the internship year it may enhance the internship experience, increase the intern's capacity as a collaborator, and contribute to a more positive and collaborative school and/or district culture.

Actions to Promote Entry

In addition to challenges in understanding and being responsive to the complexities of school and district culture, entry to the internship can be difficult for a variety of reasons. For one, the beginning phase of the internship naturally brings heightened anxiety for interns (Boylan & Scott, 2009). Anxiety is expected because the role of school psychology intern is brand new, and expectations may be unclear. For supervisors, especially novice supervisors, receiving interns may also be anxiety provoking. The intern requires a significant amount of attention and time, especially at the beginning of the year. Further, the intern's actions are seen by those in the school as an extension of the supervisor. A wise supervisor carefully gauges the intern's entry-level skills and provides appropriate scaffolding as the year begins. Despite challenges during internship entry, there are several actions that supervisors and interns can take to support the intern's acclimation to the internship site.

Before the Internship Begins

The entry process begins as early as the internship interview. During the interview, interns should be sure to ask questions to learn more about the internship site including demographics, opportunities that may be available, and perspectives on school psychology practice and supervision. All of this information can be taken into account in determining whether a particular site will be a good match for the intern's specific interests and skills. Although not every facet of the internship year can be precisely predicted, explicit dialogues between interns and supervisors may limit surprises and curb anxiety. As described in Chapter 2, the internship contract and the internship plan are two tools used to clarify and align expectations, and to specify non-negotiable aspects of the internship year.

Successful internship entry can also be facilitated by supervisors planning in advance for interns to participate in various activities that take place prior to the beginning of the school year. For instance, an intern may visit and tour the school, meet some key staff members, and have a meeting with last

Table 3.1 *The Internship: An Opportunity to Practice Interdisciplinary Collaboration*

School professionals	Examples of collaboration with school psychology interns
Administrators (e.g., principals, vice principals, superintendents, directors of psychological services)	Dr. Roberts, the school principal, sought out school psychology intern Emily's assistance when he noticed a pattern of excessive office referrals of fifth graders from the lunchroom on Friday afternoons. Emily worked with her supervisor and the principal to re-teach lunchroom expectations to the fifth graders, reward positive lunchroom behavior, and assign appropriate consequences to students not meeting expectations.
Teachers (e.g., general education teachers, special education teachers, related arts teachers)	As often as his schedule permitted and was appropriate, Jordan the intern attended grade-level team meetings for all grades, as well as special education team meetings. As the year progressed, Jordan became increasingly more comfortable at the meetings and spoke up to a greater extent; his input was highly valued by his teacher colleagues.
Administrative support staff (e.g., main office secretaries, guidance office secretaries, bookkeepers)	Whenever intern Isabella needed information about students, Mrs. Dougherty the guidance office secretary was supportive. This helped Isabella greatly when she needed to review records as part of a special education evaluation for a student.
Academic specialists (e.g., reading specialist, math specialist)	The school psychologist, Mr. Dewey, and the school psychology intern Marisa, worked together with the school's reading specialist to research core reading programs that would be most effective to use in their school.
Social workers and pupil personnel workers	School psychology intern Olivia co-facilitated a group to support GLBTQ high school students with the school social worker, Mrs. Stevens.
School counselors	The school psychologist, school psychology intern, and three of the four school counselors at Limestone High School were all a part of the school's crisis prevention and intervention team, and worked together to develop a systematic crisis plan.
Nurses	School psychology intern Alex worked in combination with the school nurse and the school social worker to make sure that a student, Mike Williams, got the reading glasses he needed. Together, they supported Mike's parents, Mr. and Mrs. Williams, who did not have transportation to get Mike to the eye doctor and could not afford to purchase new frames and lenses.
Lunch aides	Bullying was a concerning issue at Worth Elementary School. Intern Ava worked with four lunch aides to be clearer on behavioral expectations, and to increase their consistency in providing feedback to students on student behavior. The lunch aides were grateful for Ava's support and felt more effective in their role, and Ava felt she now had allies in the lunchroom to help her work with several students who needed extra assistance.
Paraeducators	Intern Chloe collaborated with a first-grade paraeducator, Mrs. Guerrero, to provide drill and practice on sight words for three students who began the year behind their peers.
Custodians	Intern Lizzy worked with Mr. Hooks, a custodian who was very popular with students and staff, to coordinate a behavioral intervention for a group of seventh grade boys. By meeting predetermined behavioral expectations, the students earned the opportunity to play basketball with Mr. Hooks.
Librarian	Mrs. Newton, the school librarian, coordinated a committee to plan Dr. Seuss Day in the school. She invited school psychology intern Sophia to be a part of the planning committee, and to take an active role in facilitating the day.
Technology specialist	Mrs. Lopez, the technology specialist, taught intern Mark how to use the district's e-mail system, and helped him learn several tricks in Microsoft PowerPoint that he used when making professional presentations to the staff, and at local and national conferences throughout the year.
Security officers	Running Town High School's security officer, Mr. Martinez, took three school psychology interns employed by the district for a ride around the community one evening after school. The interns saw several of the neighborhood's students talked about in school, and witnessed economic disparities that existed in the community.

VIGNETTE 3.1 TAMARA'S FRAGMENTED ENTRY PROCESS

School psychology intern Tamara entered a district where two school psychologists (one of whom was to be the primary internship supervisor) took maternity leave as the year began. Based on district needs and poor planning, Tamara was thrown into the two schools without the availability of direct supervisory support. Although the situation did not directly violate her contract (e.g., she still received two hours of supervision from a school psychologist outside of her buildings), Tamara had been verbally told during her internship interview that she would be at two schools, each with its own full-time school psychologist. Instead, Tamara was forced to independently enter two new schools at the beginning of her internship – not an ideal circumstance to start off the year. Fortunately, Tamara was a talented school psychologist-in-training as well as a vocal self-advocate. She worked with the internship site and her university supervisor to improve the situation. In the end, Tamara stayed in one school where the supervisor would return in a few weeks, and was moved to work four days a week in a school with a full-time school psychologist present. However, Tamara's fragmented entry process could have been prevented with better planning and more consideration for the intern's needs.

---

year's intern before the internship begins. At some districts, interns are required to attend summer events such as new staff orientations, to meet with other interns, or to participate in (or even help to facilitate) professional development sessions that occur during the summer. Such activities can help the intern network with other personnel at the district, ask any remaining questions about school or district policies or procedures, and also allay the anxiety that comes with starting a new position.

Defining the Intern Role

One challenge that interns face when entering schools is defining what it means to be an intern. Although intern role definition will be clarified in greater depth in Chapter 4, for now it is helpful to describe the process of *how* interns can describe their role to others. Even interns with a clear intuitive understanding of their roles may have difficulty verbalizing what exactly it is that they do. The role of school psychologist is not well understood by those outside of schools (e.g., "So, you're a school counselor?"), or even those within them (e.g., "School psychologists do more than test students?"). The role of school psychology intern is perhaps more confusing given that:

- the term "intern" is generically used to describe trainees in various professional fields at varying levels of training (e.g., high school, undergraduate, and graduate), and conjures distinct schemas, some of which may be negative (e.g., "Grande coffee, pronto!" or Monica Lewinsky);
- interns are both students and young professionals at the same time; and
- internships last only one full year (or two years, part time), which has implications for relationship building, and for perceptions regarding what can and cannot be accomplished.

Given these challenges, it is important for interns to be able to tell others (i.e., staff members, students, and parents) what a school psychology intern does. Having a clear understanding and definition of one's role is critical to entering schools (Marks, 1995).

Once a definition is clarified, interns should be able to briefly describe their role to others when asked what it is that they do at the school. Further, an intern's self-description should be consistent with the supervisor's description of what the intern does. In retrospect, I wish I had been more thoughtful about my role definition when I was completing a fieldwork experience at a large high school for a few hours a week. I was stopped in the hallway by a teacher who, thinking I was a high school student, asked if I had a hall pass. Unsure how to respond, I showed my university identification and disjointedly described my role until she let me move on. Although this experience did not occur during my internship, the anecdote speaks to my own lack of a defined role in a field-based experience, as well as a larger issue of a poor entry process. Most teachers, students, and administrators in the school had no idea who I was or what I did, and I was unable to explain my role coherently. What is clear to me now, but I did not know then, is that I had not successfully entered the system.

Let me provide some examples of how a new intern might describe his or her role. An intern named Sarah and her supervisor Margaret O'Donnell got a chance to discuss Sarah's internship role before staff began school for the year. At the first staff meeting, Sarah met some teachers and other staff members, and introduced herself. An example dialogue shows Sarah's preparedness to briefly discuss her role:

Intern: Hi, I'm Sarah. I'm the new psychology intern working with Maggie O'Donnell.

First-year teacher: Nice to meet you. I'm Jackie Burgess, a new kindergarten teacher. So, you are an intern?

Intern: Yes. I am finishing up the school psychology graduate program at National Louis University.

First-year teacher: Oh, excellent. I just finished my teaching certification at NLU last year! So – what will you do this year?

Intern: Well, lots of things I hope. I will be involved in things like implementing academic and behavioral interventions, and hopefully will get to run some counseling groups with Mrs. O'Donnell. I think I am going to be involved with the problem-solving team and the PBIS team. I think in the next couple of weeks I will help collect some benchmarking data for students. I'm also hoping to do some consultation work with teachers.

First-year teacher: That sounds great! I know I will need you for some consultation! It's really nice to meet you – I'm glad to know there's someone else who is new here. It feels like everyone knows each other already!

Intern: Nice to meet you too! It sounds like we can learn the ropes together!

A second dialogue exemplifies Sarah talking with another teacher who was already familiar with the school psychology internship position. In this case, the teacher already had expectations of what Sarah would be doing during the year. Sarah was prepared to have this conversation because she got to talk with last year's intern, Jeannie, and knew in advance that she would have some large shoes to fill.

Teacher: Hi, I'm Betty Travis – I teach fourth grade.

Intern: Nice to meet you! I'm Sarah, the new psychology intern working with Maggie O'Donnell.

Teacher: Oh – so you're the new Jeannie! Jeannie did a lot of work to help my students. She did a great job! We're going to miss her this year.

Intern: Yes, I'm the new Jeannie! I actually got to meet Jeannie and she told me about some of the things she did. Hopefully I will take on some of those pieces this year. I will be involved in working with some fourth-grade students to support interventions, and I think I will be working with Maggie to go to some of the grade-level team meetings. I am hoping to get involved with the implementation of PBIS this year too. I know Jeannie loved working with the fourth-grade team!

Teacher: Yeah – we have a great team, and Maggie and Jeannie really helped us last year. Let me know if you need anything as you get oriented!

As is evident from these very brief dialogues, Sarah was prepared to introduce herself and her role, and began to develop relationships that helped solidify her successful entry process.

Supervisor Actions: Scaffolding for Empowerment

There are several actions internship supervisors can take to help support an intern's acclimation to the school once the year has begun. As has been emphasized already, the field supervisor is responsible for providing structured guidance and clear expectations to the intern. Some may argue that by the time trainees reach the internship year they have been in the schools for a while and no longer require extensive hand-holding. However, even though most interns have spent parts of at least two years in schools, even the most independent of interns need some guidance as they begin the internship experience. Supervisors are challenged to decipher what is the appropriate amount of scaffolding (i.e., support) for the intern, and how best to use scaffolding to *empower* interns to be more effective problem solvers in the future. Although supervisor actions should be differentiated to meet specific intern needs, there are several general areas that are important for supervisors to consider during entry.

Administrative Support

One way for supervisors to scaffold interns is to provide guidance on the many administrative details of the internship. Although administrative pieces may be mentioned in the internship contract, some interns are left to fend for themselves once the year begins. Supervisors can support interns' entry by providing a map of the building, and introducing the intern to key administrative personnel such as building administrators, the administrative support staff, and the building custodians. In addition, supervisors can help interns obtain keys (e.g., school building, office) and an identification badge, advocate for the intern to have access to personal office space and, if applicable, a computer. Additional support might be needed regarding issues such as how and where to get fingerprinted and a background check, how to obtain a district e-mail account, how to contact human resources regarding salary and benefits, and how to access informational databases such as those related to school scheduling, or IEPs.

It is not solely the supervisor's responsibility to support the intern through every administrative detail. After all, the intern is a burgeoning professional who should be beginning to take on various responsibilities. Further, other personnel such as administrative support staff may also be in a position to guide the intern on his or her administrative way. However, administrative kinks are common, and can be detrimental to the intern starting the year off successfully. Field supervisors may be in the best position to help interns navigate around such roadblocks or, at the very least, connect them to other individuals who can.

Including Interns from the Beginning

It is helpful for supervisors to include interns in the beginning-of-year activities that occur for all staff. This seems intuitive given that the school psychology intern will be a part of the school staff for the year to come. Unfortunately, interns are sometimes unintentionally excluded from various activities that would otherwise make them feel like a welcome part of the district. A list of suggestions for how supervisors can make interns feel like a valued part of the school and district is provided in Table 3.2.

Table 3.2 *Ways Supervisors Can Help Interns to Enter and Feel Welcome in the School and District*

	Activities
• Introduce the intern at meetings (e.g., school-wide, grade-level, parent teacher association) early in the year	• Invite the intern to participate in celebrations inside and outside of school that include school staff
• Make sure the intern is included in gifts given to the entire staff (e.g., school t-shirt)	• Invite the intern to contribute to cards or gifts provided to other staff
• Have lunch with the intern the first few weeks of school	• Encourage the intern to be part of school, district, and community teams
• Invite the intern to take on responsibilities given to other staff (e.g., bus or carpool duty, lunch or recess duty, chaperone at school dance)	• Include the intern in a staff-wide photo

First and foremost, interns should be introduced at school meetings that take place at the beginning of the year. This way, even if the intern has not met every single staff member in person, his or her face is recognizable to others. Further, interns should be included in activities that include all staff such as the taking of a staff photo and the distribution of staff gifts such as a school shirt. On the first day of my internship, during staff orientation, the school principal greeted me with a firm handshake and a Cradlerock School polo shirt. From that moment, it was clear to me that I was part of the school team.

Another time supervisors can include interns is during lunch. It can be helpful for supervisors to be explicit about what they do for lunch, and invite interns to join them. For example, one of my internship supervisors and I would each lunch with the speech language pathologist on some days of the week, and with the rest of the student services department at other times. At another one of my sites, I ate lunch on most days with a small group started by the school counselor. We even had potluck Fridays! These experiences contrasted greatly with one intern I supervised who was unsure what to do for lunch. She would sit in her office by herself and eat while working, meanwhile her supervisor was in the teacher's lounge with a small group of staff members. The supervisor assumed the intern did not want to join them and the intern was not sure if she was invited.

Continuing to Include Interns Throughout the Year

In addition to taking actions at the beginning of the year to facilitate entry, field supervisors can take actions throughout the year to include their interns in school happenings. For instance, interns can be invited to participate in celebrations that take place inside and outside of school such as Secret Santa exchanges, a special education department happy hour, or a teacher's retirement party. Since interns do not always know about these opportunities, supervisors can make sure the intern is informed and invited. Further, interns can be encouraged to take on various optional responsibilities such as bus or recess duty, running part of a school-wide field day, or participating on school, district, or community teams. Many staff members will look favorably at the intern's contributions, and the intern will feel integrated into the school and larger community.

It should also be made clear by the supervisor that it is okay for interns to turn down optional opportunities. It can be challenging to contribute to every party or gift on an intern salary, and an intern's schedule may not permit being a part of teams that meet late in the evening after school. However, if the intern is not invited to participate, he or she may feel like (and may be perceived by others as) an outsider to the school community.

Supervisors Are Advocates, Not Babysitters

In identifying supervisor responsibilities surrounding interns' entry into schools, the point is not that supervisors should be babysitters, permanent hand-holders, or attached to their interns at the hip. Instead, supervisors should be advocates for their interns. An advocate supports or intervenes on behalf of the intern. Through their actions, supervisors should aim to empower interns with the skills to tackle similar problems in the future with more independence (i.e., self-advocate).

Some supervisors may think that interns desire independent functioning, and may be concerned about being too smothering of the intern. This concern contrasts greatly with my anecdotal experiences as a university supervisor. I have seen concerns frequently arise from interns about not having enough supervisory support at their internship site, but rarely have I heard about "helicopter supervisors" who are overbearing or do not let the intern spread his or her wings. In fact, I believe it is the small actions taken by internship supervisors, especially during the first days and weeks of the internship, that go a long way in making the entry process, and the year as a whole, a positive experience.

Intern Actions During Entry

There are several strategic actions interns can take, in tune with supervisor actions, to increase the likelihood that the intern successfully enters the internship site.

Proaction

One overarching theme regarding intern actions for successful entry is that interns should be proactive self-advocates rather than passive recipients during the internship year. The concept of proactive behavior is expanded upon in Chapter 5. Proactive interns are self-reflective, aware of their own goals, and actively work with field and university supervisors to ensure the year is fulfilling the intern's needs and expectations. Proactive interns share responsibility for entry with supervisors, and are active planners, coordinators, and shapers of the internship experience (a big idea stated in the book's Preface).

Move Beyond Comfort Zones

A second overarching theme regarding actions interns can take during entry is that it is important for interns to step outside of their comfort zones. The comfort zone is "a place where we feel at ease, with no tension, have a good grip on the topic, like to hear from others about the topic, know how to navigate occasional rough spots with ease [and] it is also a place to retreat" or escape when things are not comfortable (National School Reform Faculty, n.d., p. 122). The comfort zone is safe, and when interns spend a significant portion of time in their comfort zones, they may limit opportunities for professional growth. In contrast, when interns take risks and step outside of their comfort zones, it is theorized that they will augment their professional growth. The internship is an ideal time to take such risks, given that interns are still trainees and ideally have access to a great deal of supervisory support. The concept of comfort zones will be revisited in greater depth in Chapter 5.

Walk Around the School and Meet People

The learning curve for interns during the first few days and weeks of school is steep; there are new names, faces, roles, procedures, and systems. If other suggestions from this chapter have been put into action, the intern may have met some staff members already, and hopefully has been introduced at a staff meeting. Regardless, during staff week before the kids arrive, it can be helpful for the intern to get to know others in the school. Although meeting people happens somewhat informally and organically, the process may be easier for some interns than others. Therefore, it may be helpful to have a structured approach to meeting others in the school.

To begin with, interns can ask their supervisors for a staff list and school map. When the intern meets other staff members, he or she can write down information such as their role in the school, classroom location, and personal characteristics that will help the intern remember his or her new acquaintance. As teachers are preparing their classrooms, the intern can walk around the school, and peek in to quickly say "hello" and introduce him or herself. Some teachers may have more time than others to have a brief conversation, but most will appreciate the effort the intern has made. What is more, the intern will have begun to develop relationships that will facilitate entry and collaboration during the year to come.

Another way interns can introduce themselves to the staff is via a letter that can be placed in faculty mailboxes or sent out via e-mail. An example of an introductory letter sent out to staff is featured in Figure 3.1. An introductory letter is an excellent supplement to personal introductions, and is also quite useful if the intern is in more than one school. The letter gives others a chance to learn more about the intern and the intern's role in the school, and gives an impetus for in-person introductions and discussion ("So you are Sarah, the new intern working with Maggie this year. I saw your letter in my mailbox. Welcome to our school!").

Ask Questions

Perhaps the best way to demystify the school psychology internship is to ask lots of clarifying questions. Schools are unique systems with their own cultures and vernacular. Assumptions can be made by supervisors and other staff in the school about what interns know coming into the internship. Educational jargon and acronyms are tossed around with great frequency (e.g., see Torki & Nese, 2010),

August 28, 2012

Hello!

My name is Maya Villa and I am a School Psychology Intern pursuing my Master's degree at San Diego State University. I have the privilege of working with Anastasia Goodman, the School Psychologist, along with teachers and staff at Suffolk Elementary for the 2012–2013 school year.

Under the supervision of Anastasia, I look forward to working collaboratively with Suffolk's staff to provide services to children, teachers, and parents. I offer my support to the staff at Suffolk Elementary School and look forward to a wonderful school year.

Sincerely Yours,

Maya Villa
SDSU School Psychology Intern

Figure 3.1 *Example intern introduction letter*

and in a manner that can feel quite daunting for trainees. Interns are encouraged to ABC – always be clarifying – in order to learn the language spoken around them. It may be outside of an intern's comfort zone to clarify something that he or she feels should already be known. However, asking clarifying questions prevents misunderstandings and helps the intern absorb into the school culture with greater ease. The process of clarifying is revisited in depth in Chapter 4.

Summary

In this chapter, entry is defined as the process by which interns become a part of and are accepted into their internship sites (i.e., schools and districts). The ability to successfully enter into the school likely influences the intern's ability to make an impact during the internship year. Interns must be cognizant of school culture, including the unwritten rules, norms, and regularities that exist at their schools. The nature of collaboration in the school is a key feature of school culture for interns to consider during entry. In addition, interns should think critically about their own assumptions, beliefs, and values. Increasing self-awareness helps to reduce the "blinders" that may otherwise hamper the entry process.

VIGNETTE 3.2 **DOUG'S RELATIONSHIP BUILDING**

A week before the kids began school, school psychology intern Doug was introduced along with other new staff members at a full staff meeting at his school. Following the meeting, teachers were given time to get their classrooms organized. Doug had a staff list and map which were provided by his supervisor, and he began to walk around the school to meet teachers and other staff upon his supervisor's suggestion. Doing so was outside of Doug's comfort zone, in part because at his practicum site from the year before, teachers did not understand why he would enter their classrooms.

After meeting and talking briefly with a teacher named Deborah Yawkey, Doug noted on his staff list: "Kids call her Mrs. Y, she is fourth-grade team leader, is a huge baseball fan, and has twin daughters in Kindergarten." When Doug entered Mrs. Y's classroom to do an observation during the first week of school, he asked how her daughters were adjusting to school so far. Doug ended up working with Mrs. Y in several ways throughout the year including several consultations, completing classroom observations, and participating together on grade-level team meetings. They developed a close relationship. Of course, introducing himself and taking notes were not the only reasons this relationship developed, but doing so certainly got their relationship off to a strong start.

There are several specific actions that supervisors and interns can take to facilitate an entry process in which interns successfully become part of their schools and districts. Before the school year begins, interns can visit the building, meet with graduating interns, and participate in various meetings that take place over the summer. Interns and supervisors should work together to be clear on how the intern role is defined so that the intern is able to communicate that to others. Supervisors can support interns in completing administrative tasks, and include them in a variety of activities – especially those that include all staff members. Supervisors are challenged to provide sufficient support to the intern without hovering over the intern at every step, and to help interns become better critical thinkers, problem solvers, and self-advocates. Interns also have many responsibilities during the entry process including meeting staff members, asking clarifying questions, self-advocating regarding needs they may have, and challenging themselves to move beyond comfort zones.

Critical Thinking Questions and Activities

The following critical thinking questions and activities for interns, site supervisors, and university supervisors are intended to help encourage an intern's successful entry into the internship site.

For Interns:

- With a peer, practice how you would describe your role as a school psychology intern to a staff member who asks what it is that you do.
- How will you know if you have successfully entered into your internship site(s)?
- If you feel like you have not yet successfully entered into your internship site(s), what actions can you take?

For Field Supervisors:

- How do you describe the role of psychology intern to other school staff? Is your definition consistent with how your intern would define his or her role?
- What is the appropriate balance between "babysitting" and not providing enough support? How will you achieve this balance?

- How will you know if the intern has successfully entered into the internship site?
- If you feel like the intern has not yet successfully entered into the internship site, what actions can you take?

For University Supervisors:

- What is the role of university supervisors in supporting interns' site entry?
- In your training program, when and how do students learn about school culture, if at all?
- How can interdisciplinary collaboration be encouraged during students' school psychology training?

Part Two

Clarifying Roles, Developing Relationships

Chapter 4

Intern Identity and Expectations

The first section of this book (Chapters 1 through 3) is intended to orient the reader to the internship year by introducing and defining key terminology, exploring issues that commonly arise for interns and supervisors, and suggesting preventive and responsive actions for interns and supervisors to take. In this second section of the book (Chapters 4 through 8), the focus shifts to key role and relationship variables present during the internship. In this chapter, the concept of intern identity is explored, including its complexities and contradictions. The achievement of explicit expectations during the internship is discussed and exemplified. The chapter concludes with critical thinking questions and activities for interns and supervisors.

The Complexities of Intern Identity

Interns are charged with a complex undertaking. They are engaged in multiple roles simultaneously, such as being both trainees and professionals (Olk & Friedlander, 1992). Accordingly they must navigate between training and practice, worlds which sometimes are not well linked (Hughes, Kaufman, & Hoover, 2010). Moreover, interns take on a variety of tasks, many of which are new, and they are expected to develop competence, self-efficacy, and a clearer sense of professional identity during the internship. All the while, interns have an eye on the fast-approaching first year of practice and may ask themselves, "Will I be able to do this on my own next year?" Supervisors may share the same question regarding their interns' readiness to enter the field. Put succinctly, there is a whole lot for interns to learn in a limited amount of time. It follows that an intern's professional identity may be in a state of flux.

Role Conflict and Role Ambiguity

Research in the field of counseling psychology (e.g., Ladany & Friedlander, 1995; Olk & Friedlander, 1992) suggests that when trainees are engaged in multiple roles at the same time, difficulties arise. A first type of difficulty, *role conflict*, surfaces when an individual's divergent roles (e.g., supervised trainee and burgeoning professional) require expectations that are competing (Olk & Friedlander). For instance, on one hand, school psychology interns are expected to alert supervisors to areas of self-perceived weakness in need of support. On the other hand, supervision is an evaluative process during which intern competencies are assessed, therefore interns may be hesitant to share their challenges so as to avoid being poorly evaluated (Olk & Friedlander).

A second type of difficulty, *role ambiguity*, is "a lack of clarity regarding the expectations for one's role, the methods for fulfilling those expectations, and the consequences for effective or ineffective performance" (Olk & Friedlander, 1992, p. 390). Expectations may be unclear for a number of reasons. The district may never have hosted an intern before, and leadership is unclear about how to best provide support. A site supervisor may never have supervised an intern before, or may not have thought strategically about what it means to do so. There also may be any number of gaps in communication, such as between the university supervisor and field supervisors, the university supervisor and the intern, or field supervisors and the intern. In sum, role conflict and role ambiguity often stem from unclear expectations. A helpful starting point for overcoming unclear expectations may be breaking down the intern role into various components, and making explicit what is otherwise implicitly embedded within each role.

Interns are Trainees

Interns are graduate students, or trainees, enrolled in a school psychology program. In fact, consistent with guidelines from the APA (2009), CDSPP (1998), and NASP (2010c), interns are supposed to hold a title such as "school psychology intern" to designate their trainee status because they are not yet certified practitioners. Unfortunately, at some sites, interns are exploited as inexpensive sources of labor, not provided sufficient opportunities for training, or may be compelled to take on responsibilities for which they are not prepared (Sullivan & Conoley, 2008). Being thrown into a "sink or swim" circumstance without appropriate support is unethical, and is not consistent with the fact that interns are trainees. Even when an intern has advanced levels of skills in one or more areas of practice, supervisors and interns should carefully collaborate to create an experience that sufficiently supports the intern's continued professional growth.

Interns are Extensions of Supervisors

Since interns are trainees, they are in many ways extensions of their supervisors. Consistent with NASP's (2010b) *Principles for Professional Ethics*, "when supervising graduate students' field experiences or internships, school psychologists are responsible for the work of their supervisees" (p. 7). The work of interns that supervisors bear responsibility for includes products such as written reports; services delivered by the intern such as assessment, counseling, and consultation; and interns' professional interactions with children, parents, and colleagues. Given supervisors' legal and ethical responsibility for interns, providing sufficient quantity and quality of supervision, including ample scaffolding for professional growth, should be prioritized.

Perception by Association

The point that supervisors are responsible for intern actions may seem obvious to readers. What is less apparent is that others may automatically see interns as similar to their supervisor in various ways such as values, beliefs, and approaches to practice, whether or not such associations are valid. Interns who enter sites with venerated supervisors may experience a "halo effect" in which they are instantly perceived positively by others in the school. On the contrary, it may be challenging for interns to be viewed favorably if their supervisors are not well regarded by others. It should be noted that perceptions of the school psychologist, positive and negative, arise for a variety of reasons. For instance, a highly competent school psychologist who is implementing a controversial systems-level change may not be popular. Regardless of how the school psychologist is perceived, it seems likely that others may automatically meld interns with their supervisors. Such perceptions should be taken into account as the intern enters the school and engages in various professional activities.

The Supervisor's Spy?

Another aspect of interns being extensions of supervisors is that some staff may view interactions with the intern as non-confidential, assuming that anything discussed with the intern is automatically shared with the supervisor. To some staff, the intern may even be viewed as a spy. For example, a teacher may worry that an intern completing a classroom observation will report back to the school psychologist that the teacher did not have control of the classroom or did not implement an intervention with fidelity. The perception that interns share information with supervisors is based in reality. After all, supervisors are responsible for intern actions and need to be aware of the work that interns are doing. However, concerns regarding confidentiality can make it difficult for staff members to trust the intern and for collaborative relationships to be developed.

To facilitate the building of trusting relationships (a) the intern and supervisor can explicitly identify situations where concerns about confidentiality in working with staff may arise, and (b) the intern, in advance, can be upfront with staff about information that might be shared with the internship supervisor. For example, the intern may ask a teacher: "Is it okay if I observe in your class this afternoon to see how Rafael is doing academically? The observation is part of a special education evaluation, and I will touch base with my supervisor Dr. Thomas after the observation to see how that fits with the other data we have collected."

Interns are Reflections of Their School Psychology Program

The fact that interns are graduate student trainees means that they are associated with a particular university and its school psychology program. More specifically, the intern's skill level when entering the internship reflects on the quality of preparation and supervision received during pre-internship training. An intern who is a critical thinker and has a strong training background may bring to the internship innovative perspectives on practice and engage in a reciprocal learning process with his or her supervisors. Conversely, trainees that exhibit significant skill deficits may reflect poorly on their school psychology program. It is the ethical responsibility of the training program, in concert with the internship site and intern, to (a) collaboratively discuss concerns and (b) develop a plan to make sure that before entering his or her first year of practice the intern has achieved entry-level competence (Armistead, Williams, & Jacob, 2011; NASP, 2010b).

So Much to Do, So Little Time

Another implication of interns being trainees is that their role lasts only one year. Even those interns who are fortunate enough to be hired by their internship district may be placed at a different school or schools the following year.

Establishing Relationships

Because interns are at their sites for only one year, the nature of relationships they form with staff, students, and parents may be affected. For example, while a full-time school psychologist may develop a relationship with a student and the student's family over the course of many years, the intern will only work with them during a single school year. However, the brevity of the internship does not necessarily preclude interns from developing meaningful relationships. As described by Denicola and Furze (2001), "each intern will approach and deal with these issues of closeness and intimacy in his or her own way. It is helpful to be cognizant of both the rich opportunities for relationships and the limits of the training year" (p. 341). The initiation, development, and termination of relationships during the internship are challenging processes that should be explicitly strategized during supervision (see Chapter 10).

Making an Impact

The limited time window of the internship may also impinge on the perceived and actual impact that the intern can make during the year. For instance, the implementation of sustainable systems-level change may take three to five years (Hall & Hord, 2010). Consequently, although interns may contribute to processes of change, they may not see their efforts bear immediate fruit. However, as many internship supervisors would attest, interns can be significant contributors to, and perhaps even catalysts for, school and district change. Moreover, while every service delivery outcome may not be immediately visible, a training goal for interns is to provide "services that result in direct, measurable, and positive impact on children, families, schools, and/or other consumers" (NASP, 2010c, p. 8). That is, interns should conclude the year with clear evidence that they made an impact.

VIGNETTE 4.1 **JENNI'S LASTING IMPACT THROUGH A SYSTEMS-LEVEL ANTI-BULLYING CAMPAIGN**

School psychology intern Jenni joined the PBIS committee at her middle school placement and became an active team member. In the fall, the committee created and distributed a bullying survey for all middle schools in the district. In Jenni's school, the committee analyzed the data, noted locations where, according to students, bullying happened most, and worked to increase staff supervision in all identified locations. The committee devised the acronym STAND (Stand Together and Never Disrespect) to promote an anti-bullying campaign including posters, t-shirts (worn by students and staff the last Friday of every month), and a theme song as voted on by students. Eighth-grade students in a mixed-media class created their own anti-bullying videos (including student role-plays and subtitled statistics gathered from the survey), and submitted them to administration. One video was selected, mixed to the theme song, and played at a school-wide assembly in the spring. The STAND campaign delivered powerful information in a way that incorporated student voices.

Through her contributions as part of the PBIS team, Jenni made a wide-reaching impact in her school that will likely last far beyond the end of the internship year. Jenni also presented on this topic as part of her university-based internship seminar, and inspired several of her peers to think about how to approach anti-bullying efforts and systems-level change during their internships and early careers.

In addition to their immediate impact, interns should think about the long-term outcomes of their work. Critically thinking interns may ask themselves: "If I came back to this school or district or community in five years, would there be evidence that I was once here? What actions can I take that will have a positive impact on this school, district, or community?" Making a significant footprint, even if it is not instantly evident, is still possible in a limited time frame.

Interns are Burgeoning Professionals

Although school psychology interns are still graduate students, they are also blossoming professionals who work in schools on a full-time basis. Children, especially younger students, likely do not distinguish between the intern and other staff members. Competent interns will quickly gain the trust of staff members, and may be treated as on equal footing with their colleagues. In fact, some staff members may even defer to the intern, especially in areas where the intern is perceived to have expertise (e.g., issues related to mental health). Although the fact remains that the intern is engaged in a supervised *training* experience, the reality is that the intern is on the cusp of being a full-time *professional*. Therefore, as a key meeting point between training and professional practice, the internship is an ideal time for interns to continue their professional identity development.

Professional Identity Development

Establishing a professional identity involves conceptualizing oneself as a professional, integrating skills and attitudes as a professional, and perceiving oneself in the context of a professional community (Gibson, Dollarhide, & Moss, 2010). Professional identity development is an intrapersonal and interpersonal process, and includes the integration of personal characteristics and professional training (Gibson et al.). An intern's professional identity development is considered one of the most important goals of the school psychology internship (Sullivan & Conoley, 2008).

It is reasonable to presume that an intern's professional identity development begins long before the internship commences, and will continue throughout his or her career (Kaslow & Rice, 1985). In fact, assumptions and beliefs ingrained at the core of the intern's identity may have been in place for many years prior to beginning school psychology training, and perhaps even provided the impetus for choosing to pursue a career in school psychology. For university educators and field supervisors, one goal of internship training may be to disrupt trainees' belief systems in order to broaden trainee perspectives and encourage trainees to become more critical thinkers regarding professional practice (M.R. Shinn, personal communication, February 17, 2011). In other words, field and university supervisors may consider professional identity development to be a key facet of the internship year, and actively work with interns to continue the professional identity development process.

Critical Incidents: Developing Perspectives on Practice

Conceptualizing the role of school psychologist – including what school psychologists do and *how* they do it – is a part of professional identity development. In addition to classroom learning, field-based experiences such as observing and rehearsing models of practice demonstrated by field supervisors can influence trainees' future school psychology practices (Tarquin & Truscott, 2006). Professional identity development for interns is presumably linked to *critical incidents* (CIs), or "significant learning moments, turning points, or moments of realization" which occur during training, and make a significant contribution to trainees' professional growth (Howard, Inman, & Altman, 2006, p. 88). Reflecting on CIs, which may be a part of supervision expectations (Harvey & Struzziero, 2008), has been linked to increased self-awareness, increased reflective practice, and professional growth for school psychologists-in-training (Griffin & Scherr, 2010), and in turn may lead to an enhanced sense of professional identity.

Cultural Identity Development

Cultural awareness is an essential training component for psychologists (APA, 2003), is described as a critical component of internship training (Canady et al., 2011; Magyar-Moe et al., 2005), and may be viewed as related to professional identity development. After all, cultural competence is considered to be one of the four foundational domains of competency delineated in the NASP *Blueprint III* (Ysseldyke et al., 2006). However, understanding the nuances of culture, cultural diversity, and working with culturally and linguistically diverse families and children is not a straightforward task. As explained by Ortiz, Flanagan, and Dynda (2008), school psychologists "must seek to understand the manner in which culture influences both their own view of others and others' view of them" (p. 1721). Therefore, developing cultural competence begins with analyzing and understanding one's own culture and its impact on others (Harris, 1996).

The development of cultural competence is a lifelong process, and the internship may provide an excellent opportunity for such training. For example, Canady and colleagues (2011) described an activity called a Cultural Roadmap that provides opportunities for interns to become skilled at a non-linear process to learn about cultural groups. The Cultural Roadmap activity contrasts with other activities that focus solely on learning specific facts about a cultural group or groups. In brief, interns learn a set of questions to be used to gain knowledge of other cultures; research a general overview about a specific cultural group; meet with community representatives, gatekeepers, and other subgroups; and produce a final product that addresses an area of concern for the culture (Canady et al.). The reader is referred to the original article for a more in-depth description of how to incorporate a Cultural Roadmap activity in internship training.

Although the Cultural Roadmap training approach seems promising, the exercise seems to lack a consideration of one's own culture and its impact on others. One way that awareness of one's own culture can be incorporated as part of internship training is through explicit discussions in supervision (Fukuyama, 1994). Keep in mind, however, that for supervision around cultural issues to be successful, supervisors too must address the development of their own cultural competencies (Harvey & Struzziero, 2008). In sum, developing cultural competence is an essential task during internship training, and is a central component of interns' professional identity development. Interns and supervisors are encouraged to work together to incorporate cultural awareness and understanding as part of the internship experience. Issues of cultural competence and supervision are revisited in greater depth in Chapter 6.

Achieving Separation-Individuation

Although interns are extensions of their supervisors, they tend to establish their own distinct identities as the internship year progresses. Kaslow and Rice (1985) analogized professional identity development to child development, and theorized that interns move through a process of separation-individuation from "professional adolescence" to "professional adulthood" (p. 253). Three developmental phases of internship (Early Phase, Separation, and Individuation) are described in Table 4.1, along with challenges interns may face in each stage and actions supervisors can take to support the interns' professional identity development.

During the Early Phase (encompassing the time prior to the internship through the beginning of the year), interns experience a great deal of stress; there are many new expectations and tasks. As interns move towards the Separation Phase they become more independent, but still experience self-doubt and become more acutely aware of gaps between the world of training and the realities of practice. By the end of the year, interns reach the Individuation Phase, marked by increased autonomy and a greater sense of professional identity. Through all three phases, interns experience feelings such as confusion, anxiety, and stress, and benefit from ongoing supervisory support including explicit modeling, guidance, and feedback. Interns' continued need for supervision indicates that irrespective of an intern's increasing role individuation, identity development, and competence, a supervisor's ethical responsibility for intern actions does not change.

An example of an intern's movement through the developmental phases of the internship (demonstrated through her increasing participation on the school problem-solving team) is shown in Table 4.2. The intern, named Rose, began the year unsure of her role on the problem-solving team. She was hesitant to speak up during meetings despite her well-developed knowledge of problem solving, opinions about cases discussed, and thoughts on how to improve the team's functioning. Her supervisor, Sharon, encouraged Rose to participate in meetings, gave her explicit responsibilities, and provided structured guidance and feedback. Rose took on more independence as the year went on, and became a highly valued team member. In fact, by the end of the year, Sharon viewed Rose as a vital advocate in promoting effective problem solving in the school.

The Complexities of Internship Supervision

In addition to being trainees and almost-professionals, interns are supervisees. Boylan and Scott (2009) argued that supervision expectations are often unclear to interns, creating a great deal of anxiety and apprehension. When interns and supervisors engage in clear discussions about supervision expectations, it can go a long way towards alleviating intern anxiety and increasing effective learning. The complexities of internship supervision will be considered in significantly greater depth in Chapter 6. For now, some questions that can illuminate supervision expectations and trigger discussion about processes of supervision are listed in Table 4.3. The questions about supervision are organized into four thematic categories: Logistics, evaluation, developmental considerations, and troubleshooting.

Logistics

Different supervisors approach the process of supervision in different ways. For example, some supervisors prefer regularly scheduled closed-door time with their supervisees, while others improvise supervision meetings as time becomes available during the week, or when the intern requests assistance. Interns may be engaged in various types of supervision (e.g., one-on-one, group with a supervisor, non-hierarchical peer group), and there may be multiple supervisors, each with unique styles. Without explicit discussions about how supervision will be provided, interns simply will not know what to expect or how to be well-prepared supervisees. Discussions about logistics get at the nuts and bolts of supervision such as who is the primary supervisor, when and where supervision will take place, and how many hours per

Table 4.1 *Developmental Phases of Internship: Challenges for Interns and What Supervisors Can Do*

Phase of internship (time of year)	Descriptive hallmarks	Challenges for interns	What supervisors can do
Early (pre-internship/beginning of year)	• Stressful time for interns: Encountering new experiences, new expectations, and beginning to develop a sense of professional identity • Interns depend on supervisors and other staff for frequent feedback	• Internship application and selection process • Intern–supervisor relationship building • Confusion regarding administrative tasks • Apprehension about clinical skills • Feeling the need to prove themselves • Being evaluated	• Create a nurturing and warm environment with appropriate limits • Provide orientation meetings, information packets, and other adjustment activities • Answer questions, normalize anxiety, and validate perceptions • Encourage former and current interns to meet • Allow a few weeks prior to formal assessment process • Provide constructive feedback and sensitive evaluations • Allow time for interns to reflect and integrate what they are learning • Develop a trusting supervisor–supervisee relationship
Separation (middle of the year)	• Interns less frequently check in with supervisor(s), are less dependent, and more autonomous than at the beginning of the year • Interns' sense of professional identity continues to develop • Area(s) of interest, or depth, may be selected and pursued	• Self-doubt, including questioning professional identity and clinical skills • Experience of tension between university and practice settings	• Emphasize continued availability to support supervisees • Acknowledge intern's unique identity and individual needs including strengths, weaknesses, and goals • Serve as a scientist-practitioner role model
Individuation (end of the year)	• Interns achieve their own individuality, sense of professional identity, and function more independently • Interns are more autonomous in service delivery, and take on more leadership actions • Planning for next year begins	• Expectation to function independently without competence in all areas • Confusion or turmoil regarding professional next steps • Termination with students and staff	• Encourage interns to take initiative, but continue to provide support • Provide information and support regarding professional opportunities for the upcoming year • Explicitly discuss termination process • Plan a farewell occasion such as a dinner or party

Note: Adapted from "Developmental Stresses of Psychology Internship Training: What Training Staff Can do to Help," by N. J. Kaslow and D. G. Rice, 1985, *Professional Psychology: Research and Practice, 16*, pp. 253–261.

Table 4.2 *Developmental Phases of Internship Exemplified*

Phase of internship	Intern behaviors	Supervisor behaviors
Early	Rose was a vocal contributor to her school-based problem-solving team during her second-year practicum, but hesitant to contribute at problem-solving team meetings at the start of her internship due to doubts about her clinical skills, and worrying what her supervisor might think.	During a supervision meeting early in the year, Rose's site supervisor Sharon clarified the problem-solving team process at the school, and expressed hope that Rose would be a contributor this year. Prior to the second meeting, Sharon and Rose discussed what cases would be on the agenda, and shared perspectives. Sharon encouraged Rose to participate in the meeting, and gave Rose encouraging feedback immediately following the meeting.
Separation	By the December, Rose became a strong contributor during problem-solving team meetings. She increasingly took the lead on presenting cases, and helped the team work through the problem-solving process. However, Rose was frustrated because team members often did not satisfactorily identify problems, and instead tended to jump directly into suggesting interventions. The problem-solving process looked different from what Rose learned during her school psychology coursework.	Sharon asked Rose's perspective regarding the problem-solving team's functioning, and they both shared similar concerns. Together they planned to address these issues in the next problem-solving team meeting; Sharon took the lead, and Rose made supporting contributions.
Individuation	By the end of the year, Rose attended and led some problem-solving team meetings without her supervisor present. At the same time as finishing her internship, Rose actively applied for school-based positions for next year.	Rose and Sharon debriefed on the meetings during supervision time. Rose took the lead in prioritizing what she wanted to discuss. Sharon checked in regarding Rose's job prospects, provided feedback on her CV and cover letters, and offered suggestions of potential job interview questions.

week supervision will occur. Other considerations include how the supervisor approaches supervision, including models and techniques, and the coordination of supervision across various supervisors.

Evaluation

It is the responsibility of field and university supervisors to evaluate interns (a) formatively and summatively, (b) formally and informally, and (c) along numerous dimensions such as competence, professional dispositions, and ethical practice (Boylan & Scott, 2009; Sullivan & Conoley, 2008). Although it is normal for interns to feel anxious about being evaluated (Kaslow & Rice, 1985), providing a structured approach to evaluation including setting clear criteria for assessment, providing ongoing feedback that is explicit and constructive, and using a variety of techniques, mitigates apprehension (Boylan & Scott, 2009).

Developmental Considerations

As described in Chapter 1 and in this chapter, frameworks of development provide a lens to view interns' personal and professional growth during the internship year. Developmental models of supervision (e.g., Harvey & Struzziero, 2008) describe how interns' level of skills in various areas can be matched

Table 4.3 *Examples of Questions to Clarify Internship Supervision Practices*

Category of concern	Examples of questions that can be clarified
Logistics	• How often and for how much time will the intern and supervisor meet for supervision? • What model of supervision and supervision techniques will be used by the supervisor? • How should the intern prepare for supervision meetings? • What happens during a site visit?
Evaluation	• How will formative and summative evaluation be incorporated as part of supervision? • What are the intern's goals, and how will the intern and supervisor know if those goals have been met? • How is evaluative feedback communicated? • How do field requirements relate to university requirements?
Developmental considerations	• Does the supervisor know the intern's current level of skills in various areas of practice? • How are appropriate levels of independence and scaffolding determined and provided? • How does the supervisor support the intern's development in an area where the supervisor may not be competent? • How are supervision interactions different during the beginning, middle, and end of the year, if at all?
Troubleshooting	• What should an intern do if he or she disagrees with a supervisor's perspective on a case? • What should an intern do if he or she receives different messages from different supervisors? • What should the intern do if he or she is receiving too much or not enough supervision? • How can the supervisor and intern improve their relationship?

with developmentally appropriate supervision strategies. Supervisors can make explicit how developmental progress will be determined (e.g., how progress is tied to evaluation data and the intern's goals), and discuss how supervision may look different based on intern skills in a particular clinical area, or time of year (e.g., see Alessi et al., 1981).

Troubleshooting

Supervision issues that are difficult to navigate, both for supervisors and interns, sometimes arise during the school psychology internship (Harvey, Monahan, & Lineman, 2011). Such circumstances include ethical dilemmas such as the intern not receiving enough supervision time, or precarious interpersonal situations such as a poor supervisor–supervisee relationship. Interns and supervisors may be well served by being upfront about what to do if challenging situations should arise. For example, during a site visit I recently conducted, the field supervisor told the intern: "If you are not sure why I took an action, please ask. Talking through my decisions helps me continue to grow as a school psychologist." Such discussions also present excellent opportunities for teaching interns to be problem solvers, critical thinkers, and ethical practitioners.

Clarifying Internship Expectations

Given the complexities of intern identity and processes of supervision described thus far, the need for explicit and clear expectations during the internship seems apparent. In fact, the importance of clearly communicated expectations during the internship is asserted by several authors (e.g., Boylan & Scott, 2009; Harvey & Struzziero, 2008; Lamb & Swerdlik, 2003; Sullivan & Conoley, 2008), and the need for (a) clear training goals and objectives and (b) timely and specific supervisory feedback are highlighted within the APA's (2010) ethical code. Although the importance of clear internship structures appears evident, *how* to achieve clarity is less apparent. Therefore, the second part of this chapter focuses more precisely on how interns and supervisors can communicate effectively to elucidate expectations and demystify the school psychology internship.

The Influence of Language

Words shape our experiences, actions, and the actions of others. The misuse of oral or written language, whether by mistake or deliberate (i.e., for purposes of persuasion), can contribute to poor decision making in clinical practice (Gambrill, 2012). There are numerous examples of fallacies, or mistakes in thinking, related to the use of language. Examples of some of the language fallacies described by Gambrill are presented in Table 4.4. The table includes a brief definition of each term and examples of how the errors may arise when interns and supervisors negotiate internship expectations.

The information in Table 4.4 serves several purposes. First, it is helpful for interns and supervisors to be aware of potential errors of language, including giving them specific names, in order for them to avoid committing such fallacies while communicating (Gambrill, 2012). Second, many of the errors listed can be addressed by *clarifying*, using questions or statements that help break down the inferential or abstract into observable and measurable terms. Third, it is important to stress that language fallacies are often committed by mistake. For instance, communicators make assumptions about meaning even though what is meant by the speaker and what is understood by the listener may not be one and the same. Some communicators may even pretend to understand in order to avoid embarrassment. To prevent pitfalls of communication, it is important for interns and supervisors to be conscientious in their verbal and written interactions.

Clarifying Down the Ladder of Inference

To illustrate fallacies of misunderstanding, Argyris (1990) and later Senge, Kleiner, Roberts, Ross, and Smith (1994) described a heuristic called the ladder of inference, illustrated in Figure 4.1. At the bottom of the ladder is sturdy ground, including observable and measurable data as might be captured by a video recorder. Moving up the ladder, an observer filters the data through his or her own lens; adds meaning (e.g., personal, cultural, professional) to the data; makes assumptions about what is observed based on the added meaning; draws conclusions; changes his or her beliefs; and takes actions based on his or her beliefs. New beliefs affect the observer's future perceptions, a process called the "reflexive loop" (Senge et al., p. 243). When perceptions and actions are far removed from the bottom of the ladder, the observer may find himself or herself on shaky ground. In other words, the observer takes actions based on inferences rather than facts. Applied to the school psychology internship, when expectations are not clearly discussed, interns and supervisors may inadvertently find themselves atop the ladder of inference, engaged in misinformed actions.

An illustration of the ladder of inference concept applied to the school psychology internship is featured in Figure 4.2. Early in the internship year, an intern named Tricia got nervous at IEP meetings – she stammered in her speech, turned red, and looked extensively at her notes rather than making eye contact with parents. Both Tricia and her supervisor Anne recognized Tricia's nervousness, but the beliefs and actions that each of them developed in response to the performance diverged as they moved up the ladder of inference. Tricia was self-critical, labeling herself as incompetent, and assuming others (including her supervisor) viewed her in that light. Although Tricia recognized her continued need to practice presenting evaluation data, she worried about potential implications of requesting Anne's guidance and support. On the other hand, Anne empathized with Tricia's experience. However, given Anne's own prior experiences, she chalked up Tricia's nervousness to Anne being too overbearing as a supervisor. Actions resulting from inferences suggest that Anne will take a more hands-off supervisory approach, and Tricia may not receive the modeling and scaffolding support that might otherwise contribute to her growth of skills.

Table 4.4 *Fallacies Related to Language that Can Obscure School Psychology Internship Expectations*

Fallacy	Definition	Example
Predigested thinking	Oversimplifying complex topics, issues, or perspectives	An intern reports in her university seminar that her district "does not do RTI" so she cannot be involved in "RTI activities" during the internship.
Jargon	Using complicated, technical, or obscure language	On the internship plan, it is written that the intern will engage in "Data-based decision making and accountability" but what this means is not clarified.
Use of emotional words, buzzwords, or imagery	Using words, metaphors, or imagery that are emotionally laden or convey strong feelings	A site supervisor tells the intern, "Students frequently come to our office when they are in crisis. We do our best to prevent and put out fires, and make sure no one gets hurt."
Labeling	The misapplication or inaccurate use of a classification term	An intern tells her supervisor, "I want to do a group with Aspergery-type kids this year."
The assumption of one word, one meaning	Failure to recognize that the same word may mean different things to different people, or in different contexts	The intern and supervisor agree on a goal for the intern to get exposure working with "diverse children and families". The intern is interested in working with bilingual students, but the supervisor thinks the intern wanted to work with economically diverse populations.
Misuse of verbal speculation	Relying on conjecture and assumptions rather than observable and measurable facts	An intern tells his supervisor that he feels he has made significant growth in his counseling skills this year, but no assessment has been conducted.
Use of vague terms	Use of terms that are broad, unclear, or may have multiple meanings	The university supervisor tells students in the internship seminar that he expects they will engage in "evidence-based practice" during their internship experience, and does not clarify further.
Conviction through repetition	Hearing, seeing, or thinking about a statement multiple times, which increases a belief that the statement is true	The site supervisor frequently tells the intern, "Forget what you learned in school – now you are in the real world."
Bold assertions	Firmly and confidently declaring a position or stating a conclusion regardless of evidence	The intern states that he feels ready to conduct a threat assessment independently even though he has not done so before.
Primacy effects	The first thing we hear or see influences what we attend to and the attributions we make	An intern gets nervous presenting aloud at meetings (e.g., stumbling, turning red, relying heavily on notes), especially at the beginning of the year. The site supervisor rates the intern poorly in this area on an end-of-year evaluation rubric even though the intern has made significant growth during the year.

Note: The text in columns 1 and 2 is adapted from *Critical Thinking in Clinical Practice: Improving the Quality of Judgments and Decisions* (3rd ed., pp. 133–148), by E. Gambrill, 2012, Hoboken, NJ: John Wiley and Sons.

As argued by Rosenfield (2004) with regard to school consultation, the ladder of inference is a helpful heuristic to aid school psychologists "in unpacking . . . inferential language used in discussing problems" (p. 344). Rosenfield (1987) described requesting clarification as an essential skill for facilitating effective communication. Clarifying can be done through a statement (e.g., "Tell me more about what you mean by data-based decision making and accountability"), or a question (e.g., "What do you mean when you say 'diverse families and children'?"). Clarifying brings forward valuable information, and moves the communicators down the ladder of inference towards explicit goals,

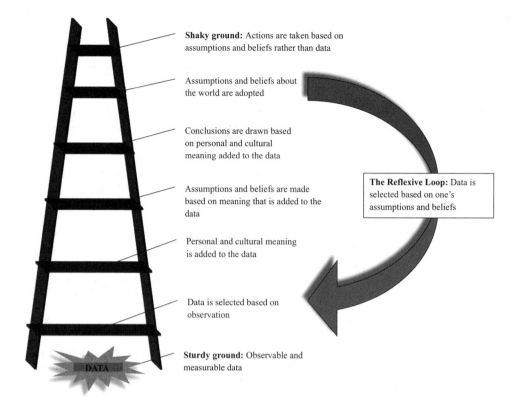

Shaky ground: Actions are taken based on assumptions and beliefs rather than data

Assumptions and beliefs about the world are adopted

Conclusions are drawn based on personal and cultural meaning added to the data

Assumptions and beliefs are made based on meaning that is added to the data

Personal and cultural meaning is added to the data

Data is selected based on observation

Sturdy ground: Observable and measurable data

The Reflexive Loop: Data is selected based on one's assumptions and beliefs

DATA

Figure 4.1 *The ladder of inference*

VIGNETTE 4.2 **ROGER'S MISUSE OF VERBAL SPECULATION**

Late in the spring, Roger reported to his supervisor Mary that he felt he had made significant growth in his knowledge and application of counseling skills. Roger in fact *had* made significant strides in counseling during his internship. He had co-facilitated a bereavement group with the school counselor at the middle school level, and worked individually with three high school students with minutes for counseling written in their IEPs (although goals of the counseling were somewhat unclear to Roger). He engaged in brief discussions with his site supervisor about the cases, but mostly discussed his work with the school counselor and his university supervisor. Roger also completed several relevant outside readings and learned new counseling strategies that he successfully applied in action. Mary assumed Roger had done an excellent job in his counseling work, and affirmed Roger's assertion. However, Mary had not observed or listened to audiotapes of Roger counseling, they had only briefly discussed counseling techniques in supervision, she had not completed an evaluation of Roger's counseling skills, and he had not self-assessed his counseling skills.

In retrospect, it may have been beneficial for Mary to clarify Roger's speculation (e.g., "Tell me more about your perceived skill growth . . .", or "How do you know you've made growth in your skills?"). In so doing, the dyad would have identified concrete examples of Roger's growth as well as experiences that Roger can continue to work on with supervisory support. Without clarification, it is not readily apparent what skills Roger needs to continue to work on for the remainder of the year, and as an early career school psychologist. Moreover, if Roger had not been becoming a more skilled counselor, the combination of verbal speculation and a faulty assumption might have been harmful to his professional development, and could have resulted in negative outcomes for children.

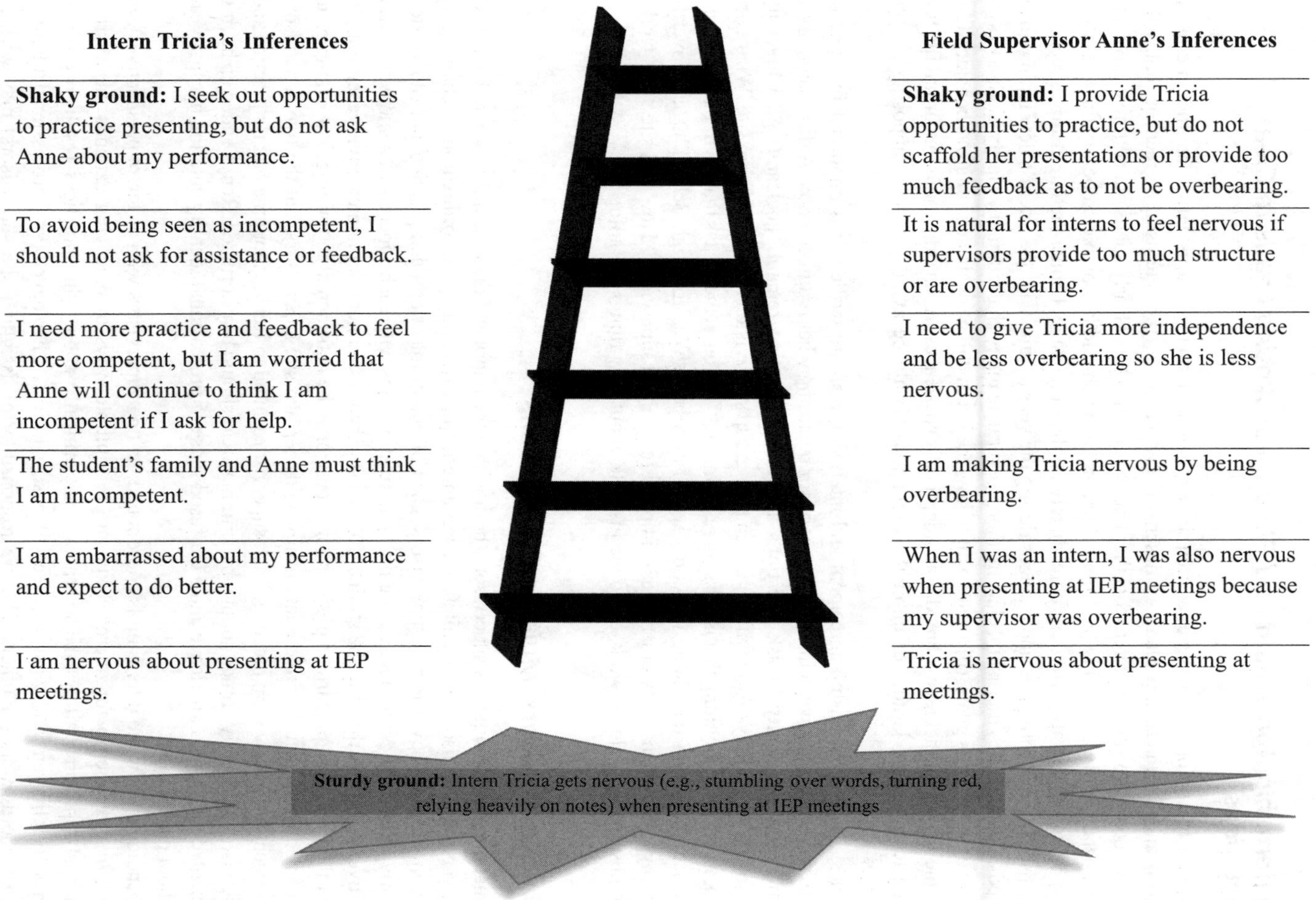

Intern Tricia's Inferences

Shaky ground: I seek out opportunities to practice presenting, but do not ask Anne about my performance.

To avoid being seen as incompetent, I should not ask for assistance or feedback.

I need more practice and feedback to feel more competent, but I am worried that Anne will continue to think I am incompetent if I ask for help.

The student's family and Anne must think I am incompetent.

I am embarrassed about my performance and expect to do better.

I am nervous about presenting at IEP meetings.

Field Supervisor Anne's Inferences

Shaky ground: I provide Tricia opportunities to practice, but do not scaffold her presentations or provide too much feedback as to not be overbearing.

It is natural for interns to feel nervous if supervisors provide too much structure or are overbearing.

I need to give Tricia more independence and be less overbearing so she is less nervous.

I am making Tricia nervous by being overbearing.

When I was an intern, I was also nervous when presenting at IEP meetings because my supervisor was overbearing.

Tricia is nervous about presenting at meetings.

Sturdy ground: Intern Tricia gets nervous (e.g., stumbling over words, turning red, relying heavily on notes) when presenting at IEP meetings

Figure 4.2 *The ladder of inference applied to school psychology internship expectations*

expectations, and actions. Looking again at Figure 4.2, Tricia or Anne could have clarified at the bottom of the ladder by explicitly discussing Tricia's performance at the IEP meeting, as well as their shared concerns.

The Internship Agreement and Plan: Clear Writing Leads to Clear Expectations

Internship expectations should be written in explicit and unambiguous terms on the internship agreement and the internship plan. As described in Chapter 2, the internship agreement holds the university, internship site, and intern together under a contract that clearly spells out administrative and logistical details of the internship. An internship agreement should be completed before the internship program begins so that all parties are immediately on the same page. Unlike the internship agreement, the internship plan is formative and changes during the year in tune with the intern's developing goals and needs. Ideally, the internship plan includes several features that augment clarity such as (a) a statement of the intern's goals, (b) a statement of how the intern will be evaluated, and (c) a consideration of how the intern will achieve a breadth and depth of experiences. As in oral communication, the use of vague terminology, jargon, or implicit assumptions should be avoided when composing written documents.

Further, after the internship agreement and internship plan are written, it is important for there to be a verbal discussion between intern and supervisor regarding what is agreed upon. A discussion gives all parties the opportunity to ask questions about anything that remains unclear (e.g., University supervisor: "The plan says Amy will engage in peer group supervision at the internship site. What does that look like?"), add anything that is missing (e.g., Intern: "The agreement says that I will be at Western Middle School, but on the phone we said I would also be at Western High School"), or to overtly address any concerns that may otherwise be implicit (e.g., Field supervisor: "How will site visits work? Do you observe Amy doing work, or do we just talk about how things are going?").

Multiple Supervisors, Multiple Expectations

Coordination across an intern's supervisors (both within the internship district, and between the district and university) can also help facilitate clearer internship expectations. Coordination is challenging because interns may have several supervisors, each of whom may approach practice and supervision differently. Further, the intern may have different relationships with each supervisor, some which may be positive and others that may be strained. When supervisors do not communicate with each other it may put the intern in a precarious position, or even worse, be detrimental to training. For example, an intern named Renya had positive relationships with her two site supervisors, but the two supervisors had divergent perspectives on practice. Each supervisor vented to Renya about the other's practice and the supervisors frequently argued about what training areas should be prioritized. Renya ended up having a fragmented internship experience and a confused sense of professional identity entering her first year as a school psychologist.

Depending on how the internship is coordinated, having supervisors with different perspectives can be a *positive* experience for interns. Exposure to multiple ways of practicing expands the intern's professional repertoire, allows the intern to think critically about what practices result in positive outcomes for children, and what practices fit best with his or her developing professional identity. Internship coordinators (or others who are responsible for assigning site supervisors) may wish to purposefully select supervisors who expose interns to different school contexts and approaches to practice, get along with each other, and will be in frequent communication during the year. Ongoing communication between supervisors can promote clear expectations, diminish feelings of confusion and contradiction, and create an integrated web of support for interns during their capstone experience.

Expectations from the University

The university supervisor should also make expectations clear. At the very least, university educators can establish clear internship guidelines in their school psychology program handbooks. Many training programs even provide students with an internship manual to explain procedures and guidelines for the internship year. Handbooks or manuals can include information about how to secure an internship, templates and examples of an internship agreement and internship plan, guidelines for site visits, procedures for university supervision, a clear description of how successful completion of the internship will be evaluated, and steps for obtaining state and national certification.

In many school psychology training programs, students are required to participate in a university-based internship seminar. The course syllabus can be explicit about what is expected of interns in the seminar, and should be consistent with expectations listed in the university handbook or internship manual. Through the seminar, the instructor (often the university internship supervisor) can provide information and answer questions about processes that may be considered confusing, such as taking state or national examinations, and procedures for attaining certification. It may also be helpful for the instructor to invite a former intern or interns to present at an early internship seminar regarding what new interns need to know, and to answer new interns' questions.

When internship seminars are offered, university supervisors should think carefully about how seminar expectations are aligned with the field components of the internship. Items for consideration are numerous, and may include:

- How often and what time does the seminar meet? Does the schedule interfere with the interns' professional responsibilities?
- What assignments should be included in the seminar? Do assignments support the interns' field experiences?
- What time, if any, is provided for peer group supervision, and how is it structured?
- How are field supervisors included as part of the university seminar, or the overall university-based internship supervision process?

By contemplating such questions, university supervisors can contribute to a transparent and integrated internship experience.

Summary

Interns are student trainees, emerging professionals, and supervisees all at the same time. Having multiple facets of identity presents numerous challenges for interns, including conflicting or ambiguous expectations. As trainees, interns are extensions of their supervisors and reflections of their school psychology programs. As soon-to-be professionals, each intern's professional identity, including cultural identity, is formatively developing towards an individuated sense of self as a professional school psychologist. As supervisees, interns are engaged in supervision processes both in the field and with their university. It is useful for interns and supervisors to explicitly discuss logistical details of supervision, procedures for evaluation, developmental considerations, and how sensitive concerns will be navigated should they arise.

In order to establish clear internship expectations, matters of communication are critically important. Errors of language – both verbal and written – should be avoided. Using clarifying questions and clarifying statements can help interns and supervisors break down vague or inferential language, and make expectations observable and measurable. Unambiguous written language should be used on the internship agreement and internship plan. Further, all supervisors should engage in ongoing communication in order to promote consistent expectations across settings. University supervisors should also be careful to provide transparent and comprehensible expectations regarding the internship.

Critical Thinking Questions and Activities

The following are critical thinking questions for interns, site supervisors, and university supervisors to ponder regarding intern identity and internship expectations.

For Interns:

■ On a continuum from trainee to professional, where would you mark your identity? How do you suppose this will change over the course of the internship year, if at all?
■ Identify five critical incidents from your training experience that have shaped your development as a school psychologist.
■ If you recognize a fallacy of language in interactions with a supervisor or written in internship paperwork, how will you respond?

For Field Supervisors:

■ What is your approach to supervision? Have you made your supervisory approach clear to your intern(s)?
■ What are school psychology internship expectations from the district level?
■ How do internship expectations differ for different interns, if at all?

For University Supervisors:

■ How are internship expectations provided to students in your program (e.g., written, oral, other)? Is the process of explaining expectations sufficient?
■ If you recognize a fallacy of language in interactions with a field supervisor or written in internship paperwork, how will you respond?
■ What are some ways you can enhance your communication interactions with field supervisors?

Chapter 5

The Proactive Intern

One of this book's big ideas is that interns should be active planners, coordinators, and shapers of the internship experience. That is, interns should self-advocate for their personal and professional needs, contribute to decision-making processes regarding the internship, take initiative, and constantly seek out opportunities for learning. This big idea does *not* mean that interns should fly solo, completing their internships independently without supervisor support. The point is that interns should actively influence the internship, as opposed to being passive recipients of their supervisors' plans. The focus of Chapter 5 is on (a) what it means to be a proactive intern, and (b) how the intern can be a proactive contributor to the internship. Actions supervisors can take to facilitate interns' proactive behavior are also explored. The chapter concludes with critical thinking questions and activities for interns and supervisors about intern proaction.

What Does it Mean to be a Proactive Intern?

Proactive behavior is a complex construct that has been extensively explored in the organizational psychology research literature (e.g., see Bateman & Crant, 1993; Erdogan & Bauer, 2005; Morrison, 1993a, 1993b; Seibert, Crant, & Kraimer, 1999), and has been applied to numerous professional fields (e.g., accounting, business, engineering, and nursing, to name a few). Proactive behavior is defined as taking "self-directed and future-focused action in an organization, in which the individual aims to bring about change, including change to the situation . . . and/or change within him- or herself" (Bindl & Parker, 2011, p. 568). Proactive behaviors are shaped by an individual's personality as well as numerous situational forces such as job demands and expectations, and are conceptually and empirically linked to superior job performance (Bindl & Parker).

Applied to school psychology interns, being proactive may be thought of as thinking critically about the internship experience and using that information to advocate for changes to enhance learning. Changes may include *changes to self* (e.g., seeking out additional professional development opportunities or resources; purposefully asking more clarifying questions; developing a process for self-assessment; or engaging in networking opportunities) and *changes to the environment* (e.g., taking on additional opportunities or activities; making scheduling changes in order to alleviate stress; or requesting additional time for supervision).

Proactive Personality

The construct of proactive personality is the dispositional tendency for individuals to take actions in order to influence their environments (Bateman & Crant, 1993). According to Bateman and Crant (1993), prototypically proactive individuals "scan for opportunities, show initiative, take action, and persevere until they reach closure by bringing about change", while those who "are relatively passive react to, adapt to, and are shaped by their environments" (p. 105). Interns with proactive personalities may have a professional advantage in how they are perceived and evaluated by supervisors. For example, in a qualitative study of the learning experiences of medical interns by Deketelaere, Kelchtermans, Struyf, and De Leyn (2006), supervisors tended to view interns' proactive attitudes as evidence of commitment and motivation, and perceived it as easier to provide proactive interns with learning opportunities.

It seems likely that school psychology interns, like other individuals in an array of professional fields and levels of training, differ in their dispositional tendencies to be proactive. Variations in proactive personality may have implications for the actions interns take or do not take, the way they are perceived by their supervisors, and the overall success of the internship year. However, personality alone does not account for the presence or absence of proactive behaviors; proactive behavior is also a function of situational variables (Bindl & Parker, 2011; Erdogan & Bauer, 2005). Therefore, it is reasonable to presume that professional practice skills such as how to be proactive can be "harvested, grown, and sustained" (Bateman & Crant, 1999, p. 66) during the internship year.

Contextual Considerations

The school psychology internship takes place in a context with its own situational variables to be accounted for. For instance, as described in detail in Chapter 4, interns are still trainees, a status that may inhibit the ability to be proactive. They may worry about overstepping the boundaries of the intern role (especially if such boundaries are not clearly delineated), may not have a sufficient understanding of their school or district culture to take certain actions, or may be concerned about processes of evaluation. Although there are some universal features of the school psychology internship for all interns, the internship is also in some ways unique for each individual. Therefore, each intern's distinct internship context provides varying opportunities for proactive behavior.

Examples of Interns' Proactive Behaviors

Although defining personality and contextual variables helps to conceptualize what it means to be proactive, it is also important to describe specific proactive actions interns can take to enhance their internship experience. For interns, being proactive includes seeking out information, seeking out opportunities, having a proactive attitude, and attending to self-care needs.

VIGNETTE 5.1 **DIFFERING CONTEXTS, DIFFERENT BEHAVIORS**

Interns Susan and Noah were in the same cohort of a training program and were interning in different school districts. Both were highly rated by their supervisors with regard to professional behaviors, and could be described as motivated interns. Neither had worked at the early childhood level during their school psychology training so far, but both wanted such an experience. During a supervision session in the early fall, Susan inquired with her field supervisor to see if an early childhood experience was possible. Together, they adjusted Susan's schedule to include a half-day a week at a preschool in the district where there was a school psychologist in the building. Susan was proactive in making a change in her environment, had the support of a flexible supervisor to do so, and there was an opportunity available nearby.

In contrast, Noah felt constrained by his already busy internship schedule (he was split between three schools over five days) and numerous responsibilities. Although he had a positive relationship with his supervisor, Noah assumed changing his schedule would not be a possibility. He also knew there was not an early childhood location in the district where he could work. As a result, Noah did not seek out his interest and did not get to engage in an early childhood experience. Noah's passivity was based on realistic assumptions regarding his internship context. However, it may have been helpful for Noah and his supervisors (field and university) to strategize ways to creatively provide Noah's desired experiences (e.g., visiting a different district, collaborating with a community agency, or working at an early childhood center on the university campus).

Seeking Out Information

One behavior that interns can engage in to be proactive is seeking out information. Information-seeking behaviors contribute to organizational newcomers' process of socialization, or "learning the behaviors and attitudes necessary for assuming a role in an organization" (Morrison, 1993a, p. 173). Socialization for school psychology interns can be defined as learning the behaviors and attitudes needed to be an effective school psychology intern and, eventually, a professional school psychologist. For interns, socialization includes entering into internship sites, establishing relationships with colleagues, developing content and applied knowledge of school psychology, and taking on professional responsibilities with increasing independence over time. Like other professional newcomers, it seems important for school psychology interns to seek information from others such as university supervisors, field supervisors, school staff, and peers to support their socialization.

What Types of Information Should Interns Seek?

According to Morrison (1995), there appear to be seven types of information that newcomers to organizations such as interns or early career professionals seek out: technical; referent; social; appraisal; normative; organizational; and political. *Technical information* refers to how one executes his or her job. *Referent information* includes requirements and expectations specific to a particular position. *Social information* is knowledge about colleagues, and one's relationship with them. *Appraisal information* refers to how one's performance is evaluated including self-assessment and evaluation by others such as supervisors. *Normative information* encompasses an organization's cultural norms, and *organizational information* gets at the structures, procedures, and services provided by the organization. Lastly, *political information* is the distribution of power in the organization. Examples of information school psychology interns may seek in each of the seven categories are provided in Table 5.1.

Passive and Active Approaches to Obtaining Information

Clearly, there is an overwhelming amount of information for school psychology interns to seek out. There are also numerous ways interns can successfully obtain information. For one, interns may receive information in a passive manner through means such as unobtrusively observing, including listening, watching, and monitoring. Being a passive recipient of information can be a helpful behavior for interns. For example, intern shadowing and observation combined with supervisor modeling are suggested to be important components of the early stages of the school psychology internship (Alessi et al., 1981). In addition, interns with supervisors who provide clear expectations and explicit, timely feedback may not always have to be proactive to gather information.

However, relying primarily on passive information seeking can be problematic, especially when not combined with any proactive behaviors. Sometimes interns are passive because they are concerned about the implications of directly asking for information. They are wary of being a burden to their supervisors or do not want to be perceived as naïve or incompetent. In fact, research on newcomers to organizations (e.g., interns) suggests that individuals would rather misinterpret or misunderstand information than endure negative perceptions that may be associated with asking questions (Morrison, 1995).

Regardless of the reason for passivity, even in contexts with formalized processes for providing information to newcomers (i.e., environments where it may be easier to be passive), proactive information seeking is demonstrated to have a positive effect on newcomers' socialization, task mastery, and role clarity (Morrison, 1993b, 1995). Therefore, interns are encouraged to combine passive behaviors with proactive behaviors in order to maximize the learning process. For example, as opposed to sitting back and watching supervisors in action, interns can take notes while they are observing and, in turn, use their notes to stimulate discussions regarding content, process, or decision making. Additional examples of proactive information seeking behaviors for interns include:

- using clarifying statements and questions to understand supervisor expectations (see Chapter 4);
- contacting/meeting with former interns from the internship site;

Table 5.1 *Types of Information Sought Out by Proactive School Psychology Interns*

Type of information	Information that may be sought by interns
Technical	• How do I perform particular parts of my job? • How do I balance job demands? • How do I obtain administrative and informational resources? • How do I work most efficiently and effectively? • What are the acronyms and technical language I need to know?
Referent	• What are the performance standards I am accountable for? • What specific responsibilities do I have? • What are my goals and objectives? • What are my supervisors' goals and objectives? • What levels of dependence or independence are expected of me? • Are there rewards (e.g., scholarships) for excellent performance? • What are my supervisors' expectations?
Social	• How do I go about developing and maintaining relationships with colleagues? • Who can I trust and not trust? • What behaviors/personalities can I expect from colleagues? • How do I best fit in with colleagues?
Appraisal	• Do I possess adequate skills and abilities as an intern, or as a school psychologist? • Are there any problems in my job performance? • Am I performing well? • What evaluation processes do my supervisors use? • How is successful internship completion determined?
Normative	• What is the history of my internship site? • What is the internship site's philosophy and goals? • What customs or rituals should I be aware of? • What behaviors and attitudes are expected at the internship site? • Is there potential for me to be hired next year?
Organizational	• What are the internship site's policies and procedures? • What is the organizational structure of the internship site? • What services are provided by the internship site? • Where are people and/or services located? • What will be my salary and benefits?
Political	• Who makes important decisions at the internship site? • Who controls resources at the internship site? • Who's who at the internship site?

Note: Adapted from "Information Usefulness and Acquisition During Organizational Encounter," by E. W. Morrison, *Journal of Applied Psychology, 78,* pp. 151–152.

- accessing and reading documents (e.g., policy manuals) from the school, district, or other site;
- asking questions to better understand how the supervisor arrived at a decision (e.g., "Can you explain how you determined that the student qualified for special education under the category of Specific Learning Disability?");
- gathering assessment data to monitor one's own performance, including feedback from supervisors, other staff, peers, and self (see Chapter 2);
- keeping abreast of developments in the field by reading professional newsletters, journals, and books, and by attending professional development workshops and conferences.

These are only a few of numerous examples of how interns may proactively seek out information.

In sum, there is a wealth of information that may be helpful to interns' socialization as interns and burgeoning school psychologists. Even though some information may be acquired through passive means, interns benefit from engaging in proactive information seeking behaviors.

Seeking Out Opportunities

In addition to seeking out information, being a proactive intern means seeking out opportunities. The countless opportunities available to interns during the internship include delivering a broad array of school psychology services (including those outside of one's comfort zone), participating in professional development, networking with colleagues, and taking on leadership roles.

School Psychology Services

With a push towards a broader role for school psychologists (e.g., see Fagan & Wise, 2007; Reschly, 2008; Sheridan & Gutkin, 2000), the array of activities interns can take part in may be quite wide. Although interns will not complete every possible school psychologist activity during the internship, they certainly can be involved in a breadth of activities. Interns can also seek out additional practice in a particular area or areas in order to achieve a depth of experience. As interns seek out practice opportunities, it should be in a purposeful manner that is consistent with their formative and summative internship goals. For example, an intern named Serena set a goal to take on a systems-level consultation case during her internship. Not having completed this activity by midyear, Serena revisited the goal with her supervisor during a midyear supervision session. Together they strategized how Serena could consult with the fourth-grade team leader who requested support in addressing increased bullying behaviors in the fourth grade.

Seeking Opportunities Outside of One's Comfort Zone

In addition to seeking out breadth and depth, proactive interns seek out experiences that are outside of their comfort zones. An activity protocol used to support the professional growth of educators called *Zones of Comfort, Risk and Danger: Constructing Your Zone Map* (National School Reform Faculty, n.d.) distinguishes between comfort zones, risk zones, and danger zones:

- *The Comfort Zone* [italics added] is usually a place where we feel at ease, with no tension, have a good grip on the topic, like to hear from others about the topic, know how to navigate occasional rough spots with ease [and] it is also a place to retreat from the danger zone.
- *The Risk Zone* [italics added] is the most fertile place for learning. It is where most people are willing to take some risks, not know everything, or sometimes not know anything at all, but clearly know [that] they want to learn and will take the risks necessary to do so. It is where people open up to other people with curiosity and interest, and where they will consider options or ideas they haven't thought of before.
- *The Danger Zone* [italics added] is an area . . . full of defenses, fears, red-lights, [and] desire for escape . . . it requires too much energy and time to accomplish anything . . . The best way to

work when you find yourself there is to own that it is a Danger Zone and work on some strategies to move into the Risk Zone (either on your own or with colleagues).

(p. 122)

A contrast of practices between two interns, Jasmine and Carla, provides a concrete example of the comfort zone concept (see Figure 5.1). Carla seeks opportunities outside of her comfort zone with more frequency than Jasmine, who tends to practice primarily from a place of comfort. In theory, by taking more risks with the support of supervision, Carla may be in a better position to achieve professional growth. The zones-of-comfort heuristic can be helpful for interns to map out what areas of practice fall in each zone, and then proactively seek out activities that are beyond their comfort zone. Supervisors can encourage interns to function more frequently in risk zones than comfort zones or danger zones, and emphasize that they will provide interns with a safety net of supervision.

Professional Development

Interns should constantly seek out opportunities for professional development. In fact, access to professional development may be required as part of the internship agreement. Professional development may take a variety of forms, and cover a multitude of topic areas. Some professional development for interns may be provided from the university. Many training programs require school psychology internship seminars that provide interns with relevant course content as well as ongoing supervisory support. For interns interning out of state, it may be possible to hook into a local university's school psychology internship seminar (university supervisors can help make this connection), or to videoconference into their home training program's seminar. Interns should keep attuned to university happenings, including speakers or workshops hosted by the training program or university, and take advantage of opportunities for learning.

Professional development activities may also be available through schools, districts, and community agencies. Some districts provide ongoing professional development sessions for all school psychologists in their district, and school psychology interns should be encouraged to participate. For professional development opportunities that are not free, some districts may provide a stipend for interns to attend. In addition to universities and school districts, school psychology organizations – local, national, and international – offer professional development workshops and conferences that interns may be able to attend. Registration fees are often reduced for graduate students, or even waived in exchange for student volunteering. Local and national professional conferences provide excellent opportunities for learning as well as for networking.

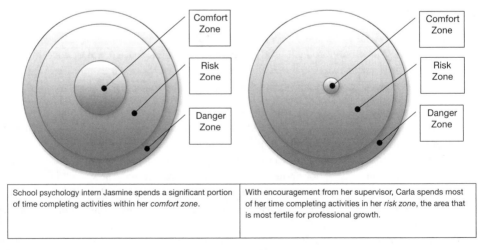

| School psychology intern Jasmine spends a significant portion of time completing activities within her *comfort zone*. | With encouragement from her supervisor, Carla spends most of her time completing activities in her *risk zone*, the area that is most fertile for professional growth. |

Figure 5.1 *Moving outside of comfort zones: A contrast of two interns*

How to Network: APPLE

Throughout their professional training, students are frequently reminded that networking is a critical task. By networking, students may learn more about their profession and find out about or even secure a job (Chin, 2009). However, like many other internship actions, *how* to engage in networking is not particularly clear. As such, networking may be a daunting task for students, especially for those students that are introverted or shy. The networking process can be demystified by illustrating how to network using the acronym APPLE: *A*cknowledge opportunities; *P*repare; be *P*ersonable; *L*eap/take risks; and *E*ngage in follow-up.

First, interns must *a*cknowledge opportunities for networking. This means seeking out chances to meet other people in both professional and social contexts. Networking does not only consist of meeting "celebrities" in the field (although this may be a part of networking), but also other graduate students, practitioners, and faculty members; such connections may grow into friendships and collaborations, and be helpful in career development. Next, interns should be *p*repared to network. Being prepared to network means the intern can briefly and confidently speak about him or herself to others, including the intern's current role and interests. To talk about oneself may feel awkward, perhaps even conceited. Thinking about what to say and practicing doing so in a way that feels genuine can be helpful. Preparation also means having materials such as business cards readily available so that exchange of information is easily accomplished.

The second P of APPLE stands for being *p*ersonable. Although some networking situations may be formal (e.g., a job fair), treating networking as a series of reciprocal discussions can make the process easier, perhaps even enjoyable. As in any conversation, it is important to remember to smile, listen, and ask questions; some social skills may inadvertently get neglected if one becomes too rigid while networking. *L*eaping is another important part of networking; leaping may mean moving outside of one's comfort zone into a risk zone. For example, while it is easy to talk with fellow students from one's own program at a conference, it is much more difficult to introduce oneself to strangers. However, networking involves taking risks, including meeting new people. Finally, *e*ngaging in follow-up is a critical component of networking. Interns may wish to stay in contact with others they have met, even with a simple e-mail saying "It was nice to meet you", "I enjoyed our conversation", and "I look forward to seeing you again soon". Follow-up efforts may also include connecting using social media resources such as Facebook or LinkedIn.

Leadership

Interns can be both learners and leaders during the internship year. At their internship sites, interns can seek out leadership opportunities such as sitting on school or district teams, consulting at the systems level with administrators, or leading professional development for staff. State school psychology organizations, as well as the APA and NASP, also offer opportunities for students to be involved in leadership activities. Examples of such activities include joining the Student Affiliates of School Psychology (SASP; the student-led organization of Division 16 of the APA) or seeking a leadership position on the SASP board; being a NASP student leader; volunteering to review convention proposals for the upcoming NASP convention; or writing an article for an organization's newsletter such as the *NASP Communiqué*. Taking on leadership roles may enhance an intern's professional identity development, increase opportunities for networking, and enrich the internship experience overall.

Achieving Balance

Hammer and Hammer (2009) suggested that in order for psychology graduate students to maximize their training experience, they should make "yes" a default response when presented with opportunities. Certainly, proactive interns are open to a variety of new experiences, even (or perhaps especially) those outside of their comfort zones. On the other hand, there is no shortage of potential experiences and activities for interns to take on during the internship year. Interns need to be strategic in seeking out

---

VIGNETTE 5.2 **HELENA'S BALANCE OF PROFESSIONAL DEVELOPMENT OPPORTUNITIES**

At Newton School District there were countless opportunities for professional development for school psychologists, including school psychology interns. In addition, the four school psychology interns at the district engaged in their own group supervision session once a month, and intern Helena's training program required a monthly internship seminar at the university. If Helena participated in every professional development opportunity, she would rarely have been in her two school buildings. Knowing this was the case, in early fall, Helena and her supervisor discussed which professional development opportunities Helena should attend during the year.

Having already determined Helena's goals, identified some of Helena's strengths and weaknesses, and developed an internship plan, they worked together to (a) match professional development opportunities with Helena's interests and needs, and (b) create a schedule that was not too fragmented. For instance, since Helena wanted to gain a depth of experience in working with students with autism, she prioritized attending a professional development session on this topic. On the other hand, she and her supervisor agreed that Helena would not attend an optional session on the topic of executive functioning because this was being covered during an internship seminar session, and would mean being out of her buildings three days in one week.

---

opportunities including (a) prioritizing opportunities based on assessed needs, and (b) self-advocating when he or she feels an experience will be particularly important. Since it often can be challenging for interns to discriminate between opportunities (i.e., is this something important for me to do, or a poor use of my time?), guidance from supervisors is vital.

Proactive Behaviors in Supervision

Proactive behaviors for interns extend to actions they can take during the supervision process. According to Corey, Haynes, Moulton, and Muratori (2010) some proactive behaviors supervisees can use to maximally benefit from supervision include:

- knowing the purpose of supervision, and recognizing that different supervisors will take different approaches to achieve that purpose;
- clarifying what the supervisor expects of supervisees and how the supervisee will be evaluated;
- being honest and forthright regarding supervisee needs; and
- preparing for supervision sessions in advance by thinking about questions, and prioritizing issues to be discussed.

When interns are proactive supervisees, the supervision process may become more individualized, applicable, and accessible. The role of the intern as supervisee is revisited in greater depth in Chapter 6.

Self-care

Advocating for self-care needs is also an essential behavior of proactive interns. Most helping professionals will find themselves working while under significant stress at some point during their training or career (Baird, 2008), and school psychologists are no exception (Huebner, Gilligan, & Cobb, 2002). In fact, Huebner et al. suggested that school psychologists may be at a greater risk for burnout than other psychological service providers, and that younger, less experienced school psychologists (including trainees) may be particularly vulnerable to burnout. Preventing or mitigating stress and burnout for school psychology interns requires putting in place protective mechanisms to increase the intern's resiliency. In contrast, an intern's failure to attend to self-care needs may be detrimental to the effective completion of professional responsibilities, including providing services to others (Barnett & Cooper, 2009; Smith & Moss, 2009).

Although "surviving" the internship requires a collaborative effort by interns, field supervisors, and university supervisors, for now the focus is on how interns may take the lead in incorporating self-care behaviors during the internship. Self-care begins with awareness of one's own needs, including recognition of the importance of one's own emotional and physical health. In addition to self-awareness, interns can engage in numerous behaviors to promote self-care such as:

- becoming more effective at time management;
- recognizing and coping with cognitions such as having realistic expectations for oneself;
- maintaining physical wellness through exercise and healthy eating;
- staying attuned with one's emotional needs at a given moment;
- seeking out support from loved ones, peers, and supervisors;
- finding time to have fun with colleagues outside of work;
- seeking out personal therapy as needed (Baird, 2008).

This section offers an introduction to the importance of self-care, and a quick glance at some self-care strategies for interns. These strategies, as well as several others (including how supervisors can support interns' self-care), are described more extensively in Chapter 8.

Additional Considerations Regarding Interns' Proactive Behaviors

Thus far, the chapter has focused primarily on what interns can do to be proactive. However, there are also numerous actions *supervisors* can take in order to encourage intern proaction. In addition, there are several cautions that should be taken into account by interns and supervisors when considering proactive behaviors.

Supervisors Can Generate Proactive Behaviors

Since proactive behaviors are a product of both intern dispositions and internship context, it makes sense to turn our attention to what supervisors can do to promote proactive behavior. Bateman and Crant (1999) identified (a) selecting, (b) training, (c) liberating, and (d) inspiring as important components of how managers generate proactive behaviors in organizations; these four areas can be applied to the school psychology internship and actions supervisors can take.

Selecting

Consideration can be given to interns' proactive behavior as early as the internship interview. For example, during the interview, supervisors might ask prospective interns to describe a time they took initiative during their practicum, or to tell about a time they encountered resistance and how they responded (Bateman & Crant, 1999). Prospective interns should think about their own proclivity to be proactive and how they might present examples of their proaction during the internship interview. Discussions about proaction should not be lip service but rather should (a) introduce proaction as an important quality of interns, and (b) help both supervisors and interns think about how to promote intern proaction during the internship.

Training

As the internship gets underway, supervisors can encourage interns to continue to think about their proactive behaviors, self-assess the extent to which they occur, and identify additional ways they might be proactive. Attempts to be proactive can be supported by supervisors, both in words and through actions. For example, if a usually reticent intern makes a valid suggestion at a meeting the supervisor may wish to publicly recognize the intern's comment, discuss ways to follow up on the idea, and provide any support needed for follow-up.

Liberating

According to Bateman and Crant (1999), proactive behaviors are often invalidated by others rather than being allowed to flourish. Internship supervisors should encourage interns' attempts at being proactive. First, supervisors can challenge themselves to loosen the reins, allowing the intern to set priorities and sometimes take the lead, especially as the year goes on. Second, supervisors can attempt to reduce overly burdensome workloads and too many short-term requirements in favor of providing interns opportunities to take initiative. An intern that is overwhelmed with too much work or is constantly putting out fires may never have an opportunity to be proactive.

Inspiring

In order to inspire proaction in their interns, supervisors can make it clear that proactive behaviors are valued at the internship site. Supervisor responses to interns' *ideas* and *mistakes* have implications for generating proaction (Bateman & Crant, 1999). With regard to ideas, supervisors can "squash the ideas (and the people) on the spot, or they can ask questions and explore possibilities" (Bateman & Crant, 1999, p. 67). The same reactions hold true for intern mistakes. A supervisor attitude of "Let's learn from this mistake" encourages further proaction, while a culture of blame can make interns feel defensive or worse, paralyzed to take action.

Passive Behavior Can Be Misleading

As mentioned earlier in this chapter, interns' proactive behaviors tend to be viewed positively by supervisors, while passive behaviors may be viewed by supervisors as signifying an intern's lack of motivation, lack of commitment, or even laziness (Deketelaere et al., 2006). However, interns may engage in passive behaviors for a variety of reasons. Some interns take a more passive stance because they are concerned with whether or not they are completing tasks correctly and are waiting for explicit supervisor feedback. Other interns may be unsure about what is expected of them, or perhaps they are unclear about where their role begins and the supervisor's role ends; as a result, they are hesitant to act in order to avoid stepping on their supervisor's toes. And yet other interns may believe that, as the old adage goes, it is better to be thought the fool than to prove it by speaking up.

In short, passive behaviors from interns may arise for a variety of reasons not related to negative intern attitudes. Changes in context initiated by supervisors or by interns, such as enhancing the clarity of expectations or encouraging proactive behaviors, can assist the dyad in turning passive behavior into proactive behavior. Further, passive behaviors may sometimes be very appropriate, such as when the intern is observing the supervisor complete a task that is outside of the intern's boundaries of competence. However, passive behavior (e.g., observation) can be combined with proaction (e.g., taking notes during the observation) to maximally benefit the intern.

Summary

Proactive behavior for school psychology interns involves thinking critically about oneself and one's internship, and advocating for changes to enhance the internship experience. Although proaction may be considered a dispositional personality characteristic that falls on a continuum, contextual factors also influence proactive behaviors. As such, it is reasonable to presume that how to act proactively can be taught and learned during the internship year.

One way interns can be proactive is by actively seeking out information. There are numerous types of information that interns may seek out to learn about internship expectations, the intern role, and the role of school psychologist. Seeking information helps interns socialize into the internship and into the profession of school psychology. A second way interns can be proactive is by seeking out opportunities. This includes engaging in a breadth and depth of school psychology activities based on interests and needs, engaging in activities outside of one's comfort zone, taking advantage of professional development opportunities, networking, and taking on leadership roles. Since so many opportunities abound, prioritizing activities is critical for interns to achieve balance. So too is engaging in proactive self-care, which acts to support one's own physical and mental health.

Proactive behaviors can be discussed as early as the internship interview, and highlighted as an important and expected behavior of interns. Supervisors can encourage interns to think formatively about and assess the extent to which they are proactive, and reflect on how they can become more proactive during the year. Proactive behaviors can be validated and supported when supervisors provide interns with opportunities for independence, respond positively to interns' ideas, and consider mistakes as opportunities for learning. It is normal for interns to engage in some passive behavior during the internship for a variety of reasons; supervisors are cautioned to be understanding of these behaviors, create open lines of communication with the intern, and encourage passive behaviors to be combined with proactive behaviors that enhance the overall internship experience.

Critical Thinking Questions and Activities

The following are critical thinking questions for interns, site supervisors, and university supervisors to ponder regarding proactive behaviors during the school psychology internship.

For Interns:

- What proactive behaviors do you currently engage in? What additional proactive behaviors would be beneficial to engage in?
- What do you need to promote your own emotional and physical wellness during the internship?
- Map out internship activities that fall in your comfort zone, risk zone, and danger zone in a diagram similar to Figure 5.1. Where do you spend most of your time? What are the implications?

For Field Supervisors:

- What actions would you take to support an intern that does not proactively seek out opportunities?
- Looking at Table 5.1, what types of information do you feel are most important for interns to seek out?
- How are interns best supported to practice in areas outside of their comfort zones?

For University Supervisors:

- How are proactive behaviors taught during the school psychology training program, if at all? If not, how might they be incorporated as part of training?
- How does interns' contact with the university during the internship support their emotional and physical health, and self-care practices?
- What opportunities do university internship seminars potentially provide interns?

Chapter 6

The Supervision Process

A brief overview of supervision is provided in Chapter 1 of this book including defining supervision, identifying types of internship supervisors, and introducing developmental models of supervision. In addition, consistent with the dynamic and integrated nature of the school psychology internship, various considerations regarding supervision are interwoven throughout the text. However, processes of supervision are explored in significantly greater depth in this chapter than in other chapters of this book.

The chapter begins by highlighting the importance of supervision as a training tool during the internship, and identifying key goals of supervision. Components and outcomes of effective supervision are described, as are processes for evaluation and remediation. Models, formats, and techniques of supervision are presented with the intent of helping supervisors think about how to most effectively structure supervision during the internship. Means for supervisors to seek out continued professional development in supervision are offered. The chapter concludes with critical thinking questions for interns, field supervisors, and university supervisors around pertinent supervision issues. Given the fundamental nature of supervision during the internship, Chapter 6 may be considered a keystone chapter in this book.

Supervision in School Psychology

While fields such as clinical and counseling psychology boast a robust base of supervision research, a research gap has existed for decades regarding supervision in school psychology (Knoff, 1986; McIntosh & Phelps, 2000; Merrell, 2008). McIntosh and Phelps (2000) suggested that the paucity of supervision research in school psychology may reflect the endeavor being perceived as daunting: There are numerous variables involved, several complications in research design, and complexity in implementation and analysis. Difficulties in conducting supervision research have also been noted by authors in related psychology disciplines such as counseling psychology and psychotherapy (e.g., Bernard & Goodyear, 2009; Goodyear & Bernard, 1998; Holloway & Neufeldt, 1995; Wheeler & Richards, 2007).

Regardless of challenges in researching supervision and its limited research base in school psychology, it is generally recognized that supervision is vital to supporting the training and practice of school psychologists (Harvey & Struzziero, 2008). For example, NASP's (2011c) *Position Statement on Supervision in School Psychology* asserts that "it is essential that all school practitioners have access to knowledgeable professional supervision", and advocates for clinical supervision to be provided to school psychologists by school psychologists at all levels of training and practice. In other words, as suggested by Knoff (1986) in a seminal article on supervision in school psychology, "supervision should be an ongoing activity from one's preservice entrance into the field to one's retirement after years of productive service" (p. 533).

Supervision During the School Psychology Internship May Be Seen as Unique

Supervision in school psychology may be viewed as different from supervision in related mental health fields given complexities of working in an educational context. Funding limitations, legislative and educational mandates, the increased need for mental health services, increasingly diverse student populations, and school psychologist roles that vary according to personal values and systemic philosophy are some of the unique contextual considerations for school psychologists (Crespi & Dube, 2005; Harvey & Struzziero, 2008). In a study of challenges to providing supervision in school psychology, Harvey and Pearrow (2010) concluded that successful school psychology supervisors must be systemic change leaders and incorporate consideration to systemic variables in supervision; in so doing, they create a supervision role that is perhaps broader than supervision in non-school settings. Furthermore, school psychologists engage in three main areas of practice – assessment, counseling, and consultation – each of which may require some unique supervision considerations as was illustrated in a special section of *The Clinical Supervisor* (Crespi & Kaufman, 2003).

Supervision during the school psychology internship is also in some ways distinct from supervision at other levels of school psychology training and practice. Although supervision during practicum is provided primarily by the university and supplemented in the field, internship supervision is predominately provided in the field and supplemented by the university. Of course, as emphasized by Knoff (1986), internship supervision is not solely the responsibility of field supervisors. The importance of a close relationship and ongoing communication between internship site supervisors and university supervisors cannot be overstated (Hebert & Patterson, 2010; Knoff, 1986). For example, while field supervisors engage in daily contact with the intern and hold immediate responsibility for intern actions, it is the university that certifies successful internship completion. Furthermore, the intricacies of the intern role such as having a hybrid identity of trainee and burgeoning professional (see Chapter 4) make the process of internship supervision particularly complex.

Finally, the receipt of intensive and individualized supervision distinguishes internship supervision from the supervision generally provided to inservice-level school psychology practitioners (Strein, 1996; Sullivan & Conoley, 2008). In other words, when graduating interns enter the field, supervision will likely look quantitatively (there will probably be less) and qualitatively (it will be more administrative than clinical in focus) different than it did during internship training. Of note, such realities are not consistent with the NASP's (2011c) *Position Statement on Supervision in School Psychology*, and may not meet post-doctoral supervision requirements for licensure for independent practice.

Goals of Supervision

Five goals of supervision in psychology are identified in this chapter, two of which are recognized as central: (a) fostering supervisees' growth and development through teaching, and (b) protecting the welfare of clients (Bernard & Goodyear, 2009; Corey et al., 2010). The first goal suggests that, through supervision, supervisee learning and development of competence is achieved via advising and instructing from supervisors (Holloway, 1995). Of note, Bernard and Goodyear (2009) point out that although supervision and teaching share similarities, they are not the same thing; "teaching is driven by a set curriculum or protocol, [and] supervision is driven by the needs of the particular supervisee and his/her clients" (p. 9). The authors also suggest that for less experienced supervisees (e.g., practicum students and interns) teaching will be a larger component of supervision than for supervisees further along the developmental continuum (e.g., inservice-level supervisees).

The second main goal of supervision is to protect the welfare of the individuals served by the supervisee. In other words, the supervisor's actions must ensure that clients (e.g., children and families) receive services that are delivered with both professionalism and competence. If the supervisor has reason to believe the supervisee's actions are not in the best interest of clients, it is the supervisor's legal and ethical responsibility to intervene (Corey et al., 2010). For example, Maureen, a female intern working at the high school level frequently wore revealing clothing, was ogled by several male students, and was teased behind her back by some of the school staff. Worried about how this might affect Maureen's relationships with staff and students as well as her ability to effectively deliver services, her supervisor intervened. She sensitively broached her concerns with Maureen early in the year, gave examples of what may be deemed appropriate and inappropriate dress in the school setting, and noted Maureen's ongoing professional dress following their conversation. Acting to ensure client welfare via prudent supervisee monitoring is consistent with the ethical responsibility supervisors maintain for supervisee actions according to the APA (2010) and NASP (2010b).

A third goal of supervision, related to promoting client welfare, is *gatekeeping* for the profession, or monitoring supervisee performance to make sure only those who are ready to obtain certification or licensure and enter the field are permitted to do so. The gatekeeping goal is particularly relevant in the consideration of supervision during the internship because the internship is likely the last stop for intensive, individualized supervision before trainees enter the field and practice independently (Sullivan & Conoley, 2008).

A fourth goal of supervision is empowering supervisees with the capacity to self-supervise in the future (Bernard & Goodyear, 2009; Corey et al., 2010; Knoff, 1986). Being able to self-supervise includes valuing and employing self-evaluation; trusting one's own clinical judgment; acknowledging one's assumptions and beliefs and how they influence practice, and proactively working to reduce bias; and recognizing limits of competence, including seeking out consultation or supervision as needed. To expand on this goal, supervisees should also learn about effective processes of supervision by way of supervisor actions so that one day they too can be effective supervisors. The reality is that many school psychology supervisors have limited or no formal training in supervision (Cochrane, Salyers, & Ding, 2010; Hunley et al., 2000; Ward, 2001), and supervisors' supervision practices are often informed by prior life experiences such as how they were supervised (Bernard & Goodyear, 2009). Therefore, it is likely that the internship supervision process modeled by site and university supervisors will be applied to the intern's future practice as a supervisor for others in a few short years.

Finally, a fifth supervision goal mentioned by Proctor (1986; as cited by Bernard and Goodyear, 2009) is to serve a restorative function, or to provide emotional support to supervisees to prevent or mitigate burnout. The restorative goal is consistent with the importance of self-care behaviors described in Chapters 5 and 8 of this book. Further, supervisors can model self-care behaviors in order to promote such actions in supervisees. An internship supervisor who does not take time for him or herself, who is often stressed or overwhelmed, or who frequently complains about being burnt out is likely not providing a good model of self-care. On the other hand, interns can benefit from discussing with their supervisors the sometimes hectic realities of being a school psychologist and how the supervisor best balances, both personally and professionally, the fulfillment of all responsibilities.

Why is it Important to Recognize the Overarching Goals of Supervision?

To some readers, the broad goals of supervision may seem intuitive or obvious. However, as the internship gets underway, goals of supervision can quickly become neglected or ignored. For instance, although it is sometimes appropriate to have "on the fly" supervision (e.g., an intern asks a supervisor to clarify a decision-making process immediately following a meeting), this type of supervision should not be the only type of supervision interns receive during the internship. In order to make sure the overarching goals of supervision receive adequate consideration, making time for scheduled, closed-door, and carefully structured supervision is important.

Components of an Effective Supervision Process

The research evidence demonstrating supervision outcomes in psychology, especially client outcomes, is limited (Bernard & Goodyear, 2009). However, in extant research there seems to be agreement of several elements that are contributors to effective supervision. Some pivotal elements of effective

---

VIGNETTE 6.1 **JOANNE'S INTERNSHIP CHALLENGES**

A doctoral intern named JoAnne had a successful entry into her internship. Her clinical skills improved greatly throughout the beginning of the year as documented by formative assessments, and she was well thought of by her supervisor and the school staff. Since JoAnne began the year with so much success, by mid-October she and her supervisor Jack had stopped planning supervision time in advance, instead meeting only when specific questions came up. However, as the year progressed, several challenges mounted for JoAnne. In January, JoAnne was unsuccessful in proposing her doctoral dissertation due to complications with obtaining Internal Review Board approval. As spring approached, JoAnne began to look for job openings but, due to budget shortfalls in her state, school psychologist positions were few and far between. All the while, JoAnne was planning her wedding to take place in June, one week following the end of her internship. JoAnne was frequently sick during the second half of her internship and missed several days of work. The quality of her work suffered, including not being prepared for counseling groups she was running, completing several assessment reports at the last minute with numerous grammatical errors, and finding herself fatigued during the school day.

　　JoAnne broke down crying one afternoon in March. She and her supervisor talked about JoAnne's stressors, and made a plan to help JoAnne achieve a personal and professional balance. Jack shared some of his self-care strategies and normalized JoAnne's stress by sharing similar experiences he faced when he was an intern and that he currently tackles in his full-time practitioner role. Jack and JoAnne agreed to meet weekly for extra supervision time on Friday mornings before school. During one supervision meeting, Jack even helped JoAnne reconceptualize her dissertation. JoAnne was able to close out the year successfully with Jack's ongoing supervisory support. Although this case ended positively, explicit consideration given to the five goals of supervision earlier in the year may have preventively supported JoAnne's emotional well-being and the quality of her service delivery.

---

supervision include a positive supervisor–supervisee relationship, multicultural competence, and reflection from the supervisor and supervisee.

Supervisor–Supervisee Relationship

A positive supervisory relationship is at the heart of successful supervision while negative or conflictual relationships may be detrimental to supervision outcomes, both for supervisees and clients (Bernard & Goodyear, 2009; Corey et al., 2010; Harvey & Struzziero, 2008). In a series of commentaries on ethical and effective supervision practices in professional psychology, Barnett, Cornish, Goodyear, and Lichtenberg (2007) suggested that a good supervisor–supervisee relationship includes a supervisor's commitment to the professional growth and emotional support of the supervisee, a collaborative working dynamic, and the establishment of mutual trust. A supervisor's explicit and clear expectations are also critical to building a strong supervisory working alliance (Harvey & Struzziero, 2008). In addition, supervisors' provision of constructive feedback in a non-judgmental, supportive manner creates a safe environment and mitigates anxiety-provoking circumstances that might otherwise silence a supervisee from discussing critical concerns (Barnett et al., 2007; Webb, 2000). Moreover, Corey et al. (2010) stressed that self-disclosure, or the willingness of supervisors and supervisees to engage in open and constructive dialogue, is an important condition of a productive relationship in supervision.

　　The supervisor–supervisee working alliance is impacted by numerous variables including the context for supervision, supervisor characteristics, supervisee characteristics, relationship dynamics, and characteristics of the organization (Harvey & Struzziero, 2008; Holloway, 1995). Characteristics of the supervisor and supervisee that are relevant include each individual's personal characteristics as well as their level of experience, development, theoretical orientation, and motivation. Variables that relate to supervisor–supervisee relationships can receive consideration as early as internship interviews (e.g., Will this candidate be a good match for our district and the supervisor[s] we can match him or her with?). Supervisor–supervisee relationship dynamics maintain importance throughout the internship year and should be given appropriate consideration by internship coordinators, and field and university supervisors.

Multicultural Competence

Attending to issues of diversity in supervision is an important component of the supervisor–supervisee relationship, and may translate into culturally competent practice by the supervisee (Barnett et al., 2007; Butler, 2003). Supervisors must develop their own multicultural competence and ensure that their supervisees are developing multicultural competence as well (Harvey and Struzziero, 2008). Bernard and Goodyear (2009) suggested that supervisors should define all interactions as multicultural in nature and check their assumptions accordingly. For example, supervisors should acknowledge that dynamics of power and privilege frequently exist within the supervisory relationship but often do not receive adequate consideration (Butler, 2003), and address this dilemma through culturally sensitive interactions with the supervisee.

Multicultural Supervision

Lopez and Rogers (2010) explored a multicultural approach to supervision and framed its importance within the context of APA's (2010) and NASP's (2010b) ethical codes which advocate for fairness, justice, and respect for people's rights and dignity. Lopez and Rogers (2010) defined multicultural supervision as "an approach . . . that (a) provides a forum for examining how human diversity influences quality of life and (b) uses that knowledge to improve effectiveness of services, with the goal of ensuring a just and fair environment for clients" (p. 120). Corey et al. (2010) outlined several multicultural supervision competencies that supervisors can incorporate in supervision practice. Although the competencies outlined by Corey and colleagues were intended for supervisors, their list is adapted with examples for supervisors *and* supervisees in Table 6.1. By highlighting specific actions, it is hoped that interns and supervisors can begin to incorporate multicultural considerations into supervision and other activities during the internship.

Lopez and Rogers (2010) concluded that multicultural supervision may lead to (a) positive outcomes for clients through effective service delivery; (b) supervisor modeling of a multicultural approach to practice for supervisees; (c) increased feelings of efficacy for supervisees in working with diverse clients; (d) increased supervisee satisfaction and perceived quality of supervision; (e) creation of opportunities to discuss and explore bias, prejudice, and oppression; and (f) increased justice within the organizational (e.g., school) system. Lopez and Rogers also pointed to obstacles in applying multicultural supervision such as variance in supervisors' abilities and readiness to engage in multicultural supervision, a lack of bilingual psychologists, and some environments (e.g., school culture) that may contrast with the goals of a multicultural approach. Obstacles notwithstanding, incorporating a multicultural approach into supervision is an ethical obligation of school psychologists that has the potential to benefit supervisors, supervisees, children, and families.

Self-reflection

Self-reflection, both from supervisors and supervisees, is another integral component of effective supervision. Supervisors should reflect on their own supervision competencies, the goals that are established and monitored with supervisees, and solicit and utilize evaluative feedback from others (e.g., supervisees, peers, metasupervisors) to improve their supervision work (Falender et al., 2004). Supervision of supervisors, or metasupervision, encourages self-reflection and includes interventions for gaps in one's supervision knowledge, skills, confidence, objectivity, and interactions (Knoff, 1986).

Table 6.1 *Integrating Multicultural Supervision into the School Psychology Internship*

Multicultural supervision competencies	Supervisor and intern actions to promote competencies
Explore cultural dynamics in supervisory relationships	Supervisors can discuss cultural similarities and differences with the supervisee in a way that avoids misunderstandings Supervisors can model appropriate and safe communication, for example seeking permission of supervisees before asking personal questions Interns can share cultural experiences that may impact their perspectives on practice
Include multicultural competencies in the internship plan	Supervisors can think about what opportunities to develop multicultural competencies will be available during the internship and encourage interns to take on these opportunities Interns can inquire about what opportunities to develop multicultural competencies will be available during the internship and engage in these opportunities Interns can seek opportunities outside of their cultural comfort zones
Encourage and empower supervisees to develop cultural self-awareness	Supervisors and interns can complete self-assessments of cultural awareness or sensitivity (e.g., see Harvey & Struzziero, 2008, pp. 93–96; Corey et al., 2010, pp. 128–129) Supervisors and interns can reflect on how culture impacted their work, and discuss in supervision
Accept multicultural limitations	Supervisors can seek support if needing to address challenging issues in the supervisory relationship beyond their own competence Interns should be careful not to practice outside of domains of multicultural competence without the support of supervision Supervisors and interns should be willing to make mistakes and learn from them
Model cultural sensitivity	Supervisors should be aware of cultural saliency instead of overemphasizing culture Interns should be clear with supervisors about what they need from supervision Supervisors and interns can practice cultural awareness and sensitivity in interactions including supervision as well as interactions with children, families, and staff
Accept responsibility to provide knowledge regarding cultural diversity	Supervisors can use supervision interactions as opportunities to teach and learn about cultural diversity Supervisors and interns can seek out ongoing professional development opportunities to learn about culturally competent practice
Treat culture as integrated in all domains of school psychology practice including assessment, consultation, and counseling	Supervisors and interns should view clients and cases as individual experiences, each deserving differentiated consideration Supervisors and interns should develop a working knowledge of cultural considerations within each domain of school psychology practice (e.g., see Jones, 2009)
Provide and model social advocacy	Supervisors can model social advocacy for interns and train interns to act as advocates for other groups Supervisors and interns can speak out on behalf of groups that have been oppressed or discriminated against Supervisors and interns can work towards reducing and ideally eliminating biases, prejudices, and discriminatory practices

Note: Adapted from *Clinical Supervision in the Helping Professions* (2nd ed., pp. 125–132), by G. Corey, R. Haynes, P. Moulton, and M. Muratori, 2010, Alexandria, VA: American Counseling Association.

Reflection is also critical for supervisees. Neufeldt, Karno, and Nelson (1996) described the reflective process in supervision for Counseling Psychology supervisees as "a search for understanding" of phenomena with attention to supervisee actions, emotions, thoughts, and interactions between the supervisee and clients (p. 8). Reflective supervisees actively seek understanding of events, engage in active inquiry, take risks, and are open to learning as opposed to being defensive. Accordingly, "reflectivity in supervision leads to changes in perception, changes in practice, and an increased capacity to make meaning of experiences" (Neufeldt et al., p. 8).

A Model of the Reflective Process in Supervision

Newman (2012) illustrated the reflective process in supervision for consultants in training (CITs) (i.e., school psychology trainees learning about school consultation) based on a reflective model of practice originally illustrated by Bernard and Goodyear (2009). Figure 6.1 demonstrates a novice CIT's reflective process as she worked through a consultation case with the support of university supervision. According to this model, reflection begins with a trigger event resulting in supervisee surprise, discomfort, or confusion. Supervisee reactions are connected to self-perceptions regarding clinical skills, personal issues, and/or a case conceptualization. In turn, supervisors can help supervisees critically reevaluate the situation in favor of a new perspective on how to approach similar situations in the future. Some techniques for promoting reflection in supervision are illustrated in Figure 6.1 (e.g., use of journaling, taping, modeling and rehearsal); these and other supervision techniques are discussed in greater depth later in this chapter.

Bernard and Goodyear (2009) summarized three important concluding points about reflective processes in supervision. First, it is likely that every supervisor stimulates at least some level of reflection with his or her supervisees. Second, in so doing, supervisors encourage supervisees to be reflective, which is consistent with the overarching goal of supervision to promote skills for the supervision of self and others. Third, reflection should not take place in a vacuum but rather be linked to evidence-based practices. If not, supervisees risk engaging in a misguided discovery process that may be detrimental to the supervisee's provision of services to clients.

Outcomes of Effective Supervision

Harvey and Struzziero (2008) synthesized research from the fields of psychology and education to highlight broad outcomes of effective supervision that can be applied to school psychologists. The authors concluded that effective supervision contributes to (a) supervisees' skill maintenance, development, and expansion; (b) reduced experience of stress; (c) increased self-reflection; and (d) increased accountability for service delivery. Applied specifically to school psychology interns, Sullivan and Conoley (2008) conjectured that effective supervision results in supervisees:

(a) developing autonomous skills in services such as assessment, counseling, and consultation; (b) learning to translate knowledge into informed, competent practice; (c) learning to apply the most recent ethics guidelines and legal standards to professional practice; (d) enhancing interpersonal skills with clients and families; (e) developing a professional identity and sense of self-confidence; and (f) receiving opportunities to share personal and professional experience.

(p. 1957)

Although there are many potential positive effects of supervision, the field of school psychology generally lacks a strong empirical base regarding supervision outcomes (McIntosh & Phelps, 2000), and studies of supervision outcomes in fields such as counseling psychology or psychotherapy often are of poor methodological quality (Ellis, Ladany, Krengel, & Schult, 1996; Wheeler & Richards, 2007). Nevertheless, (a) research evidence supporting supervision outcomes is burgeoning (Bernard & Goodyear, 2009), (b) the potential impact of effective supervision is far reaching, and (c) supervision is generally accepted as a critical pedagogical tool in school psychology and allied fields.

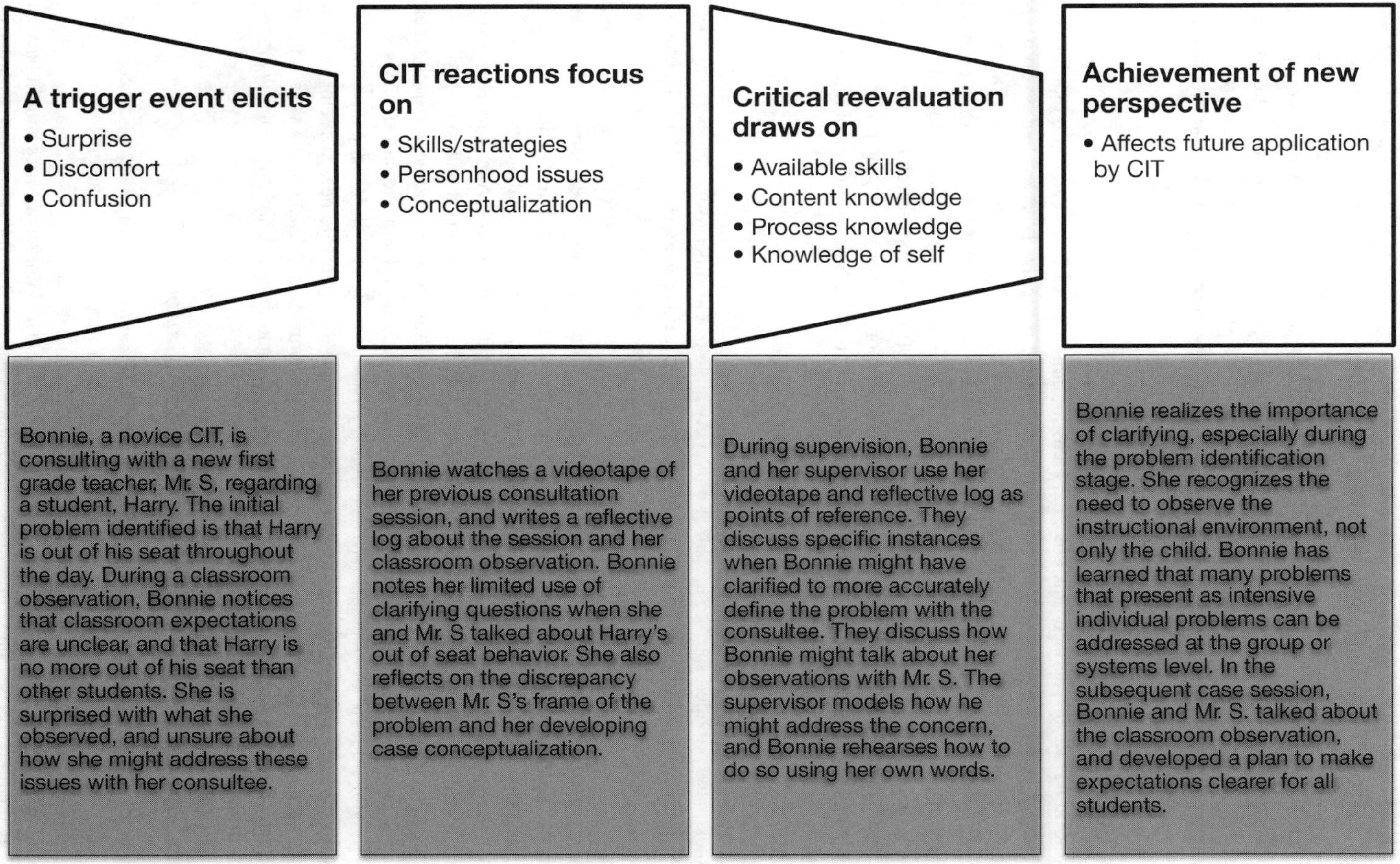

A trigger event elicits

- Surprise
- Discomfort
- Confusion

Bonnie, a novice CIT, is consulting with a new first grade teacher, Mr. S, regarding a student, Harry. The initial problem identified is that Harry is out of his seat throughout the day. During a classroom observation, Bonnie notices that classroom expectations are unclear, and that Harry is no more out of his seat than other students. She is surprised with what she observed, and unsure about how she might address these issues with her consultee.

CIT reactions focus on

- Skills/strategies
- Personhood issues
- Conceptualization

Bonnie watches a videotape of her previous consultation session, and writes a reflective log about the session and her classroom observation. Bonnie notes her limited use of clarifying questions when she and Mr. S talked about Harry's out of seat behavior. She also reflects on the discrepancy between Mr. S's frame of the problem and her developing case conceptualization.

Critical reevaluation draws on

- Available skills
- Content knowledge
- Process knowledge
- Knowledge of self

During supervision, Bonnie and her supervisor use her videotape and reflective log as points of reference. They discuss specific instances when Bonnie might have clarified to more accurately define the problem with the consultee. They discuss how Bonnie might talk about her observations with Mr. S. The supervisor models how he might address the concern, and Bonnie rehearses how to do so using her own words.

Achievement of new perspective

- Affects future application by CIT

Bonnie realizes the importance of clarifying, especially during the problem identification stage. She recognizes the need to observe the instructional environment, not only the child. Bonnie has learned that many problems that present as intensive individual problems can be addressed at the group or systems level. In the subsequent case session, Bonnie and Mr. S. talked about the classroom observation, and developed a plan to make expectations clearer for all students.

Figure 6.1 *Reflective process in supervision of school-based consultation*

Source: "Supervision of Consultation Training: Addressing the Content and Process Concerns of Novice Consultants," by D. S. Newman, 2012, in *Becoming a School Consultant: Lessons Learned* (p. 51), by S. A. Rosenfield (Ed.), 2012, New York: Routledge. Copyright 2012 by Taylor & Francis. Reprinted with permission.

Evaluating Supervision Outcomes

Evaluation may be considered "the nucleus of clinical supervision" (Bernard & Goodyear, 2009, p. 20) and is considered central to achieving supervision goals (Corey et al., 2010). That is, in order to make sure school psychology interns are meeting the goals of supervision, it is necessary to measure their formative growth of skills and ability to deliver clinically and ethically competent services to children, families, and staff. Lamb and Swerdlik (2003) suggested that when evaluation is effectively incorporated in supervision, it (a) mitigates evaluation apprehension, thereby allowing for professional growth (a formative function), and (b) facilitates the assessment of trainees' competencies, skill development, readiness to function independently, and any potentially problematic behaviors (a summative function).

Evaluation Domains

Sullivan and Conoley (2008) defined nine potential areas for ongoing assessment and skill building for school psychology interns (see Table 6.2). Sullivan and Conoley recognized that evaluation domains likely differ according to the needs of the intern, the internship site, and the training program. Therefore, interns and supervisors may wish to think about each of the nine domains and which are most relevant to use in their particular context. The examples of each domain in Table 6.2 purposefully exhibit different levels of intern functioning. Readers are encouraged to reflect on (a) how to interpret varying levels of an intern's performance, and (b) what prospective supervisor responses may be most helpful to support interns' continued skill growth in that area. Further, readers can consider how each domain links to the five overarching goals of supervision.

Evaluation Tools

Several authors have provided specific tools that university and/or field supervisors can use to support processes of evaluation during practica and internships (e.g., see Cruise & Swerdlik, 2010; Harvey & Struzziero, 2008; Kaslow et al., 2009; Sullivan & Conoley, 2008). In this book, four evaluation tools are featured as Appendices, each of which is adapted from other resources for use in the School Psychology Program at NLU. Appendix C is a field-based evaluation used to evaluate the clinical competencies of our trainees as rated by field supervisors. The field-based evaluation aligns with the domains of practice from the NASP standards (2010). Appendix D is an evaluation of trainees' professional behaviors, which may be completed by university or field supervisors. Appendix E provides information from trainees on their field experience, support from the district and site, and field supervisor(s). And finally, Appendix F provides information on how prepared trainees feel for their field experience based on their training, and on the support received from the university supervisor(s).

Each evaluation tool is included in NLU's *School Psychology Program Handbook*, explicitly discussed with trainees, and applied from program entry to exit to support trainees' development of clinical competencies and professionalism. All evaluations are completed at least twice a year, and are discussed in numerous ways including between field supervisor and trainee, university supervisor and trainee, and all three parties (e.g., during site visits).

Addressing Supervisee Problems of Professional Competence (PPC)

The majority of school psychology interns will complete their internship year ready to successfully enter their first year of professional practice. However, a small percentage of students may exhibit significant deficiencies with regard to clinical or professional competence.

Addressing problematic behaviors begins with prevention. Field and university sites should have in place clear evaluation policies and procedures, including processes for formative and summative evaluation as have already been described. It is important that evaluations address both clinical competencies and also professional behaviors. Supervisors can use evaluations to determine the level

Table 6.2 *Evaluating Intern Skills: Nine Domains for Supervisor Investigation*

Domain	Definition	Examples demonstrating varying levels of competence
Competence	Having the skills, techniques, and knowledge to take appropriate action	During a classroom observation in a middle school, intern Lola intervened immediately upon seeing two students about to get into a physical altercation. She separated the students, alerted the teacher to the situation, supported the teacher to sort out the situation, and then processed her actions with her supervisor.
Emotional awareness	Using emotions and reactions to understand and empathize with others	Intern Roberta observed that a teacher she was consulting with was feeling overwhelmed with a busy schedule. She recognized this verbally, and they rescheduled to meet later that week.
Professional identity	Consistency in thinking about problems and planning actions	When unsure how to approach a problem, intern Eddie seeks out various resources including people (e.g., his field supervisor, school-based specialists, his university supervisor, other colleagues), and literature (e.g., research articles, books, materials available online) before intervening.
Respect for individual differences	Makes an effort to understand and appreciate cultural, ethnic, linguistic, and sexual orientation differences	Intern Allison is asked by her supervisor to meet with a student who recently emigrated from Nigeria. Prior to their meeting, Allison does background research on Nigerian culture to better understand and connect with the student.
Purpose and direction	Formulates a plan, identifies goals, and monitors progress	Intern Tanya is part of a problem-solving team that identifies a student's reading difficulties. She agrees to take the lead in support of a struggling reader, but is not sure how to best monitor the student's reading progress during an intervention.
Autonomy	Makes choices and decisions independently (when appropriate)	While intern Li is administering a standardized test as part of an assessment battery, the student being tested breaks down crying uncontrollably. Li decides to stop the testing, help the student calm down, and return the student to class. She will discuss next steps with her supervisor.
Acceptance of supervision	Recognizes need for supervisory support, and seeks it out when necessary	On the second day of school, a teacher alerts school psychology intern Preeti that she overheard a student talking to his friends about having swallowed a bottle of pills before class. Unsure what to do, Preeti immediately contacts an administrator and her supervisor.
Ethics	Integrates ethical values and standards in practice	School psychology intern Nina takes home from school a folder including various case data such as test protocols, rating scales, and interview notes. She brings the folder to a coffee shop to complete the write-up of a psychological evaluation, and accidentally leaves it behind. She returns to the shop two hours later and the manager, who recovered the folder, returns it to Nina. She does not speak of this incident again.
Motivation	Is motivated and finds work rewarding and meaningful	Doctoral-level intern Sam is not enjoying his internship experience. He is introspective about whether he should have become a counseling psychologist instead of a school psychologist. He has been in school for five years and feels stuck. Although he works hard, Sam is not satisfied with his internship experience.

Note: The information in columns 1 and 2 is adapted from "Best Practices in the Supervision of Interns," by J. R. Sullivan and J. C. Conoley, 2008, in *Best Practices in School Psychology V* (pp. 1960–1961), by A. Thomas and J. Grimes (Eds.), 2008, Bethesda, MD: National Association of School Psychologists.

of severity of competence problems in order to determine the appropriate level of supervisory response (Cruise & Swerdlik, 2010). Problematic behaviors that are noted should be communicated both verbally *and* in writing to trainees, with behaviors specified in observable and measurable terms (Cruise & Swerdlik). If a remediation plan is developed, it should include these components:

- an observable and measurable statement of the concerning behavior(s);
- an acknowledgement of ethical codes that relate to the behavior(s) of concern;
- a specification of goals to be achieved by the remediation plan;
- a constructive and educative focus that specifies replacement behaviors;
- a description of interventions to be implemented with details regarding what, who, when, where, and how;
- a statement regarding how it will be determined that goals are met;
- a statement of what will happen if goals are not met.

The reader may refer to Cruise and Swerdlik (2010) and Lamb and Swerdlik (2003) for further information regarding prevention of and response to supervisee PPC. A sample remediation plan including due process rights and personal therapy, originally developed by Cruise and Swerdlik (2010), is provided in Appendix G.

The Structure of Supervision: Models, Formats, and Techniques

It can be argued that "the structure of clinical supervision profoundly influences its potential to be effective" (Harvey & Struzziero, 2008, p. 182). Whether or not explicitly recognized, supervisors have assumptions and beliefs about the world and school psychology practice that guide their use of specific models, formats, and techniques in supervision. Further, since school psychology interns may have multiple supervisors, they are likely to be exposed to many different types of supervision during the internship. Figure 6.2 illustrates the structure of supervision, as constructed by models, formats, and techniques. In addition to the supervisor's worldview, the structure of supervision is also influenced by the supervisee's developmental level in various skill areas. In other words, models, formats, and techniques may be differentially relevant or helpful depending on supervisee developmental level.

Supervision Models

Much is written about models of supervision in mental health fields, but it is still unclear if any models of supervision are better than others (Aten, Strain, & Gillespie, 2008; Kaufman & Schwartz, 2003), and there is not sufficient evidence to conclude that one model should be endorsed as most effective for school psychology supervision (Kaufman, 2010a; McIntosh & Phelps, 2000). Examples of supervisor theoretical orientations and models discussed in school psychology supervision literature (e.g., Harvey & Struzziero, 2008; Kaufman, 2010a; Kaufman & Schwartz, 2003) include psychodynamic, behavioral and cognitive behavioral, person-centered, constructivist, discrimination, developmental, integrative, and transtheoretical approaches. Although there are numerous models of supervision, "the best supervisors may be those who . . . manage a flexible blending . . . of perspectives . . . to meet the unique needs of individual interns" (Sullivan & Conoley, 2008, p. 1960).

Developmental Approaches to Supervision

A common underlying theme across supervision models is the (sometimes implicit) recognition that supervisee development of clinical skills and professional identity is a critical component of supervision (Kaufman, 2010a). Two categories of developmental models of supervision are (a) stage-based models and (b) process models. Stage-based models such as the prominent Integrated Developmental Model (IDM) (Stoltenberg, 2005; Stoltenberg & Delworth, 1987; Stoltenberg, McNeill, & Delworth, 1998) and life-span developmental models (e.g., Rønnestad & Skovholt, 1993, 2003) focus on distinctions

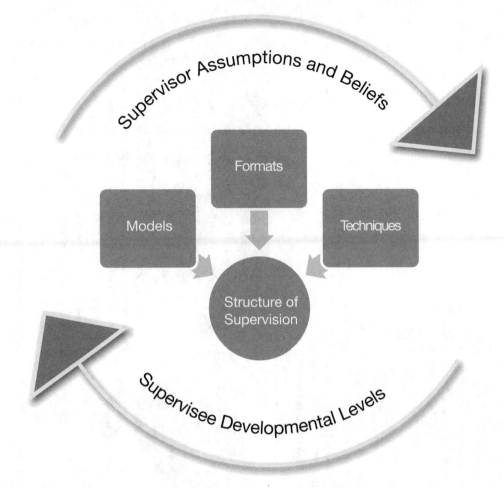

Figure 6.2 *The structure of supervision: Models, formats, and techniques*

between stages of development (e.g., beginning student versus experienced professional) rather than differences within stages. On the other hand, process developmental models focus on "processes that occur within a fairly limited, discrete period of time" (Bernard & Goodyear, 2009, p. 92) such as the one-year window of the school psychology internship.

Process Developmental Models

Process developmental approaches to supervision include reflective models of practice (illustrated in Figure 6.1), an events-based approach to supervision (Ladany, Friedlander, & Nelson, 2005), and an intricate model of counselor development (Loganbill, Hardy, & Delworth, 1982). The Loganbill et al. model describes supervisees working through eight developmental issues (competence, emotional awareness, autonomy, theoretical identity, respect for individual differences, purpose and direction, personal motivation, and professional ethics) during three recursive stages (stagnation, confusion, and integration), which are typified by attitudes towards self, supervisor, and the world. The developmental issues identified by Loganbill et al. for supervisees overlap considerably with intern skills identified by Sullivan and Conoley (2008), defined in Table 6.2.

In the Loganbill et al. (1982) model, process-related stages are revisited more than once as part of supervision, each time with "increasing thoroughness" – like tightening the bolts on a wheel until it is firmly fastened to the car (p. 17). The Loganbill et al. model is illustrated in Figure 6.3 using an example

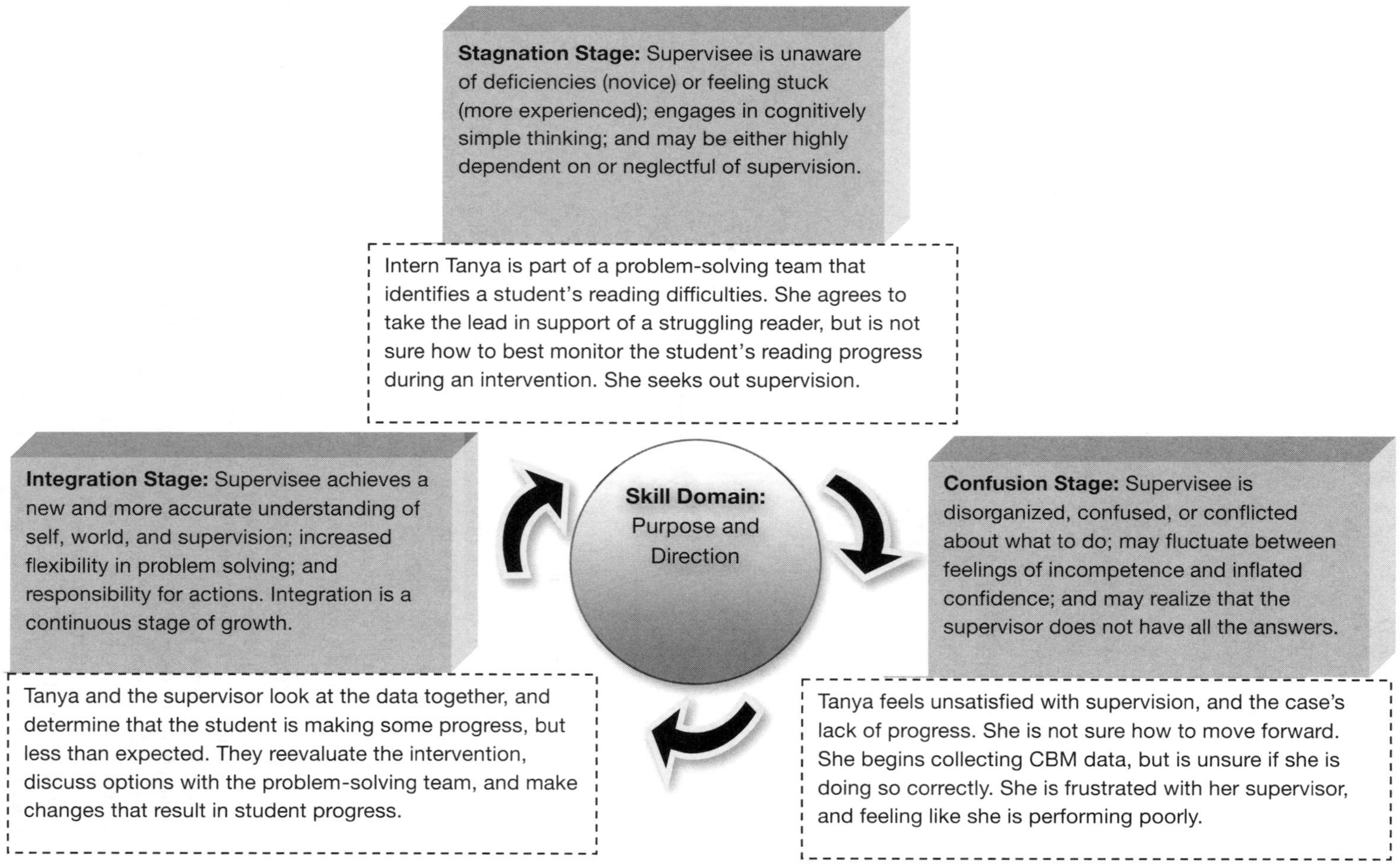

Stagnation Stage: Supervisee is unaware of deficiencies (novice) or feeling stuck (more experienced); engages in cognitively simple thinking; and may be either highly dependent on or neglectful of supervision.

Intern Tanya is part of a problem-solving team that identifies a student's reading difficulties. She agrees to take the lead in support of a struggling reader, but is not sure how to best monitor the student's reading progress during an intervention. She seeks out supervision.

Confusion Stage: Supervisee is disorganized, confused, or conflicted about what to do; may fluctuate between feelings of incompetence and inflated confidence; and may realize that the supervisor does not have all the answers.

Tanya feels unsatisfied with supervision, and the case's lack of progress. She is not sure how to move forward. She begins collecting CBM data, but is unsure if she is doing so correctly. She is frustrated with her supervisor, and feeling like she is performing poorly.

Skill Domain: Purpose and Direction

Integration Stage: Supervisee achieves a new and more accurate understanding of self, world, and supervision; increased flexibility in problem solving; and responsibility for actions. Integration is a continuous stage of growth.

Tanya and the supervisor look at the data together, and determine that the student is making some progress, but less than expected. They reevaluate the intervention, discuss options with the problem-solving team, and make changes that result in student progress.

Figure 6.3 *Stagnation, confusion, and integration: A developmental process model applied to the school psychology internship*

of intern Tanya's development of purpose and direction. Tanya's progress through the stages of stagnation, confusion, and integration are illustrated so the reader can see how her skills progress with each recurring stage. Theoretically, "stages of the process can be gone through again and again", (Loganbill et al., p. 17) and ideally, Tanya will experience skill growth in this and other domain areas over the course of the internship year.

Since the supervisor is expected to maintain awareness of eight issues over three stages in the Loganbill et al. (1982) model, over 24 positions are considered. Needless to say, the model is quite complex. However, the model (a) offers supervisors insight into the multitude of concerns supervisees face, (b) offers a starting point for deciding how to evaluate intern skills, (c) provides an impetus for supervisors to differentiate the process of supervision given divergent supervisee needs, and (d) demonstrates that ongoing practice and supervisory support is needed over an extended period of time for supervisees to develop competence.

Internship Stages

To wrap up the consideration of developmental approaches to supervision, a sequential, goal-directed teaching model of supervision described by Alessi et al. (1981) and expanded on by Harvey and Struzziero (2008) is illustrated in Figure 6.4. Harvey and Struzziero (2008) described five stages of supervisor–supervisee supervision interactions: (a) shadowing and modeling; (b) observation of assessment and professional skills; (c) guided independent practice; (d) increasing independent practice; and (e) professional independence.

Supervisors may consider this model an "I do, we do, you do" approach to internship supervision, which begins with intern entry and observation of supervisor behaviors ("I do"), moves to the intern and supervisor working together in parallel ("we do"), and concludes with an intern's achievement of increased independence ("you do"). Harvey and Struzziero (2008) noted that "supervisors should not expect that interns will function completely independently by the end of the internship" (p. 206).

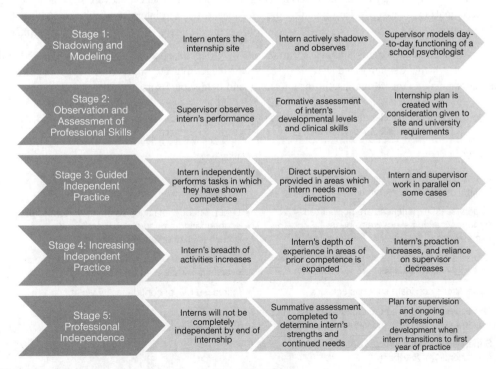

Figure 6.4 *Five stages of the school psychology internship*

Therefore, at the end of the year, it may be beneficial for the intern and supervisor to discuss the intern's transition into the first year of independent practice including how the intern may access various supports such as mentorship, supervision, and professional development. Such a dialogue may act to enhance the intern's feelings of readiness to enter the field.

Supervision Formats

In addition to supervision models, there are several supervision formats that school psychology interns may encounter during the internship including individual, group, and peer group supervision.

Individual Supervision

The most common format for supervision is *individual supervision*, or a single supervisor working with a single supervisee to work on case planning and to support the supervisee's formative development of clinical skills. Individual supervision can be time consuming but allows the supervisor and supervisee to focus on the supervisee's distinctive needs, and permits close monitoring of the supervisee's developmental progress and of the services provided by the supervisee. Individual supervision can also take place in a small group, where the supervisor works with each supervisee individually in a rotation; this may be more time efficient than one-on-one supervision (Harvey & Struzziero, 2008). Consistent with NASP (2010c) and APA (2009) guidelines, the majority of supervision hours during the internship will likely occur in individual supervision.

Group Supervision

Another supervision format is *group supervision*, which is defined by Bernard and Goodyear (2009) as:

> the regular meeting of a group of supervisees (a) with a designated supervisor or supervisors, (b) to monitor the quality of their work, and (c) to further their understanding of themselves . . ., of the clients with whom they work, and of service delivery in general . . . Supervisees are aided in achieving these goals by their supervisor(s) and by their feedback from and interactions with each other.
>
> (p. 244)

There are numerous benefits and a few limitations of group supervision identified by Bernard and Goodyear, which are summarized in Table 6.3. The advantages of group supervision outweigh potential limitations making this format useful for university and field supervisors.

Table 6.3 *Summary of Benefits and Limitations of Group Supervision Identified by Bernard and Goodyear (2009, pp. 245–247)*

Benefits	Limitations
• Supervisors' economic use of resources such as time, money, and expertise	• Supervisees may not get individual needs addressed (e.g., if time is not managed well)
• Supervisees' experiences are normalized through vicarious exposure to peers' experiences	• Group phenomena such as competitiveness or scapegoating among group members can potentially hinder learning
• Supervisees learn from each other's experiences and application of skills	• Everything that is discussed may not be relevant to every supervisee at every interval
• Supervisees can learn supervision skills	• Increased risk of confidentiality violations
• The supervisor can see the supervisee in a different way than is possible in individual supervision	
• Supervisees receive greater quantity, quality, and diversity of feedback	

Although there is great potential variability in the structure of group supervision (Mastoras & Andrews, 2011), there are some principles that may help guide its implementation. Harvey and Struzziero (2008) suggested supervisors limit group size to between four and eight supervisees and aim for relative homogeneity of developmental levels and topical interests when composing a group. Processes of group development are also important to consider (for further description of group theory, see Haboush, 2003). Finally, Harvey and Struzziero (2008) acknowledged the importance of having a formal group structure which may include supervisee case presentations and requests for assistance, peer clarification questions and feedback, supervisee response, and post-supervision feedback from the supervisor to supervisees that presented cases.

Peer Group Supervision

Peer group supervision is a type of group supervision, but differs from other supervision formats because it is non-hierarchical and does not include a formal evaluation process (Bernard & Goodyear, 2009). Counselman and Weber (2004) offered insights regarding peer group structure including the importance of developing a group contract, sharing tasks of leadership, and having a plan for case presentations. Even though the research on peer supervision groups is thin, the approach seems like a promising one for interns. First, the internship provides an opportunity for interns to learn a peer supervision process they can apply in their future practice. Since school psychology practitioners do not always receive systematic professional supervision or mentoring at the inservice level (Chafouleas, Clonan, & Vanauken, 2002; Curtis, Castillo, & Gelley, 2012), knowing how to effectively access peer consultation is essential. Second, the non-evaluative nature of peer group supervision can facilitate interns' openness to share with one another, thereby acting as a supplement to other forms of internship supervision. Third, opportunities for peer group supervision may naturally arise during the internship, especially if there are several interns at one internship site or if the intern attends a university-based internship seminar with other interns.

A Structure for Group or Peer Group Supervision

In the university-based internship seminar I instruct, I incorporate a formalized group supervision process. Supervisors may find this model relevant to use for field- or university-based supervision. Students work in groups of three or four and I rotate to participate in each group, making this approach a hybrid of group and peer group supervision. Consistent with characteristics of well-functioning peer supervision groups (e.g., Counselman & Weber, 2004) students are expected to: (a) develop a working group contract; (b) stay on task during group discussions; (c) work collaboratively through problems; and (d) follow a format for group supervision. Any violations of the group contract are expected to be addressed by the group.

The following steps in the supervision process adapted from the work of Wilbur, Roberts-Wilbur, Hart, and Morris (1994) provide the format for the supervision:

- Step 1: *Request for Help.* The intern states what assistance is being requested from the supervision group. Summary information may be presented using audio/video tapes, data from the case, written summaries, and/or verbal statements. Following the presentation of information, the supervisee should state what they are requesting assistance with (e.g., "I need the group's help to . . .").
- Step 2: *Asking Questions.* The group members should *paraphrase* and *clarify* regarding the information presented in Step 1 to make sure they accurately understand the presenting concern(s). Peers should avoid asking relevant questions (e.g., those related to the topic, but not stemming directly from information provided by the presenter) and irrelevant questions (e.g., those not related to the topic). Questions should be asked one at a time in an orderly manner until there are no more questions (i.e., the request for assistance is clear).
- Step 3: *Feedback.* Group members respond to the information provided in Steps 1 and 2 by stating how they might handle their peer's concern (e.g., "If I was working with that teacher, I might . . .").

The presenter should remain silent but take notes regarding the comments or suggestions. Feedback should be provided one at a time in an orderly manner, until there is no additional feedback.

■ *Pause/Break.* A break of a few minutes between Steps 3 and 4 allows for the presenter's reflection on the group members' feedback.

■ Step 4: *Response Statement.* The group members remain silent and allow the presenter to respond to each person's feedback, one at a time. The presenter may choose to state whether the feedback was helpful or not, and why it was helpful or not. The response statement concludes with the presenter summarizing the next steps for his or her work.

■ Step 5: *Discussion (optional).* If time is available, issues discussed in small groups may be discussed with the full class.

Supervision groups are more organic and flexible than may be apparent when looking at the steps in this process. For instance, the group must determine the order in which they will present, sometimes clarifying questions arise at steps other than Step 2, and the format can be used with or without a supervisor present. Anecdotally, I have noticed that having some structure tends to support positive group dynamics, effect problem solving, and provide opportunities for vicarious learning.

Techniques

Supervision is considered an intervention in and of itself, but is also composed of several interventions (also called methods or techniques) that are delivered by supervisors (Bernard & Goodyear, 2009). Purposeful supervisors select techniques based on supervisee and supervisor goals, supervisee experience and learning preferences, and the supervisor's theoretical orientation and model of supervision. In other words, "techniques . . . must be malleable and conducive to reaching a variety of supervision goals" and supervisors should be technically eclectic in their practice (Bernard & Goodyear, p. 219). Supervision techniques are used to (a) assess supervisee needs, (b) change, shape, or support supervisee behavior, and (c) evaluate supervisee performance, and may be differentially suited to achieving these different goals (Bernard & Goodyear).

A number of techniques commonly used in supervision are featured in Table 6.4, with a consideration of their advantages as well as challenges in their application. Although there are multiple supervision techniques that may be helpful training tools, supervisors do not always apply a wide array of strategies, or choose the ones that are most effective. For example, Romans, Boswell, Carlozzi, and Ferguson (1995) found that directors of counseling, clinical, and school psychology training programs rated co-facilitation (e.g., co-therapy) to be the most effective supervision strategy, but implemented that technique less than all others. On the contrary, self-report techniques (e.g., case consultation) were rated as the least effective but were the most commonly applied. Similarly, in a survey of internship supervision practices in school psychology, Ward (2001) found that both university- and field-based supervisors spent the largest chunk of their supervision time on supervisee case presentations.

Ward (2001) also noted differences between the activities of field and university internship supervisors. Field supervisors reported more involvement in clinical supervision activities (e.g., reviewing reports, modeling, live observation) while university supervisors spent more time in less-individualized activities including general group supervision and sharing of resources. Ward concluded that "together, the field-based and university supervisors provide interns with a more extensive supervision experience than either supervisor could provide on his/her own" (p. 281). Surely, the combination of field and university supervision has the potential to be a powerful tool to support interns. However, if supervisors are not thoughtful about what techniques they implement – including when and with what purpose – supervision may be an improvised process of trial and error rather than a structured intervention.

Training and Skill Development for Supervisors

There appear to be supervision gaps at all levels of school psychology training and practice. A survey of NASP members by Curtis and colleagues (2012) found that only 56% of school psychologists responding to their survey received administrative supervision (i.e., supervision focused on administrative issues as opposed to school psychology–specific clinical skills) and only 28.5% reported receiving systematic professional support, mentoring, and/or peer supervision to support their school psychology practice. In an earlier study, Curtis et al. (2008) found that only 7% of all school-based practitioner respondents reported receiving clinical supervision from an individual with a school psychology degree. In other words, most practicing school psychologists do not receive clinical supervision, and those who do receive it from someone who is not trained to be a school psychologist. Given these data, it seems likely that school psychologists do not receive metasupervision when providing field-based supervision to practicum students or interns.

The findings from Curtis et al. (2008, 2012) are consistent with data presented by Ward (2001) who surveyed school psychology internship supervisors (239 field-based and 41 university-based) and found that most (both field *and* university) had received little or no training in supervision, and did not engage in formal metasupervision. Further, Ward reported that the vast majority of field and university supervisors had undertaken no graduate coursework in supervision, and that the most common type of supervision training for both types of supervisors was informal discussions with colleagues. Such gaps are inconsistent with the increasingly common expectation that supervision coursework and metasupervision be included as components of graduate training in psychology (Falendar et al., 2004).

For supervisors who have not taken or will not take a course in supervision, other opportunities for professional development may be available, some of which may provide continuing professional development credits. Opportunities may include attending presentations or workshops, engaging in self-study (e.g., completing relevant readings), or participating in a peer supervision network (Harvey and Struzziero, 2008). Some universities or state associations also run training for field supervisors. For example, Harvey and colleagues (2010) described a supervision institute for practicum and internship supervisors in Massachusetts, which documented several positive outcomes for attendees, and the state of Illinois has hosted an annual Intern Supervision Day for internship supervisors, and new interns for over 12 years (Kelly, Cruise, Newman, Swerdlik, & Simon, 2012).

In addition, metasupervision is an underutilized way that supervisors can continue their ongoing professional development. Peer networks can provide opportunities to engage in peer group supervision including consultation on complex supervision issues and matters outside of one's boundaries of competence. No matter how knowledge and skill support is obtained, supervisors should remember that professional development on the topic of supervision should be ongoing. Attending presentations or workshops, engaging in self-studies, and conversing with colleagues offer starting points for supervision training. Supervisors are encouraged to seek out multiple opportunities and to continue to engage in learning over time.

Summary

There is a dearth of research on supervision in school psychology, but it is generally accepted that supervision is a pivotal training tool. School psychology internship supervision may be considered distinct from supervision in other mental health fields as well as from supervision at other levels of school psychology training and practice.

Goals of supervision include supervisee skill growth; supporting client welfare; gatekeeping for the profession; teaching supervisees skills to self-supervise; and providing restorative support. Three pivotal, interrelated components of effective supervision include a positive supervisor–supervisee relationship, attending to multicultural considerations in supervision, and engaging in ongoing self-reflection. When effective supervision is in place, positive outcomes for supervisees include expansion of knowledge and applied skills, reduction of anxiety, increased self-efficacy, enhanced accountability and ethical practice, and the continued development of professional identity. Formative and summative evaluations help supervisors and supervisees gain awareness of supervision outcomes and the intern's progress from the beginning to end of the internship. For interns who demonstrate problems with regard to their development of competence, a plan for remediation may be necessary.

Table 6.4 *Supervision Techniques*

Technique	Definition	Advantages	Challenges
Case consultation	Discussion of supervisee's cases including supervisee's description of major case issues and broad case conceptualization	• Effective in individual and group formats • Can be applied in consideration of numerous issues • Easily combined with other techniques	• Supervisee self-report may not be accurate due to supervisee's limited awareness or understanding, or desire for positive evaluation
Co-facilitation	Supervisee and supervisor(s) work together on a particular case including planning, implementation, and follow-up	• Supervisor gets first-hand perspective of supervisee skills • Supervisor can model skills	• Potential for role confusion • Supervisor may dominate, not letting supervisee get experience • Clients may favor supervisor over supervisee
Live observation	Supervisor(s) observe the supervisee's work, either behind a one-way mirror, on a video, or in person. May include in vivo supervisor feedback such as interruptions or built-in breaks	• Supervisor gets first-hand perspective of supervisee skills • Allows supervisors to provide feedback before, during, or after • Use of one-way mirror is amenable to group supervision processes	• Interruptions may be distracting or anxiety provoking to supervisee • Permission from clients may be necessary
Audio- and videotaping	The supervisee is recorded while applying skills in action. Supervisee process notes are often required in conjunction with recordings	• Tapes can be watched, paused, and replayed as needed allowing for discussion, modeling, and rehearsal • Observable and measurable recordings provide accurate supplements to supervisee and supervisor perceptions • Easily available on devices such as cellular phones, computers, and cameras	• Potential for technological difficulties • Videotaping is more robust than audiotaping because it provides information on body language and other environmental factors • Permission from clients is necessary

Technique	Description	Benefits	Limitations
Computer and online	Use of technology for supervision in any of a variety of forms such as supervisor instant messaging during live observation, e-mail supervision, videoconferencing, and use of simulation activities	• Allows supervision and learning over far distances • Novel, engaging, and relevant to technologically savvy supervisors and supervisees	• Potential for technological difficulties • Ethical challenges such as maintaining confidentiality • May be difficult to form the supervisor–supervisee relationship • Limited research base regarding effectiveness
Role play	Acting out challenging case scenarios with the supervisee. May include role reversal (e.g., supervisee plays the role of client to explore case issues, or the role of supervisor to explore supervision process issues)	• Effective in individual and group formats • Promotes perspective taking • Provides supervisee opportunities to practice skills in a safe space	• May feel awkward or artificial • Skills may not transfer to real situations
Modeling and rehearsal	Supervisor teaches the supervisee through his or her behavior, and/or demonstrates how to do something. Modeling is often combined with supervisees' rehearsal, or practice of skills	• Supervisees see and hear how to do something rather than only talking about how to do something • Promotes conscious reflection from the supervisor(s) regarding modeling behaviors • Provides supervisee opportunities to practice skills in a safe space	• May inhibit supervisees from finding their own voice • Supervisees may not apply what was modeled or rehearsed in actual cases
Written information (e.g., process notes, progress notes, and transcription)	Written notes may cover case issues and case progress, perceptions regarding growth in skills, challenges, successes, and supervision needs. Partial or full transcriptions can be produced using audio or videotapes of sessions	• Promotes supervisee reflection on a number of issues • Encourages supervisee and supervisor preparation for supervision • Provides documentation of case progress as well as supervisee skill growth	• May be time consuming for supervisee and supervisor • Supervisee notes may not be accurate due to supervisee's limited awareness or understanding, or desire for positive evaluation

Supervision is structured by particular supervision models, formats, and techniques. Research does not support one model of supervision over others, but most approaches have developmental underpinnings. Process developmental models may be particularly relevant to internship training given their focus on supervisee development during a limited period of time. Supervisors may wish to use an "I do, we do, you do" approach to supervision in order to allow interns to develop autonomy with appropriate amounts of scaffolding along the way. There are a number of techniques that supervisors can use to structure supervision, and being eclectic (purposefully selecting approaches to match with supervisee needs and the supervision context) is a helpful approach. Supervision may also take place in a variety of formats such as one-on-one, in a group, or non-hierarchically with peers. It is recommended that supervisors, especially novice supervisors, continue to seek out professional development to hone the supervision practices that they provide.

Critical Thinking Questions and Activities

The following are critical thinking questions for interns, site supervisors, and university supervisors regarding the role of supervision during the school psychology internship.

For Interns:

- What trigger events (see Figure 6.1) have stimulated reflection for you during your internship thus far? How were trigger events addressed in supervision, if at all?
- Reflect on your skill development in the domain areas identified in Table 6.2. Which areas do you feel are your strengths? How might you improve in areas that are challenging for you?
- What have you learned about supervision from observing supervisors in the past or during the internship? How do you predict this will influence who you are as a supervisor in the future?

For Field Supervisors:

- How do you incorporate multicultural supervision practices as part of the supervision you provide?
- Looking at Table 6.4, what new techniques might you apply as part of supervision? How might you combine several different techniques? Are different techniques more or less relevant for particular domains of school psychology practice? Do you use the same approaches with all supervisees?
- What opportunities are available for you to continue your own professional development as a supervisor?

For University Supervisors:

- Reflect on the structure of supervision in your training program. What models, formats, and techniques are used to support school psychology interns? Other trainees?
- How might you decrease the anxiety many interns experience regarding evaluation?
- How can the university support field supervisors' continued professional development?

Chapter 7

Breadth, Depth, and Competence

As has been defined in previous chapters, *breadth* of experience refers to an intern's involvement in a number and assortment of opportunities, and *depth* of experience is the progression of training in a particular domain from early coursework to skill application, working with differing populations at different levels of service (Haworth & Brantley, 1981). With sufficient breadth and depth of experiences that are (a) aligned with the 10 domains outlined in NASP's Standards and (b) completed in conjunction with ongoing supervision, it is expected that the intern will develop the competencies needed to begin practice as an entry-level school psychologist.

Explicitly considering breadth, depth, and competence fits within the "culture of competence" that currently impacts the broad field of professional psychology (e.g., see Belar, 2009; Fouad et al., 2009; Kaslow et al., 2009) and the sub-discipline of school psychology (e.g., see Daly, Doll, Schulte, & Fenning, 2011; Phelps & Swerdlik, 2011). The competency movement recognizes the need to (a) clarify foundational competencies (i.e., the knowledge, skills, attitudes, and values underlying psychology practice) and functional competencies (i.e., the major functions of psychologists); (b) specify benchmarks for attaining competency at varying developmental levels; and (c) provide formative and summative evaluation of performance for psychology trainees and practitioners (Fouad et al., 2009; Kaslow, 2004).

As discussed by Kaslow (2004), when psychologists apply a competency-based approach they must be careful not to reduce "the profession to a collection of specific skills that might or might not require extensive educational/experiential training, and as a result, train technicians rather than professionals" (p. 779). Similarly, Belar (2009) expressed the view that too narrow a focus on articulating and evaluating competencies may result in a "stove-piping" phenomenon whereby psychologists mechanically list competencies, but do not sufficiently recognize their interrelated and interactive nature. Such concerns are consistent with this book's big idea that the development of a school psychology intern's professional skills should be treated as an integrated process rather than a series of isolated activities. Therefore, although this chapter contains a number of examples of potential activities that school psychology interns may take on, it is purposefully designed to be integrated, non-prescriptive, and practical.

The chapter begins by clearly defining the terms *competence* and *competencies*. Competency documents influencing professional psychology and the subfield of school psychology are briefly reviewed with consideration of how they may help shape the school psychology internship. Examples of activities completed by one intern, Raven, are provided to demonstrate how competence can be integrated into internship training. The importance of breadth and depth during the internship is explored in detail. With regard to depth, interns are encouraged to develop a *Hedgehog Concept*: the overlap between what they excel at more than anything else, what they are passionate about, and what will make them marketable upon internship completion. The chapter closes with critical thinking questions and activities for interns and supervisors regarding breadth, depth, and competence.

What is Competence?

According to Kaslow (2004), *competence* is "an individual's capability and demonstrated ability to understand and do certain tasks in an appropriate and effective manner consistent with the expectations for a person qualified by education and training in a particular profession or specialty thereof" (p. 775). Further, competence implies being able to (a) engage in critical thinking and analysis; (b) apply professional judgment in decision making; and (c) adapt decisions based on specific situations. Competence is developmental, meaning that expectations regarding competence should differ for individuals at different stages of training and practice (Fouad et al., 2009). For example, what it means to be a competent practicum student likely differs in some ways from what it means to be a competent intern as well as what it means to be competent to enter professional practice. Finally, competence is context dependent; that is, different settings or environments may differentially impact the development and/or the evaluation of competencies (Kaslow, 2004). *Competencies* are "elements of competence that are observable, measurable, containable, practical, derived by experts, and flexible" (Kaslow, 2004, p. 775). Competencies correlate with one's performance and therefore can be formatively and summatively evaluated as well as augmented through training.

Competency Guidelines Influencing School Psychology

In a recent consideration of evolving issues concerning the school psychology internship, Phelps and Swerdlik (2011) identified four documents that are particularly relevant to a discussion of competency attainment: the *Competency Benchmarks* (Fouad et al., 2009) and the *Competency Assessment Toolkit* (Kaslow et al., 2009), both derived from APA workgroups, and NASP's *Blueprint III* (Ysseldyke et al., 2006) and *Standards for Graduate Preparation of School Psychologists* (NASP, 2010c). Although the documents are briefly summarized in the sections that follow, a detailed exploration is beyond the scope of the chapter. Readers are referred to the original resources for a more in-depth description of standards, domains, and competencies.

APA Competency Documents

The *Competency Benchmarks* (Fouad et al., 2009) describe 15 competencies (7 foundational and 8 functional) intended to be relevant to all psychology disciplines. Each competency is further divided into essential components, and behavioral anchors are provided across three developmental levels (readiness for practicum, internship, and entry-level practice). The related *Competency Assessment Toolkit* (Kaslow et al., 2009) identifies 15 assessment measures (both formative and summative) that can be used by multiple informants to evaluate competence, including readiness for practicum, internship, and professional practice. The measures identified in the *Toolkit* are listed and briefly described in Table 7.1, and can be seen as consistent with assessment processes discussed at various other junctures in this book. The assessment approaches are described and scrutinized in greater detail in the original *Toolkit* including psychometrics as well as steps for implementation, strengths, and limitations. Although the *Toolkit* has been criticized for potentially presenting an oversimplified view of assessment (Daly et al., 2011), supervisors and interns may find one or more of these approaches useful for evaluation.

NASP Documents

Both *Blueprint III* (Ysseldyke et al., 2006) and the *Standards for Graduate Preparation of School Psychologists* (NASP, 2010c) have been referenced and described throughout the book thus far. The NASP documents are similar to the *Competency Benchmarks* in several ways, including the delineation of foundational and functional competencies, and taking into account developmental levels. Although *Blueprint III* is developmentally oriented, specific benchmarks for the developmental levels of novice, competent, and expert are not provided. However, *Blueprint III* does make explicit that novice levels of competence should be expected for trainees following the completion of coursework (pre-internship), competence to enter professional practice expected by the end of the internship year, and expertise after practicing in the field for several years, and perhaps achieved in only in a few domains (Ysseldyke et al., 2006).

Table 7.1 *Assessment Tools that May Help Evaluate Interns' Competency Development*

Tool	Brief summary
360-degree evaluations	Multiple raters evaluate the intern across foundational and functional competency domains. Raters may include supervisors, peers, colleagues, supervisees, and the intern. Ratings are summed, feedback is provided to the intern, and an action plan for improvement is developed.
Annual/rotation performance reviews	Faculty, field supervisors, and possibly peers provide an integrated, summative evaluation to the intern regarding foundational and functional competency domains. Multiple sources of data are used for review, integrated, and assessed with regard to developmental level (e.g., readiness to enter professional practice).
Case presentation reviews	The intern discusses a case s/he is working on in a predetermined format. Presentations may include client and/or system characteristics, assessment methods, intervention design and implementation, progress monitoring, and outcomes. Presentations are followed by interactive discussion by the intern and evaluators.
Client process and outcome data	Client outcomes are evaluated using any of a number of measures (e.g., working alliance, symptom checklists, rating scales, diagnostic interviews). Intern and evaluator(s) determine measures, explain purpose to clients, and gather data. Data are analyzed and used to enhance quality of services delivered to clients.
Competency evaluation rating forms	The intern is rated by supervisors on behavioral indicators for selected foundational and functional competency domains in order to indicate attainment. The intern and supervisors discuss evaluation results and pinpoint areas of need.
Consumer surveys	Surveys are completed by clients regarding satisfaction with services received and the intern's competency results are summed, and shared with the intern by supervisors.
Live or recorded performance ratings	Evaluator(s) observe the intern in person or via a recording, and rate the intern's performance in relevant competency areas. The observation format is determined in advance, and both the intern and client(s) consent to the observation.
*Objective structured clinical examinations *and* standardized client interviews	Specially trained actors play the role of clients with particular psychological symptoms. The intern interacts with the actors, and completes notes, or prepares other written material regarding the interaction with the "client". Performance may be evaluated by the "client", the assessor, and the intern.
Portfolios	A collection of products are gathered by the intern providing evidence of competency attainment. The portfolio format (e.g., electronic or hard copy) is determined in advance as are elements to be included, and the intern is evaluated based on his or her work.
Record reviews	Client records (e.g., assessment reports, case files, counseling notes) developed by the intern are reviewed by the assessor to determine the presence of notes, as well as quality and accuracy. A standardized rating system/protocol can be developed for record review.
Self-assessment	The intern evaluates his or her own strengths and areas of need (e.g., limits of expertise) across foundational and functional domains of competence. The intern should be aware of the rationale for self-assessment, methods for self-assessment, and competencies to be evaluated, and should reflect on the self-assessment with field and/or university supervisor(s).
Simulation/role plays	A situation resembling actual practice (including competencies) is constructed – either in vivo or computer based – and the intern's practice in the simulation observed and evaluated. Immediate feedback may be provided to the intern.
Structured oral examinations	The intern is asked a series of questions orally in a systematic manner, and is expected to respond orally. Responses are evaluated using predetermined criteria to assess foundational and functional competencies.
Written examinations	The intern completes a paper- or computer-based examination which may include questions of varying types (e.g., multiple choice, essay, problem-solving vignettes or scenarios). Results may provide data regarding the intern's knowledge in a number of foundational and functional competency areas.

* Indicates categories were combined given their similarity; the reader is referred to Kaslow et al. (2009) for further distinction.

Note: Adapted from "Competency Assessment Toolkit for Professional Psychology," by N. J. Kaslow, C. L. Grus, L. Campbell, N. A. Fouad, R. L. Hatcher, and E. R. Rodolfa, 2009, *Training and Education in Professional Psychology*, 3, pp. S27–S45.

With regard to development of competence, NASP's (2010c) *Standards for Graduate Preparation of School Psychologists* states that training programs should ensure "candidates demonstrate basic professional competencies, including both *knowledge* and *skills*, in the 10 domains of school psychology as a result of their graduate preparation" (p. 4). Further, it is explicitly stated that interns should provide "services that result in direct, measurable, and positive impact on children, families, school, and/or other consumers" (p. 8). Taking the *Blueprint III* and the *Standards for Graduate Preparation* documents together, by the end of the internship year, school psychologists should (a) have some exposure to each NASP domain area, including the development of basic competencies (i.e., breadth), (b) pursue *at least* one area that is more well developed than others (i.e., depth), and (c) directly contribute to service delivery resulting in positive outcomes for clients.

Specialist Versus Doctoral-Level Competencies

School psychology, unlike other subspecialties in psychology, produces graduates at both the specialist and doctoral levels. Although NASP differentiates between specialist and doctoral-level internship hours requirements (i.e., 1,200 hours for specialist-level interns and 1,500 hours for doctoral level), differences between competencies at these two levels are not explicitly stated. Since the APA competency documents are primarily intended for doctoral-level trainees (as opposed to non-doctoral), a potential challenge in alignment with NASP competencies arises (Daly et al., 2011). Perhaps one way doctoral-level competencies can be distinguished from specialist-level competencies is based on skill depth or specialization (Phelps & Swerdlik, 2011), a topic that is revisited in more detail later in this chapter.

Application of Competencies During the School Psychology Internship

The four documents may be used by university educators, field supervisors, and interns for several purposes including (a) assessing readiness to begin the internship; (b) goal-setting; (c) identifying, preventing, and responding to problematic professional behaviors; (d) designing internship training experiences; and (e) assessing a graduating intern's readiness to enter the field (Phelps & Swerdlik, 2011). The example of school psychology intern Raven helps highlight the use of competency documents to inform what happens during the school psychology internship. Given the book's focus on *school psychology* interns, competencies are primarily considered with the frame of the two NASP documents.

Why Breadth is Important

As introduced in Chapter 2, there is an expectation in school psychology training that interns should be exposed to a variety of services so that they can effectively practice across domain areas once they enter the field (Harvey & Struzziero, 2008). Participating in a breadth of experiences is important, given school psychologists' increasingly versatile role, and the quick turnaround from trainee to practitioner (e.g., at the specialist-level, it is typically two years of coursework plus a nine-month internship). Gaining exposure to a variety of roles may increase an individual's ability and desire to practice in a broader way when entering the field. Breadth should be sought in the context of internship goals, and it should be recognized by interns and supervisors that it is not possible for an intern to engage in *every* activity a school psychologist may encounter in his or her work.

Linking Breadth and Competence

Consistent with the idea that interns should gain exposure to activities across the 10 domains identified in the NASP Standards, interns should be involved in a great number and variety of activities during the year. Interns and supervisors are encouraged to move beyond listing activities to be completed (e.g., "You need to do a Functional Behavior Assessment [FBA] before the year is over") to consider the meaning behind them (e.g., "Would an FBA be appropriate in this case? How do we know? How does

VIGNETTE 7.1 **RAVEN'S INTEGRATED INTERNSHIP ACTIVITIES**

A specialist-level intern named Raven completed her internship at a small suburban school district, including spending time at the elementary and middle school levels. Four of the more involved activities Raven participated in during the year are described in detail in Table 7.2, along with their alignment with domain areas from the NASP (2010c) *Standards for Graduate Preparation of School Psychologists.* Even from this small sample out of all activities Raven completed during the year, it is apparent that she worked towards attainment of internship breadth. Whether or not Raven achieved depth is not readily apparent from Table 7.2. Each highlighted activity supports Raven's growth in a manner that integrates several different NASP (2010c) domains, or areas of competence. None of the four activities integrates all 10 domains, but each activity spans several. It is also possible to parse out specific competencies that fall under each NASP domain area. Interested readers are referred to the NASP (2010a) *Model for Comprehensive and Integrated School Psychological Services* which offers examples of professional practice activities representative of some professional competencies for school psychologists, and Harrison and Prus (2008) who aligned an earlier version of NASP's (2000a, 2000b) domains with sample competencies.

Table 7.2 *Integration and Breadth During Raven's Internship*

Detailed description of activity	NASP domains
Raven and her field supervisor consulted together with the assistant principal at her middle school around a school-wide cyberbullying concern. Together they engaged in an ongoing problem-solving process that included: • clearly defining what was meant by cyberbullying; • conducting a needs assessment regarding students', teachers', and parents' perceptions of the problem and its prevalence; • analyzing the data; • making relevant changes to school policies including clarifying the protocol for reporting cyberbullying and intervening; • educating school staff, parents, and students about cyberbullying and its consequences; • evaluating changes in perceptions and prevalence over the year.	• Data-based Decision Making and Accountability • Consultation and Collaboration • Interventions and Mental Health Services to Develop Social and Life Skills • School-wide Practices to Promote Learning • Preventive and Responsive Services • Family–School Collaboration • Research and Program Evaluation
Raven's supervisor asked her to take the lead (with ongoing supervision) on a case regarding a kindergarten student, Maria, who had not spoken for the first two days of school. Raven consulted with Maria's teacher, Mrs. Livingston, who reported that although Maria did not talk verbally, she communicated non-verbally by pointing and nodding or shaking her head. Raven and the teacher contacted Maria's parents, and learned that Maria spoke primarily in Spanish at home. Raven conducted a literature review to learn more about selective mutism, and the potential intersection with English Language Learning (ELL). She learned that ELL students may go through a "silent period" where they focus on listening strategies to facilitate comprehension (Elizalde-Utnick, 2007). In addition to learning English, Mrs. Livingston and Raven noticed that Maria often appeared terrified during opportunities for verbal communication. Raven, her supervisor, and Mrs. Livingston consulted with the English as a Second Language teacher, and also planned a behavioral intervention that included contingency-based positive reinforcement to (a) decrease Maria's anxiety about speaking,	• Data-based Decision Making and Accountability • Consultation and Collaboration • Interventions and Mental Health Services to Develop Social and Life Skills • Family–School Collaboration Services • Diversity in Development and Learning • Research and Program Evaluation

Detailed description of activity	NASP domains

and (b) increase Maria's non-verbal and verbal communication (in Spanish and English). Maria made significant progress on behavioral goals, monitored together by Raven and Mrs. Livingston.

At her middle school, Raven worked with a veteran school counselor, Amy, to design and facilitate a grief and loss counseling group for seventh graders who had recently experienced the loss of a loved one (e.g., a parent, sibling, or grandparent). First, they screened seven participants they thought would be a good fit for the group, and selected six (one student was referred for individual counseling services outside of the school setting). Next, Raven and Amy collaboratively developed an informed consent letter that was sent home to parents including information about the purpose of the group, the facilitators, and the meeting schedule. They developed pre- and post-assessment measures to be completed by Raven and Amy, the group participants, and caregivers. The assessments measured students' development of coping skills at school and home, as well as progress towards individual goals set by each group member. Since they did not have an evidence-based curriculum readily available, Raven and Amy consulted with a local community counseling resource center regarding potential activities to implement, and Raven also conducted additional background research.

- Data-based Decision Making and Accountability
- Consultation and Collaboration
- Interventions and Mental Health Services to Develop Social and Life Skills
- Preventive and Responsive Services
- Family–School Collaboration
- Research and Program Evaluation
- Legal, Ethical, and Professional Practice

Raven and her supervisor participated in grade-level problem-solving team meetings at the elementary school. A third-grade teacher, Mr. Douglas, expressed concerns about four students in his class that were struggling readers. Two of the students were ELLs. Raven volunteered to follow up with Mr. Douglas through a formal consultation process. After contracting to work together, they decided that Raven would observe the class during reading. Raven noticed that Mr. Douglas rapidly introduced the text, made few connections to students' prior knowledge, and did not introduce any vocabulary words. He had the students briefly read independently, and rapidly asked comprehension questions using the Socratic method. Several of the students, including the four of concern, were visibly terrified to be called on. Mr. Douglas asked for Raven's honest feedback, and she shared her observations in a constructive and non-evaluative manner. They collaboratively developed alternative strategies for reading instruction including accessing students' prior knowledge, identifying and pre-teaching challenging vocabulary, and having students demonstrate comprehension in a variety of ways. By collecting data on reading comprehension, Raven and Mr. Douglas noticed significant reading progress for three of the four students (including both ELLs) in a short period of time, as well as several other students in the class. The student who did not make progress received a tier-three intervention, and eventually was determined eligible for special education services; Raven contributed to the special education evaluation process.

- Data-based Decision Making and Accountability
- Consultation and Collaboration
- Interventions and Instructional Support to Develop Academic Skills
- School-wide Practices to Promote Learning
- Diversity in Development and Learning

the FBA link to a pragmatic Behavioral Intervention Plan?"). In short, completing a breadth of activities in a rote fashion does not necessarily link to competence. As discussed by Daly et al. (2011), university educators must move from primarily identifying or delineating competencies towards putting them into use in ways that improve graduate preparation and eventual school psychology practice. Developing competence involves increasing critical thinking skills in action, and flexibly adapting skills for particular situations (Kaslow, 2004). An individual who is trained to think through *why* and *how* in addition to *what* may develop a more nuanced and less prescriptive understanding of school psychology practice.

Who Knows What Next Year Will Bring?

Gaining a breadth of experiences during the internship is also important because it is unclear where the intern will be practicing next year. Exposure to an array of school psychologist roles and functions as well as a diversity of clients (e.g., differing ages, cultures, disabilities, and economic backgrounds to name a few) during the internship expands the number of positions the intern may be qualified for when entering the field. For instance, an intern who has never worked with students with severe and profound disabilities may not be considered for a position where this is an aspect of the school psychologist's role. If an individual *is* hired to work in a context or with a population they have not experienced before it can be daunting (and potentially unethical, if practicing beyond boundaries of competence), especially if limited or no clinical supervision supports are in place. Even minimal exposure to some activities during the internship may increase an individual's preparedness to enter his or her first year of professional practice.

Why Depth is Important

As trainees progress in their level of knowledge and applied skills through the training sequence, there may be particular areas that are focused on to a greater extent than others. Like breadth, depth should be explicitly linked to the intern's goals for the internship year. In addition to the intern's interests and goals, depth may also stem from (a) opportunities available at the internship site (e.g., an intern who spends a significant portion of time at a therapeutic day school may develop depth in relevant NASP domains and competencies); (b) supervisors' approaches to practice (e.g., a supervisor spends a good deal of time doing group counseling and the intern is involved in planning, implementing, and evaluating group counseling throughout the year); and (c) the foci of the school psychology training program (e.g., a particular program emphasizes coursework and applied experiences in school neuropsychology). Trainees do not always know what area(s) of depth they are interested in pursuing when entering a training program. However, by the time they are applying for internships, trainees should be able to seek a match between their own developing interests and what is offered by the internship site and supervisors.

Linking Depth and Competence

Just like breadth, depth inherently links to competence. Competence develops over time, as does expertise, which may only be achieved in a few domains over the course of a school psychologist's career (Ysseldyke et al., 2006). To achieve competence and eventually expertise in a particular domain requires more intensive, supervised training and practice in that area. It is helpful for the intern and supervisors to discuss and prioritize areas of depth that relate to the intern's goals and internship plan, jointly develop a plan for achieving depth from early on in the year, and establish indicators or benchmarks for what it means to be competent in a particular domain. The competency documents highlighted in this chapter provide a starting point for making such a determination.

Specialization

The concept of depth is expansive. Depth can mean gaining conceptual and applied knowledge with a specific population, in a particular domain of practice (e.g., NASP, 2010a or Fouad et al., 2009), in one or more competencies subsuming a domain (e.g., see Harrison & Prus, 2008), or an integrated combination of all of these. Depth may be considered analogous to the notion of specialization, or intensive training in a particular area of practice within school psychology.

Reynolds (2011) suggested university educators incorporate specialization into school psychology training programs given several challenges that make it "increasingly difficult to maintain professional standards and to know all that is required to practice as a school psychologist . . ." (p. 924): the explosion of knowledge in the field; the half-life of knowledge and need for continuing education; advances in scientific methods; challenges in research consumption; and increasing demands for schools as points of service delivery. Through specialization, interns begin to master one or more areas with greater intensity than others, and school psychologists can become "highly trained professional specialist[s]" rather than "jack of all trades and master of none" (Reynolds, p. 929). On the other hand, breadth and depth/specialization may be seen as complementary rather than dichotomous entities. Seeking breadth does not preclude mastering a given domain or domains. One can participate in a number and variety of experiences and simultaneously seek out one or more areas more extensively than others. Further, while some interns may wish to pursue highly specialized positions following training (particularly doctoral-level interns), many others will wish to practice in schools (or other settings) where broad competence, which develops over time, is necessary.

Depth at the Doctoral Level

In Chapter 2, it was suggested that doctoral-level interns may be in a unique position to achieve depth of training compared to non-doctoral trainees given they (a) take more coursework; (b) likely spend more time in fieldwork, including the potential to engage in a number and diversity of experiences within a specific domain; and (c) engage in research, which may connect to an area of depth. Further, the NASP (2010c) *Standards for Graduate Preparation of School Psychologists* specifies that school psychology doctoral programs should offer "greater depth in one or more school psychology competencies", and that while "doctoral programs are typically characterized by advanced competencies in research . . . the program may identify additional competencies" that are emphasized in training (p. 4). In other words, achieving depth is not only a viable option given coursework, fieldwork experiences, and research, but an expected aspect of doctoral-level school psychology training.

Two additional points about depth deserve mention. First, depth does not equate to the accrual of hours (McCutcheon, 2009), nor is achievement of depth guaranteed by receiving doctoral-level training (Miller et al., 2010). To achieve depth necessitates planning, goal setting, purposeful intervention, and supervision. Second, attaining depth is considered a best practice for trainees at both the doctoral *and* non-doctoral levels (Prus, 2009); specialist-level interns are expected to achieve depth too. The attainment of depth at the non-doctoral level may look somewhat different than at the doctoral-level (e.g., there may not be the same expectation or opportunity for research); however, specialist-level interns should pursue and achieve depth in at least one area by the internship's conclusion.

Depth and the Hedgehog Concept

In his book *Good to Great*, author Jim Collins (2001) describes the *Hedgehog Concept*, an idea derived from an ancient Greek parable ("The fox knows many things, but the hedgehog knows one big thing"), which was later developed into a well-known essay by Isaiah Berlin. Foxes are quick, clever, and crafty and are seemingly at an advantage in overtaking the ostensibly simple hedgehog. However, the hedgehog does one thing really well – he rolls into a ball with spikes protruding – a method that is consistently successful in diverting even the swiftest of foxes. Collins proposed that "great" businesses were distinguished from "good" businesses based on having a unified and clear vision, a hedgehog of what they can be best at and can produce long-term success. Three considerations inform the hedgehog: what you can be the best in the world at; what you are deeply passionate about; and what drives your economic engine. The overlap between these three components defines the ideal point of functioning for a business or an individual. Although Collins's book was originally intended for the field of business, I believe the Hedgehog Concept can also be applied to school psychology interns and the notion of seeking and achieving depth. The Hedgehog Concept as it applies to school psychology interns is illustrated in Figure 7.1, and an example of intern Ellie's personal hedgehog is detailed in Figure 7.2.

What Can the Intern Be Best In the World at?

A first consideration in defining an intern's hedgehog is to determine something that he or she might be the best in the world at. Being competent at something is *not* the same thing as potentially being the best in the world in that area. For instance, a doctoral-level intern named Ellie was competent at statistics. She successfully completed three statistics courses in graduate school, and was able to effectively consume, conduct, and distribute quantitative research. Nevertheless, she readily acknowledged that she was not born to be a statistician. Statistics was not part of her hedgehog. In contrast, during her school psychology training Ellie became interested in supervision of psychological services. As an

Figure 7.1 *The Hedgehog Concept applied to school psychology interns*

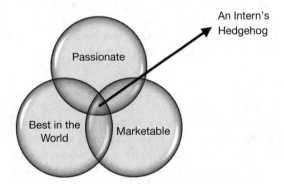

As an advanced doctoral student Ellie realized that she loved supervising first- and second-year practicum students. During her internship her enthusiasm peaked when working with a district-level school psychologist. She could not wait to get to work each morning. Ellie determines that she will pursue systems-level activities in the future.

Ellie's Hedgehog

Ellie excels at providing supervision and understanding systems-level processes. She often thinks "this is what I was born to do!" and seeks out more opportunities in these areas during her internship.

In addition to general competencies, by gaining a depth of conceptual and applied knowledge in supervision, systems-level change, and professional development during training, Ellie has increased her marketability for jobs. In the future, she will likely pursue a position at a systems-level (e.g., the head of psychological services unit).

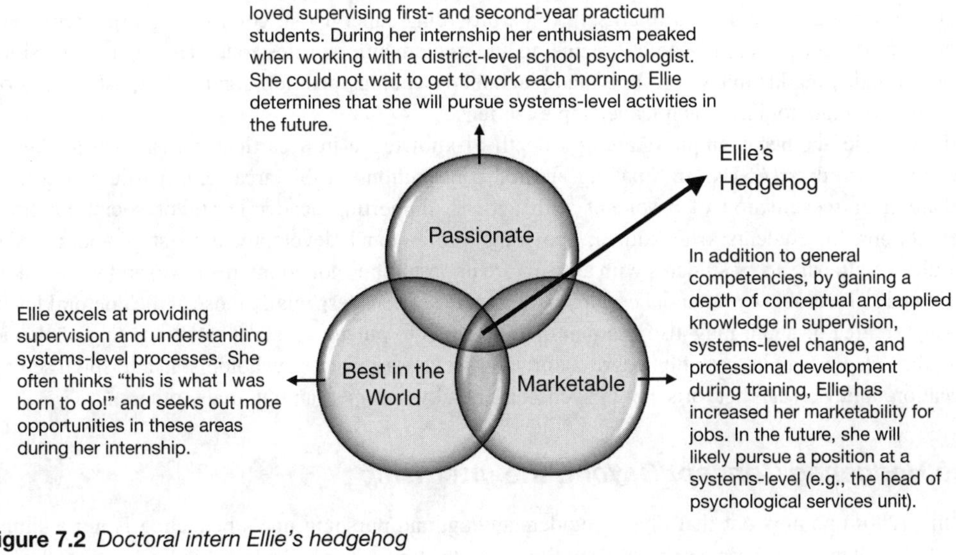

Figure 7.2 *Doctoral intern Ellie's hedgehog*

advanced graduate student she supervised a few first- and second-year students in her program during their practica, and received metasupervision from a course instructor. Ellie also completed a research project investigating supervision practices at her internship school district, and presented at a state conference. Ellie would likely acknowledge that although she has a way to go before she is the "best supervisor in the world", her supervision knowledge and skills are a personal strength, and will continue to develop over time with training and practice.

What is the Intern Deeply Passionate about?

A second consideration is what ignites the intern's passion. When someone is passionate about something, they wake up in the morning and cannot wait to take on that particular task. Passion may arise for numerous reasons such as believing one's work makes a positive difference, and feeling work tasks and expectations are optimally matched with of one's skills (e.g., see Csikszentmihalyi, 1990). Feeling passionate about one's work may be considered antithetical to the experience of burnout as described in Chapter 8. Passion is discovered rather than motivated or manufactured. Supervisors cannot make interns feel passionate about a particular area. However, supervisors can help the intern to discover what it is about the job that they absolutely love to do. To extend the example of Ellie, one rotation during her internship was completed under the supervision of a school psychology supervisor who worked as a director of special education services. The supervisor's role had a systems-level focus including coordinating professional development for school psychologists and special education staff, providing metasupervision, and introducing systems-level change. Ellie was sparked by observing her supervisor, and by working together with the supervisor on various systems-level projects. She realized that she eventually wanted to pursue work at an administrative level.

What Will Make the Intern Marketable?

The final third of the hedgehog was originally conceptualized by Collins (2001) as products or services that can generate significant financial success for an organization. Obviously the "economic engine" (Collins, p. 95) element of the hedgehog does not directly apply to the internship in the same manner conceptualized for business. An intern's goal is likely not to make a large financial profit during the internship year, and if it is, there is a good chance that he or she will be disappointed. However, interns do want to end the year with skills that make them desirable candidates for future employment. Although breadth is one piece of marketability (i.e., I have gotten a great deal of experiences and would be a good fit for many different positions), gaining depth in a particular area helps an intern stick out from the pack. To continue to build on the example of Ellie, the leadership skills she developed during her school psychology training and internship (e.g., providing supervision, contributing to systems-level change efforts, conducting research, organizing and implementing professional development sessions) made her highly marketable when applying for school psychology positions, and distinguished her from her peers who did not have such leadership experiences.

To provide another example, gaining a depth of knowledge in a particular area such as Autism Spectrum Disorders (ASDs) and making applied contributions in this area (e.g., participating in an evaluation or reevaluation of a student with autism; supporting academic and/or social-emotional interventions for students with autism; providing professional development to staff about ASDs; consulting with parents of students with autism) are opportunities not all interns have, and would likely be viewed as favorable by potential employers. For some interns (especially those at the doctoral level), seeking an area of depth may also sharpen qualifications to pursue specialty positions (e.g., behavior specialist, response to intervention coordinator, assessment associate, psychologist in a hospital setting, education policy researcher, or school psychology faculty member, among many others).

The Hedgehog Concept Beyond the Internship

Collins (2001) pointed out that finding, understanding, and pursuing one's hedgehog is not a simple task. In fact, it took businesses an average of four years to clarify their hedgehog. Finding one's hedgehog is a process that is ongoing for students throughout their school psychology training and beyond. The internship provides a unique opportunity for interns to focus in on their hedgehog given that they are experiencing the day-to-day life of a school psychologist for the first time and are ideally devoting at least some time to discussing professional interests and goals in supervision. The internship is a time for both personal and professional development. Consistent with the notion that school psychologists are lifelong learners (Armistead, 2008), the hedgehog continues to evolve following internship completion. For example, it seems like a potentially excellent fit for Ellie to pursue work as a coordinator of school psychology services after practicing as a school psychologist for a few years. School psychologists continue to develop pockets of expertise over time (Ysseldyke et al., 2006), a process that can be informed by what they can be best in the world at, what they are passionate about, and what continues to make them professionally relevant and marketable.

Summary

By the end of the internship year it is expected that school psychology interns will achieve both breadth and depth of experiences (Prus, 2009), and entry-level competencies across all NASP (2010c) domains. Competence refers to the intern's ability to understand and complete tasks as would be expected at a particular developmental benchmark (e.g., beginning the first year of professional practice). Competence includes critical thinking, problem solving, and flexible decision making. Competencies are the atoms of competence that can be developed and evaluated. Four documents assist interns and supervisors to incorporate considerations of competence during the internship: APA's *Competency Benchmarks* (Fouad et al., 2009) and *Competency Assessment Toolkit* (Kaslow et al., 2009), and NASP's *Blueprint III* (Ysseldyke et al., 2006) and *Standards for Graduate Preparation of School Psychologists* (NASP, 2010c). These documents describe foundational and functional competencies, and are useful in supporting competency planning and assessment. Interns and supervisors are encouraged to treat competency attainment as an integrated and meaningful process rather than a rote list of technical skills and activities to be completed during the internship year.

Gaining experiential breadth during the internship is important because of the increasingly broad expectations for the school psychologist's role, the brevity of school psychology training, and not knowing where the intern will be working next year. Like breadth, depth of experience can increase an intern's marketability. Developing a specialized skill or set of skills may differentiate the intern from other candidates, or increase preparedness for specialized positions. Although doctoral students may more easily achieve depth (i.e., they spend more time in coursework and fieldwork, they conduct research, and doctoral programs may offer specialized foci), non-doctoral interns are also expected to seek and achieve depth by the internship's end. Depth can be thought of using the Hedgehog Concept: the ideal alignment of something the intern can be the best in the world at one day, is passionate about doing, and will make him or her professionally marketable. The Hedgehog Concept may be considered applicable to school psychologists throughout their careers.

Critical Thinking Questions and Activities

The following are critical thinking questions for interns, site supervisors, and university supervisors to ponder regarding breadth, depth, and competence.

For Interns:

- What does it mean to be a competent intern? A competent entry-level school psychologist?
- How does internship depth link to prospective job opportunities?
- What is your hedgehog? How do you suppose your hedgehog will evolve during your career?

For Field Supervisors:

■ Looking at the overview of assessment approaches from the *Competency Toolkit* (Kaslow et al., 2009), what new approaches may be beneficial to incorporate into internship evaluation processes?

■ In what ways can you encourage interns to think about *how* and *why* instead of *what*?

■ Have an explicit conversation with your intern about his or her hedgehog. How can you support the intern to become clearer about his or her hedgehog?

For University Supervisors:

■ How is competence assessed at different developmental benchmarks in your training program (e.g., readiness to enter practicum; readiness to begin internship; readiness to enter practice)?

■ What areas of depth, if any, are foci in your school psychology training program? Does it matter if areas of depth are implicitly or explicitly identified?

■ Realizing that accrual of hours may not link to competence, how can the requirement for interns to document hours be made into a meaningful process?

Chapter 8

Survival

It is hard to imagine a helping professional who is not in some way emotionally affected by his or her work. Reactions may range from positive (e.g., pride about helping a client) to negative (e.g., distress). On the negative end of the continuum, work-related stressors have the potential to adversely affect one's ability to deliver services to clients (i.e., PPC) (Barnett, 2008; Elman & Forrest, 2007; Smith & Moss, 2009). For interns, the combination of learning a new role, applying newly learned skills, and having a great number of responsibilities may make the internship an "emotionally hazardous" or highly stressful experience (Solway, 1985, p. 50). Interns who are able to successfully "survive" and thrive during the internship apply effective strategies to cope with stressors, and also receive support from supervisors, peers, and others.

The purposes of this chapter are (a) to illuminate specific stressors faced by school psychology interns, and (b) to explore potential coping mechanisms, including self-care strategies as well as a variety of supports from supervisors, peers, and loved ones. The chapter begins with general definitions of stress, distress, burnout, and PPC, as well as unique considerations about stress for school psychology interns. Strategies are presented in order to empower interns, supervisors, peers, and loved ones with concrete skills for stress prevention and management. The chapter concludes with critical thinking questions and activities for interns and supervisors.

Stress, Distress, Burnout, and PPC

In literature investigating the impact of stress on psychologists' personal and professional functioning, the terms *stress*, *distress*, *burnout*, and *impairment* are often interchanged (Smith & Moss, 2009). What is more, for a number of reasons, the traditional term "impairment" has been replaced in the professional psychology literature by the term PPC (see Elman & Forrest, 2007; Kaslow et al., 2007). Although these concepts are interrelated, a subtle difference between them is the potential severity with which they may impact one's ability to deliver psychological services, with stress being the least severe and PPC the most. *Stress* is a term that is difficult to define with precision. In fact, according to the American Institute of Stress's (2011) website, stress "is such a highly subjective phenomenon that it defies definition". For instance, stress experienced by one psychologist as harmful (e.g., leading to PPC) may be a helpful motivator to another psychologist, or perhaps not experienced as stress at all by a third. Broadly speaking, stress can be considered "a biological and psychological response to the demands made upon individuals by their environment, perceptions, and relationships" (Hess & Copeland, 2006, p. 255). Stress is an experience that likely occurs for all school psychology interns at some point during the internship year. However, as is evident in the definition provided, the impact of stress differs for each intern and internship context.

Distress is an experience of intense stress that is not easily relieved, and that moderately affects one's well-being including personal or professional functioning (Munsey, 2006). When distress occurs over time and is not adequately addressed it may result in *burnout*, defined as a prolonged response to work-related stress (i.e., a lack of fit between person and job) that includes feelings of exhaustion, cynicism, and inefficacy (Maslach, 2003). Finally, *PPC* is defined broadly as when a psychologist's "performance or behavior does not meet professional and ethical standards" (Jacobs et al., 2011, p. 177).

The experience of stress, distress, burnout, and PPC for a school psychology intern named Lena is illustrated in Figure 8.1. It should be noted that although the terms are visually divided by levels of severity, precisely where each phenomenon ends and the other begins is not rigidly defined (APA, 2006; Barnett, 2008; Smith & Moss, 2009). The diagram is intended to convey the slippery slope by which an intern's normal experience of stress may rapidly progress to a point of PPC that may negatively impact clients.

PPC are Ethically Problematic

As explained by Barnett (2008), "If left unchecked, distress may grow and have an increasingly negative impact on the psychologists experiencing it, and as a result, on those they serve" (p. 858). Working professionally without attending to PPC violates the overarching aspirational principles that undergird APA's (2010) and NASP's (2010b) codes of ethics. APA's (2010) *Ethical Principles of Psychologists and Code of Conduct* calls for psychologists to be self-aware of stress, engage in self-care behaviors, and use appropriate strategies to maintain clinical competence. Principle A of APA's (2010) Code, Beneficence and Nonmaleficence, explicitly calls for psychologists to "strive to be aware of the possible effect of their own physical and mental health on their ability to help those with whom they work".

Beyond guiding principles, specific and enforceable ethical standards from APA (2010) directly relate to PPC. For example, Standard 2.06, Personal Problems and Conflicts, states:

(a) Psychologists refrain from initiating an activity when they know or should know that there is a substantial likelihood that their professional problems will prevent them from performing their work-related activities in a competent manner.

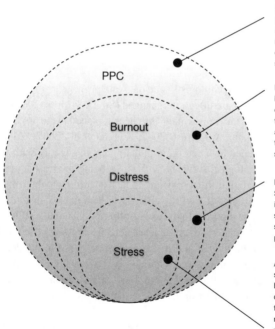

The day before an IEP meeting, Lena realized she had not completed the write-up of a psychological report that was due. She hastily put together the evaluation that evening. The morning before the meeting, Lena's supervisor noticed several errors in the report, including use of another student's name and incorrect test score reports.

Lena dragged herself out of bed each day to head to her internship. She felt cynical about her choice to become a school psychologist, and that her work was not making a difference to anyone. Lena emotionally distanced herself from the students and staff at her school as well as her supervisor.

Lena's feelings of stress continued to escalate. She missed several days of her internship due to illness as well as a few university internship seminar meetings. Lena inadvertently neglected some internship responsibilities such as returning phone calls and attending meetings.

At the beginning of the year, intern Lena was surprised by the amount of work required during her internship. She experienced difficulty completing work in a timely manner. Lena began to stay at work late and to neglect some responsibilities at home. Even though her partner was very supportive, Lena felt awful about the lack of time she had to spend at home with her three young children.

Figure 8.1 *Slippery slope to PPC during the school psychology internship*

(b) When psychologists become aware of personal problems that may interfere with their performing work-related duties adequately, they take appropriate measures, such as obtaining professional consultation or assistance, and determine whether they should limit, suspend, or terminate their work-related duties.

In short, psychologists should not engage in work activities if their performance is impacted by PPC, and if they are already engaged in professional activities when they begin to exhibit PPC, they should seek assistance or perhaps terminate their work (of course, with the client referred to another qualified professional).

Related to this, Standard 3.04, Avoiding Harm, states: "Psychologists take reasonable steps to avoid harming their clients/patients, students, supervisees, research participants, organizational clients, and others with whom they work, and to minimize harm where it is foreseeable and unavoidable." Clearly, before stress escalates, it is critical to take action that prevents harm to others. Finally, Standard 2.03, Maintaining Competence, states that "Psychologists undertake ongoing efforts to develop and maintain their competence". Maintaining competent practice includes engaging in self-care and seeking support from supervisors and peers, and therefore such actions may be considered ethical imperatives – both for practicing psychologists and for the psychology trainees (e.g., interns) they supervise.

Stress and Burnout for School Psychology Practitioners and Interns

There is some research on stress and burnout specific to the field of school psychology. Huebner (1993) surveyed a national sample of NASP members looking at symptoms of burnout and the relationship between burnout and job functions. Compared to consulting psychologists' ratings of burnout in a comparable survey, school psychologists experienced higher levels of emotional exhaustion (e.g., feeling overwhelmed by job demands) and depersonalization (e.g., developing cynical, negative attitudes towards clients), and lower levels of personal accomplishment (e.g., feeling incompetent to help clients). When compared to clinical and counseling psychologists, while school psychologists experienced lower levels of depersonalization, they also experienced similar levels of emotional exhaustion and lower levels of personal accomplishment. These data suggest school psychologists may be at a greater risk for burnout than other mental health professionals (Huebner, 1993).

In exploring these issues further, Huebner, Gilligan, and Cobb (2002) conceptualized stress and burnout among school psychology practitioners and trainees using three variables: personal risk and resiliency factors, organizational context, and professional roles and functions. Risk and resiliency factors include demographic variables and personality characteristics. For instance younger, less experienced individuals are more likely to experience symptoms of burnout, as are those with particular personality factors such as introversion and disagreeableness (Huebner et al., 2002). In terms of organizational context, the following factors may relate to burnout: relationships with colleagues, the amount of risk involved in work, being able to work efficiently without barriers, time management, and recognition received for one's work. Role conflict (i.e., divergent roles with competing expectations), role ambiguity (i.e., lack of clarity regarding role expectations), and role overload (i.e., too many demands and too little time) may also influence the experience of stress and burnout. As discussed in Chapter 4, school psychology interns may be particularly vulnerable to these three factors. Finally, job roles and functions may relate to stress and burnout. Work should not be too easy (leading to boredom) or too difficult (leading to anxiety or frustration), but ideally well matched to interns' developing knowledge and skills. In sum, it is critical to assess interns' roles and functions in conjunction with personal factors as well as organizational context in order to more clearly gauge an individual's burnout risk.

Unique Stressors for School Psychology Interns

Given the unique characteristics of being an intern (see Chapter 4), it is likely that the intern role brings with it distinctive stressors. Solway (1985) defined three main categories of stressors for psychology interns: clinical; institutional; and personal. *Clinical stress* results from interns' transition from a trainee or student role to now taking on significant professional responsibilities. Examples of clinical stresses include having to prove one's skills in a new context, developing new relationships with supervisors, and learning new techniques. *Institutional stress* relates to the internship training context or environment, and includes adjusting to new colleagues, organizational goals, administrative policies and procedures, and accessing administrative resources. Finally, *personal stress* refers to factors indirectly associated with the internship, but that affect an individual intern's adjustment. Examples of personal stressors include moving to a geographically new location, developing new friendships, navigating financial matters, and balancing one's personal life with internship demands.

Preventing and Remediating Stress, Distress, Burnout, and PPC

With stress during the school psychology internship more clearly defined, the discussion now turns towards a consideration of actions that interns, supervisors, peers, and others can take to prevent and mitigate the potentially negative impact of intern stress.

Intern Self-care

Self-care behaviors are actions interns can take to establish and promote physical and emotional wellness, and to allay stress. It is of little debate that self-care behaviors are critical to professional and personal well-being. However, there is a gap between psychologists' perceptions and practices regarding self-care (APA Advisory Committee on Colleague Assistance, ACCA, 2009).

Barriers to Self-care

Most psychologists readily acknowledge the stressful nature of working in a helping profession as well as the importance of self-care behaviors, yet many continuously overextend themselves and put clients' needs above their own (ACCA, 2009). Barnett and Cooper (2009) suggested several reasons this may be the case including (a) an illusion of invulnerability (e.g., "I'm knowledgeable about mental health prevention and intervention given my training background, so I'm not at risk"); (b) an increased vulnerability to distress and PPC for those who become helping professionals; and (c) the isolating nature of psychologists' work, which results in an inability to vent, share, or debrief with others. Additionally, a common misperception by psychologists is that engaging in self-care is a selfish behavior (Barnett, 2008). Tamura, Vincent, Bridgeman, and Hanbury (2008) identified several additional barriers to engagement in self-care behaviors unique to psychology trainees. For one, many students feel they must work non-stop to get ahead in their careers. Processes such as the pressure-filled APA internship match (e.g., see Hatcher, 2011) may inadvertently encourage such perceptions. Additionally, self-care may not be promoted by training programs as important, and faculty or peers may even question the dedication of those who are not workaholics. Further, some trainees may not be aware of the importance of self-care, or how to engage in self-care behaviors.

Self-awareness

Barriers notwithstanding, the reality is that caring for oneself promotes better care for clients served. As pointed out by Barnett (2008):

> It is recommended that all psychologists see themselves as potentially at risk for distress and impairment. While you need not live in constant fear of this occurring, a state of general vigilance is recommended. Being aware of your vulnerabilities as well as the challenges and demands of your professional and personal lives will help minimize the risk of blind spots, promote prevention activities, and minimize the risk of adverse consequences occurring.

(p. 873)

Stress may have emotional, physical, and social impacts on psychologists, so ongoing monitoring in these areas is critical (Baird, 2008). A checklist of warning signs of distress, burnout, and PPC adapted from descriptions by Barnett (2008) and Baird (2008) is presented in Table 8.1. The checklist is intended to promote awareness regarding symptoms that may indicate movement beyond typical levels of stress, and to encourage a process of ongoing monitoring by both interns and supervisors. The reader should note that the list of items is intended to be representative of typical concerns rather than to be comprehensive, and that the three dimensions of concerns considered (i.e., emotional, physical, and social) are interrelated.

Self-care Behaviors

Self-care behaviors are ongoing activities that psychologists (inclusive of interns, practitioners, and faculty) engage in to prevent and mitigate stress, thereby promoting their own emotional, physical, and social wellness (Barnett, 2008). There is a burgeoning research base regarding the self-care behaviors that psychologists find most helpful. For instance, Stevanovic and Rupert (2004) surveyed a random sample of licensed psychologists in Illinois, and found the most important career-sustaining behaviors (CSBs) to be (a) spending time with partner/family; (b) maintaining a personal–professional life balance; (c) maintaining a sense of humor; (d) maintaining self-awareness; and (e) maintaining professional identity. Of note, the authors also found that psychologists with higher levels of job satisfaction seemed to value CSBs more than individuals with lower levels of job satisfaction, and that women in their study engaged in more CSBs than men; the latter finding suggests that female psychologists differ from males in how they approach work-related stress (Stevanovic & Rupert).

Turner et al. (2005) investigated self-care strategies used by psychology interns. The most frequently applied strategies were (a) active problem solving; (b) social support from family and friends; (c) exerting control over internship choices; (d) maintaining awareness of internship impact; (e) use of humor; and (f) seeking out other interns for consultation. All of these self-care strategies were rated to be at least somewhat effective. Data from both Stevanovic and Rupert (2004) and Turner et al. (2005) point to both internal (e.g., maintaining a sense of humor, maintaining self-awareness) and external (e.g., spending time with loved ones, seeking peer consultation) strategies as valuable, and demonstrate the importance of seeking a personal–professional balance.

Consistent with this research, Huebner et al. (2002) described self-care strategies for preservice-level school psychology trainees and inservice-level school psychologists including seeking peer consultation and ongoing professional development, maintaining self-awareness of stress and burnout, designing a stress management plan, participating in supervision, and expanding job functions and roles. A summary

Table 8.1 *Summary of Warning Signs of Distress, Burnout, and PPC Identified by Baird (2008) and Barnett (2008)*

Emotional symptoms	Physical symptoms	Social symptoms
• Irritable with clients • Less empathy for clients • Bored or disinterested with clients • Not listening to clients or colleagues • Enjoying work less than in the past • Frequent feelings of depression, anxiety, and/or agitation • Attempts to squeeze too much into each day • Frequent cynicism	• Exhaustion/fatigue • Disturbed sleep • Changes in eating patterns (may be related to weight gain or loss) • Frequent headaches, body tension, or pain (e.g., back, jaw, neck, shoulders, stomach) • Self-medication (e.g., alcohol, too much caffeine, over-the-counter or prescription drugs)	• Isolation from friends, family, or significant others • Irritable with friends, family, and/or significant others • Failure to take breaks or time off • Seeking emotional support or nurturance from clients • Enjoying life less than in the past • Feeling like no one understands what you are going through

Table 8.2 *Intern Self-care Strategies to Prevent and Mitigate Stress*

Clinical	Institutional	Personal
• Seek peer consultation • Seek clinical supervision • Engage in a variety of functions and roles • Be active in professional organizations • Seek professional development readings • Carefully select clinical activities based on time limitations	• Collaborate with other school personnel to try new activities • Strive for cooperation and support not competition with other interns • Determine when saying "no" to opportunities is okay • Seek administrative consultation and supervision • Schedule work breaks • Proactively seek clear expectations	• Self-evaluate current levels of stress and burnout • Develop a stress management plan • Maintain a personal and mental self-care plan • Maintain a sense of humor • Seek personal therapy, if needed • Make non-negotiable time to spend with family and friends (e.g., vacations *without* work) • Attend to physical, cognitive, emotional, and financial needs (see Table 8.3)

of various self-care strategies for interns are highlighted in Table 8.2. The strategies are aligned with the categories of stress described earlier in the chapter: clinical, institutional, and personal.

Physical, Cognitive, Emotional, and Financial Self-care

Extending on from Table 8.2, four main categories of personal self-care strategies identified by Baird (2008) – physical, cognitive, emotional, and financial – are elaborated in Table 8.3. *Physical self-care* involves actions such as monitoring and responding to stresses that manifest in the body. *Cognitive self-care* involves overcoming unrealistic beliefs or expectations about oneself (e.g., "I am not allowed to make mistakes"), clients and work (e.g., "Theo should immediately behave better as a result of our work together"), and the world (e.g., believing a "dysfunctional" school context is typical of all schools or districts). Strategies such as questioning one's own assumptions and expectations, proactively seeking supervisory support regarding cognitive perspectives, and making comparisons across a wide variety of experiences help to promote cognitive self-care. *Emotional self-care* strategies include self-checking one's own emotional state, seeking personal therapy if needed, engaging in rituals such as deep breathing between counseling sessions, meditating, or praying. Finally, *financial self-care* includes assessing one's personal values and goals, and how such values balance with monetary compensation. Ideally, intrinsic rewards received from working in a helping profession (e.g., achieving alignment between personal values and professional practices) counterbalance what may sometimes be considered poor extrinsic incentives.

Supervisor Support

In addition to interns engaging in self-care strategies, supervisors play a critical role in helping prevent and reduce intern stress. Preventively, supervisors can attempt to ensure adequate training is provided prior to and during the internship so that interns have prerequisite knowledge and skills to effectively meet expectations; being effective at one's job alleviates job stress (Huebner et al., 2002). Related to this, internship field supervisors can be part of internship interview processes to help determine whether particular candidates will be a good match with the internship site and field supervisor(s). Supervisors can also promote intern self-care through modeling self-care strategies, providing information about self-care, and accounting for organizational and professional factors that encourage or hinder self-care (Turner et al., 2005).

Table 8.3 *Summary of Intern Self-care Strategies for Physical, Cognitive, Emotional, and Financial Needs Identified by Baird (2008)*

Physical	Cognitive	Emotional	Financial
• Exercise • Eat a healthy diet • Monitor stress in the body • Get a massage	• Set realistic expectations about self, clients, work, and the world	• Monitor emotions through a self-check • Seek therapy, if needed • Cleansing rituals (e.g., deep breathing between work activities) • Meditation and prayer	• Conduct a cost–benefit analysis of work and health • Seek expert financial guidance, if needed • Ask yourself, what does it mean to have enough?

Learning by Example?

Ironically, while it may seem obvious to readers that the school psychology internship year is in some ways stressful, this is not always recognized via field and university supervisors' actions. For instance, some supervisors may encourage or reinforce interns' workaholic behaviors, or model poor self-care behaviors that are then emulated by interns (Tamura et al., 2008). One intern I recently supervised felt obligated to arrive at her school at 5:30 each morning and not leave until late in the evening because this is what she observed of her supervisor and thought was expected of her. Another intern who experienced symptoms of burnout tied to a number of accumulated stressors was told by her field supervisor: "Grin and bear it – I am getting you ready for the rigors of school psychology practice." University supervisors may also be guilty of being poor role models regarding self-care behaviors, stress management, and job enjoyment. Perhaps one result is that school psychology faculty roles are perceived by students as too demanding or not enjoyable, which in turn may contribute to the current shortage of school psychology educators (Little & Akin-Little, 2004). Given the importance of self-care behaviors throughout the professional life span, it is important for field and university supervisors to be cognizant of the type of self-care role modeling they are providing for interns.

Other Supervisor Behaviors

Many processes of supervision described throughout this book are relevant to preventing and mediating intern stress. Regarding clinical stresses, both field and university supervisors can care for interns by (a) establishing and maintaining a strong supervisory relationship, (b) engaging in open communication, (c) providing explicitly clear expectations, (d) developing and formatively discussing the intern's goals and internship plan, and (e) pushing interns to move outside of comfort zones while simultaneously providing a professional safety net. Supervisors can also help interns navigate institutional stresses such as facilitating the intern's entry into the internship (see Chapter 3), letting the intern know it is acceptable to sometimes say "no" to taking on responsibilities, and encouraging cooperation and collaboration with other professionals.

Supervision is Not Counseling

Some interns may seek supervisors' guidance regarding personal stresses. At times it is appropriate for supervisors to support intern supervisees regarding personal stress. However, there are also instances when interns' personal stress (and stress reactions) may be more appropriately addressed in personal therapy than supervision. In such instances, it is supervisors' ethical responsibility to direct interns to seek therapy (APA, 2010). As described by Corey et al. (2010):

> It is the supervisor's responsibility to help trainees identify how their personal dynamics are likely to influence their work with clients, yet it is not the proper role of supervisors to serve as personal counselors for supervisees . . . supervision can be useful in helping supervisees become aware of

personal limitations or unresolved problems that intrude into their work with clients. With this awareness, supervisees are then in a position of seeking personal therapy to work through a problem rather than using supervision as a substitute for therapy.

(p. 168)

A vignette contrasting two interns – Tisha and Brian – may provide clarification about the sometimes ambiguous boundaries between supervision and therapy.

VIGNETTE 8.1 **TISHA'S AND BRIAN'S PERSONAL STRESS**

Tisha and Brian were interns in the same school psychology training program working at different school districts in the same state. As interns began to look for jobs, the stagnant economy resulted in only a few positions being available. The 20 students in the school psychology program were applying to the same positions and feelings of competition were rampant. The monthly university seminar, which brought together all 20 interns, seemed to fan the flames of stress. For example, the university supervisor put each intern on the spot, asking them about their progress in the job hunt in front of all other students. Those interns who had secured positions felt embarrassed to share their good news, and those who did not yet have positions felt ashamed.

Tisha felt a great deal of stress, and sought out guidance from her field supervisor, Ingrid, with whom she had a strong relationship. Ingrid offered a variety of perspectives to Tisha including encouraging her to be more flexible in her job search, and reassuring her that it was acceptable to seek some distance from the competitive interactions happening between peers. Brian also had a strong dynamic with his supervisor, Maria, and sought out her guidance about how to best proceed with finding a job in such a stressful context. In broaching his concerns, Brian also mentioned other personal strains resulting from the job-search stress including not sleeping well, getting in frequent spats with his spouse, and finding himself quickly losing patience with a few high school students he was working with. Maria offered guidance similar to Ingrid, but also suggested that some of the concerns expressed by Brian may be better addressed through private counseling rather than supervision.

Peer Support

Seeking and receiving support from peers is another way for interns to effectively prevent and mediate stress. In fact, data reported by APA's ACCA (2009) from a survey of 430 psychologists suggested that the most frequent coping response to professional stress was talking to a colleague, and 91% of respondents found that strategy to be at least somewhat helpful.

There are multiple potential avenues for interns to seek out peer support. In contrast to the vignette about Tisha and Brian, a strong climate of peer support permeates many training programs. Faculty can set the tone for such a climate from students' initial entry into the school psychology program by encouraging positive collaborative interactions among trainees. When peer support is a training program norm, interns tend to help each other continue to develop clinical skills, navigate program or university requirements, and study for exams such as doctoral comprehensive examinations, and state and/or national certification. Further, in a collaborative climate, interns are more likely to discuss their personal and professional challenges with others engaged in a comparable experience. Fellow interns understand better than anyone the unique challenges faced during the school psychology internship.

Some interns may work in the same school or district as other interns from the same or different training programs. Establishing a community with fellow interns at the district can be supportive in many ways, especially in navigating institutional stresses. Interns from other programs may offer some unique perspectives on practice based on their distinct training experiences. Other individuals at the district may also provide peer support. For example, early career psychologists easily remember what it was like to be an intern, and can provide a great deal of advice and guidance during the internship. A first-year school psychologist who had graduated from my training program the previous year supported me in many ways during my internship, and I think I also supported her as she transitioned from her internship to early career. Peer support may also come from trainees from other disciplines (e.g., a school counseling intern or a student-teacher), or other staff that the intern develops a strong relationship with over the course of the year.

Support from Loved Ones

Family and friends are one of the most frequently accessed and valued sources of support for psychology interns (Turner et al., 2005). Since loved ones are likely not embedded in the school psychology internship context, they may be able to offer alternative perspectives and insights regarding the intern's experiences. Loved ones also are likely to appreciate hearing about and celebrating the intern's successes throughout the year. Other times it may be frustrating to communicate with family or friends about graduate school or the internship experience because they simply do not understand precisely what the intern is going through. It is difficult to convey the great deal of work involved in internship training, let alone to explain the emotion and stress involved in events like intervening during a crisis, or proposing and defending a dissertation. As a result, interns may feel unsupported or isolated, and communicating with loved ones may increase, rather than reduce, stress.

To maximize the value of support from loved ones, maintaining open communication and clear expectations before, during, and following the internship is critical. For example, interns should explicitly address pending realities regarding the internship schedule, workload, and financial compensation (or lack thereof). Such areas can contribute stress to personal relationships throughout the year, and discussing them and developing strategies early on is a preventive approach. In addition, Baird (2008) proposed a series of questions to help interns assess the effects of the internship on life and relationships. Following are a few examples of items adapted from Baird that interns may contemplate to continuously monitor the health of their personal relationships:

- When was the last time you did something with just yourself and your significant other?
- When was the last time you did something with just yourself and one or more good friends?
- How often in the past month have you not done something with family or friends due to a work conflict?
- Do you listen to loved ones as well as you would like?
- How does work interact with your personal life?

An intern can think about these items, as well as others, and share his or her thoughts with significant others to evaluate his or her personal–professional balance. If the internship is taking a toll on one's personal life, seeking therapy may be appropriate.

A Word from Interns and their Loved Ones

To understand more specifically what supports interns need from their loved ones, I surveyed school psychology graduate students in my training program regarding (a) what qualities and actions from loved ones (i.e., significant others, family members, close friends) were most helpful throughout their time in the school psychology program, and (b) what advice their loved ones would provide to other loved ones of school psychology graduate students. The sample of respondents was one of convenience, consisting of 12 students at various points in the training program who responded to the questions within a one-week period via an online survey. Although not analyzed in a formal manner, the responses demonstrate some common themes, which are compiled in Table 8.4, along with representative quotes.

Clearly, it can be challenging to be a loved one of a student in a school psychology program, especially during the internship year. It is my hope that the themes identified in Table 8.4 are helpful for both

Table 8.4 *Characteristics and Actions of Supportive Loved Ones*

Theme	Examples
Understanding the stressful nature of being a graduate student (including time, energy, and other commitments)	• "Flexibility and being available when I actually have time. Understanding that this is very important to me, and though it is not life or death, it's a big deal right now." • "Just being aware and understanding that my time is limited." • "[Loved ones] can be most supportive by expecting a little moodiness or social disconnect. Intermittently reaching out . . . in a caring, non-demanding manner . . . the student will be reminded of their support system yet have the option to get back in touch when they have replenished resources."*
Pragmatic support	• "As a wife and mother of two teenage boys, I most appreciate . . . when they pick up after themselves . . . and when I am given time, guilt-free, to go to the coffee shop." • "As a mother of four children, it was most helpful when my support system would help care for my children so that I can have time to do work . . . it became part [of the] routine when the children would spend time with grandparents, aunt, or dad while I was able to have that time alone." • "Financial support from my parents – welcoming me back home to live with them." • "Help with chores . . . and purchasing chocolate." • "Recording the TV shows I'm missing because I am studying or doing work."
Understanding/ appreciating the field of school psychology	• "Understand that school psychologist does not mean counselor." • "Telling me that the profession I am going into is commendable and all my efforts will be worth it."
Listening	• "Don't try to help, just listen." • "Close friends . . . have been 'sounding boards' allowing me to bounce my ideas off them." • "Reassure the student that [you] are there for support. Let the student know they can always talk to you, don't just assume they will come if they need help."* • "Letting me vent when things aren't going perfectly and listen to my successes as well."
Providing encouragement	• "My husband's continuous belief in me . . . trust that I can make it and the fact that he is there to support me ethically and financially." • "Showing encouragement that I can do this." • "[Offering] encouragement to continue even when I felt burnt out and stressed." • "Above all, hearing encouraging words such as 'you're really going to make a difference in the lives of children'." • "Taking me out to dinner to celebrate the end of the quarter/year or other accomplishments."
Maintaining a long-term focus instead of a short-term focus	• "My parents have said that all the time and hard work will all be worth it in the end when I have a successful and fulfilling career." • "I can advise my friend to make sacrifices to complete the program because in the long run the profession will provide her with many rewards."* • "Although it may . . . get overwhelming, just know that it is not long term where you may have to carry a bit more of 'the load'."

* Indicates a direct quote from a loved one (e.g., significant others, family members, or close friends). All other quotes are from school psychology graduate students at varying levels of training.

interns and loved ones. For interns, the themes may provide a way to talk with their loved ones about what supports might be most helpful during the internship year. In other words, interns can share this list with their parents, children, spouses, boyfriends, girlfriends, and close friends to discuss these themes, as well as other supports perhaps not specified on this list. For loved ones, this list provides an "insider" perspective into the world of being a graduate student or intern as well as specific examples of actions they can take to provide support for the ones they love.

Summary

All interns will likely experience stress at some point during the internship year. Ideally, interns will engage in self-care behaviors as well as receive supports from supervisors, peers, and loved ones to prevent and cope with stress. A diagram summarizing the balance of stress and support during the internship year is presented in Figure 8.2. Sufficient supports act as supportive mechanisms for interns. When sufficient supports are not in place, stress may escalate into distress (i.e., intense stress not easily relieved), burnout (i.e., prolonged response to stress including exhaustion, cynicism, and inefficacy), or PPC (i.e., professional functioning becoming ineffective). Beyond the obvious negative impact for the intern, PPC is unethical given the potentially detrimental results for clients. Personal factors, organizational factors, and professional roles and functions all contribute to school psychology interns' risk for moving beyond typical levels of stress. Types of stressors for interns include clinical (e.g., new skills, new relationships, new supervisors), institutional (e.g., new context, new colleagues, new goals), and personal (e.g., new friendships, finding a personal–professional balance, dealing with financial matters).

There are several actions interns can take to prevent and respond to stress. First of all, interns should maintain awareness of their emotional, physical, and social well-being and immediately respond to concerns that arise. In addition to self-initiated actions (e.g., exercising, healthy eating, maintaining a sense of humor, engaging in rituals), interns can proactively seek support from supervisors, peers, and loved ones. Supervisors support interns in a number of ways such as modeling healthy self-care behaviors and making internship expectations explicit and unambiguous. Peers (e.g., other school psychology interns, interns from other disciplines, early career practitioners) may provide invaluable supports to interns, with an "insider" perspective that can be otherwise difficult to find. Finally, loved ones including significant others, family members, and close friends provide support to interns during the internship. Supportive behaviors from loved ones include understanding what it means to be a school psychology intern (including time commitments), listening, providing pragmatic assistance, offering encouragement, and maintaining a long-term focus even when the short term is challenging (e.g., "All the time and hard work will be worth it in the end").

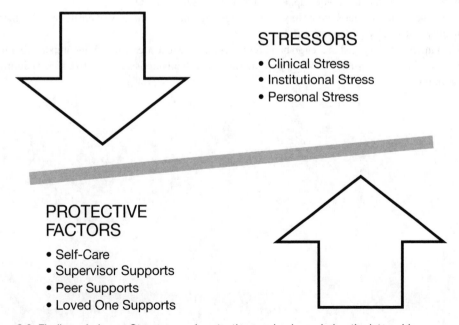

STRESSORS
- Clinical Stress
- Institutional Stress
- Personal Stress

PROTECTIVE FACTORS
- Self-Care
- Supervisor Supports
- Peer Supports
- Loved One Supports

Figure 8.2 *Finding a balance: Stressors and protective mechanisms during the internship*

Critical Thinking Questions and Activities

The following are critical thinking questions and activities for interns, site supervisors, and university supervisors to ponder regarding stress and self-care.

For Interns:

- In what ways does your work as an intern affect your emotional well-being? Physical well-being? Social relationships?
- How will you determine if your experience of stress has moved beyond what is typical (e.g., distress, burnout, or PPC)?
- Have a conversation with a loved one about the internship experience (e.g., what you do on a daily basis, what stressors you face, what is rewarding to you) and discuss what supports would be most helpful from that person during the year.
- Set up a group composed of interns from your university, the interns at your internship site, or other peers with the purpose of providing peer support during the internship year.

For Field Supervisors:

- How would your intern describe your self-care behaviors? Given the intern's perception of your self-care, how valuable do you suppose he or she views self-care to be?
- How can an intern's personal problems be addressed in supervision without a supervision session becoming a therapy session?
- How will you determine if your intern's level of stress has moved beyond what is typical (e.g., distress, burnout, or PPC)?
- What steps will you take if an intern begins to exhibit PPC?

For University Supervisors:

- How is self-care taught and/or modeled in your training program? Based on what is taught and/or modeled, how valuable do you suppose students view self-care to be?
- Assess the nature of peer support in your training program. How might you create or strengthen the quantity and quality of peer support?
- When interns are engaged in the job hunt, it may contribute to a stressful and/or competitive training program climate. How might you support interns (individually and as a collective group) during the search process?

Part Three

Moving Beyond the Internship

Chapter 9

The Job Hunt

Applications, Interviews, and Employment

The first section of this book (Chapters 1 through 3) focused on orienting interns and supervisors to the internship year, and the second section of the book (Chapters 4 through 8) covered the critical relationships that are developed during the internship. The third and final section of this book focuses on closing out the internship year and helping the intern transition into a successful first year of professional practice. Thinking about life beyond the internship is a topic that likely produces mixed emotions for interns. Feelings of accomplishment may be paired with disappointment regarding how quickly the year is ending and how much remains to be done. Anxiety about what next year will hold is hopefully accompanied by feelings of anticipation and excitement for new challenges to come.

In this chapter, the processes of searching, applying, and interviewing for jobs are demystified in order to support interns' eventual job procurement. The job process is divided by stages spanning pre-internship through the end of the internship, with each stage subsuming several actions interns can take during the job hunt. Focused attention is given to compiling, shaping, and submitting a professional application; requesting letters of recommendation; and preparing for and completing job interviews. The importance of patience and persistence are emphasized, with the ultimate payoff being the landing of a job. Actions for supervisors to take during interns' job hunt process are also included in this chapter. The chapter ends with critical thinking questions and activities for interns and supervisors.

The Job Timeline

A timeline for the job application and interview process is presented in Figure 9.1. This timeline also provides an organizational structure for the chapter, with each part of the process elaborated in detail in ensuing sections. Although the job timeline is illustrated in a simplified manner to provide an overall sense of what should be happening and when, this schedule is a general one that may differ in some ways according to individual circumstances. For instance, some interns may get offered jobs early in the spring (e.g., interns who get offers from their internship districts) while others may not secure a position until August or later. Though there may be some variance in this process, the job timeline offers guidance regarding actions interns can take before their internship even begins through its end.

Pre-preparation Stage: Pre-internship Through October

The process of securing a job can be thought of as beginning long before the intern sends out applications. The *pre-preparation* stage spans pre-internship through early fall of the internship year. The internship application, interview, and hiring process completed the year prior to the internship may be seen as a dress rehearsal for applying and interviewing for jobs. First, internship preparation offers the trainee opportunities to begin compiling and organizing a portfolio of professional materials including cover letters, a résumé and/or curriculum vitae (CV), work samples, and letters of recommendation. Such materials provide a foundation for materials used during the job application process. Second, internship interviews allow the individual to practice orally representing his or her school psychology knowledge

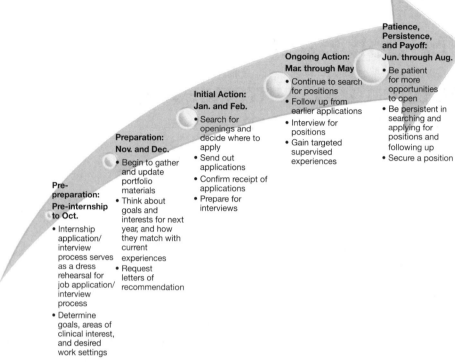

**Patience,
Persistence,
and Payoff:**

Jun. through Aug.

- Be patient for more opportunities to open
- Be persistent in searching and applying for positions and following up
- Secure a position

**Ongoing Action:
Mar. through May**

- Continue to search for positions
- Follow up from earlier applications
- Interview for positions
- Gain targeted supervised experiences

**Initial Action:
Jan. and Feb.**

- Search for openings and decide where to apply
- Send out applications
- Confirm receipt of applications
- Prepare for interviews

**Preparation:
Nov. and Dec.**

- Begin to gather and update portfolio materials
- Think about goals and interests for next year, and how they match with current experiences
- Request letters of recommendation

**Pre-preparation:
Pre-internship to Oct.**

- Internship application/ interview process serves as a dress rehearsal for job application/ interview process
- Determine goals, areas of clinical interest, and desired work settings

Figure 9.1 *The job process from start to finish*

and skills in a manner similar to that expected during job interviews. Although internship applications and interviews provide some important preparatory experiences for the eventual job hunt, there are also numerous differences between internship and job processes as is discussed later in this chapter.

During the pre-preparation stage interns also engage in internship planning, goal setting, and ongoing formative evaluation. In so doing, they are gaining skills that should begin to inform where they want to work, and how they will present themselves as job applicants. Part of the pre-preparation stage includes self-reflection regarding professional development, including specific areas of interest that may be sought out in future positions. For example, a doctoral-level intern named Cordell had strong direct service practitioner skills, but his favorite parts of his doctoral-level training inclusive of the internship were completing program evaluations, providing professional development for school staff, and working on his doctoral dissertation including collecting data at his primary internship site. Based on his experiences as well as discussions with his field and university supervisors, Cordell decided early in the fall of his internship year that he would pursue a post-doctoral research position the following year.

Granted, not all students will have determined a clear job path by the end of the pre-preparation stage. In fact, flexibility is an important characteristic for graduating interns to have throughout the job process. Nevertheless, thinking critically about one's identity as a school psychologist (including professional interests and skills) is beneficial at all stages of training, and fall of the internship year may be an important benchmark for decision making regarding forthcoming professional pursuits.

Alternatives to School-based Jobs

During the pre-preparation stage or later in the job timeline, some interns (in particular those at the doctoral level) may determine they want to apply for jobs other than school-based positions. Wasik, Song, and Knotek (2009) offer some questions graduating students can consider when contemplating career options:

- Who do I want to influence?
- What types of professional practice do I want to engage in?
- What kinds of issues affecting children and youth do I want to address?

Depending on the answers to these questions, interns may find themselves interested in practicing at the district, state, or national level; in a research position; working at a college or university; in a nonschool clinical setting; or pursuing a post-doctoral fellowship.

District-level practice may include being responsible for a unique program (e.g., director of the preschool intervention team), or having administrative responsibilities for a department or unit (e.g., director of psychology services, or director of intervention and support). Typically, district-level positions require a school psychologist with a good deal of prior experience. State or national positions may be options for some graduating interns, including positions in state departments of education or in public or private organizations focusing on education policy decision making or reform. Research positions may be a viable option for some school psychology graduates who are interested in data-based decision making, evaluation, and the application of science and the scientific method. For example, Nebbergall (2011) described her transition from school-based practice to a rewarding educational research position.

Post-doctoral or academic positions may be the right fit for some graduating interns. Post-doctoral positions provide an opportunity for doctoral interns to get another year of supervised clinical experience, which is required in most states prior to applying for licensure (see Chin, 2009 for further description of post-doctoral positions in psychology). Teaching, service, and scholarship are core components of academic positions, with emphases varying per program and institution (see Wasik et al., 2009, and Newman & the NASP Early Career Workgroup, 2010 for further description of academic positions in school psychology). Finally, nonschool clinical practice may be a desirable option for some entry-level school psychologists. Nonschool work may include community mental health clinics, hospitals, forensic psychology, or private practice. In short, although the majority of school psychology interns will go on to work in schools, some may choose rewarding alternative career paths.

Preparation Stage: November and December

As fall transitions into winter, interns move into the *preparation* stage, a time during which they update the professional materials in their portfolios, think about their current experiences and how they might be purposefully supplemented, and request letters of recommendation from supervisors and others.

The Professional Portfolio

The professional portfolio is a compilation of several formative and summative documents including the résumé and/or CV, work samples, and letters of reference (Crespi, Fischetti, & Lopez, 1998). During the preparation stage interns begin to edit, sharpen, and update already existing pre-internship materials. Interns should ask themselves: "How have I changed professionally from when I originally created these documents to this point in time?" and "How do I demonstrate my growth of skills so that it is evident to potential employers?" Such questions fit with developmental frameworks and models described at various points within this book.

One way interns can demonstrate professional growth is by highlighting in their professional materials increases in breadth and depth of their skills and experiences. Regarding breadth, an intern will want to show potential employers that during the internship he or she has gotten a range of applied experiences and worked with a variety of different students and families. As for depth, graduating interns should be able to demonstrate certain skills that they obtained more experience in than others; these may be considered areas of burgeoning proficiency or expertise.

To illustrate how professional materials may change, a few excerpted bullets from a pre-internship and pre-job CV for a trainee named Joelle are compared in Figure 9.2. Since Joelle demonstrated extensive involvement in problem solving during her internship, she was able to remove that bullet in

CV for Internship Application	Adapting the CV for a Job Application
Joelle W. Lawrence, M.Ed.	**Joelle W. Lawrence, Ed.S.**
SUPERVISED PRACTICUM	SUPERVISED INTERNSHIP
Waukegan School District 60 Fall 2010 – Summer 2011 Waukegan, IL • Participated on a school-based problem solving team • Contributed to school-wide PBIS including planning, implementation, and evaluation • Assisted supervisor in completing play-based assessments for preschool students	Waukegan School District 60 Fall 2011 – Summer 2012 Waukegan, IL • Co-facilitated the school-based problem-solving team including creating meeting agendas; collecting, organizing and presenting data; following up on case progress; and providing professional development to team members • Represented our school on the district-level Positive Behavior Intervention and Support (PBIS) team including participating in monthly meetings, and consulting with building principal regarding PBIS implementation SUPERVISED PRACTICUM Waukegan School District 60 Fall 2010 – Summer 2011 Waukegan, IL • ~~Participated on a school-based problem solving team~~ • Contributed to school-wide PBIS including planning, implementation, and evaluation • Assisted supervisor in completing play-based assessments for preschool students

Figure 9.2 *Changes in a CV from internship application to job application*

her practicum description on her job CV (crossed out on the right side of Figure 9.2). On the other hand, Joelle kept one bullet about PBIS involvement from her practicum CV to demonstrate how she increased her depth in this area during her internship (e.g., she was involved at both the building and district levels), and kept another bullet about play-based assessment because she did not have this experience during her internship year. From the brief excerpt of Joelle's CV, the reader can see that she has taken on several different experiences (breadth) and has increased her level of involvement in the same area (PBIS) from practicum to internship (depth).

Résumés and CVs

Even though they are often thought of as interchangeable, résumés and CVs are not exactly the same. The primary difference is that a résumé tends to be shorter (one or two pages) than a CV (usually more than two pages), which covers skills and experiences more expansively (Peña, n.d.). The CV, while longer than the résumé, should not be overly wordy or lengthy; redundant or irrelevant information should be avoided. Job notices will usually specify whether they want applicants to submit a résumé or a CV as part of the application.

Peña (n.d.), in collaboration with the NASP Student Development Workgroup, created a sample CV template that is featured in Appendix H. This template provides helpful examples for interns to compose or improve their CVs. Interns are also encouraged to search online for relevant examples of CVs, especially those that may match their own job aspirations. For instance, when I applied to an academic position in a school psychology program I structured my CV to mirror exemplars I found online of school psychology faculty members. Of note, I had to adapt my CV in some ways to look different from the one I included when applying for school-based positions (e.g., I put a greater emphasis on scholarship in my academic CV).

In addition to using template examples, there are several big ideas interns can keep in mind when creating or updating a résumé or CV:

- Every résumé or CV does not need to be identical. Résumés or CVs should demonstrate the unique experiences and skills of the applicant, and match with the opportunity being applied for.
- Instead of listing all experiences in a single section called "Professional Experience", particular areas can be highlighted to demonstrate the applicant's unique skills and experiences (e.g., "Teaching Experience"; "Research Experience", or "Leadership Experience").
- Aesthetics and consistency of formatting are important. Sections should be clearly divided by using borders and other formatting tools (e.g., bolding, italicizing, and strategic spacing). Formatting should be consistent throughout the résumé or CV including fonts used, heading structures, and use of space.
- The résumé or CV should not list "everything but the kitchen sink" (Plante, 1998, p. 509), only the most relevant and current experiences.
- The résumé or CV should be updated as soon as new experiences are completed because it is easy to forget to include relevant activities.
- Honesty is essential. Exaggerations or lies may be questioned during the job interview.

Interns should seek out feedback and assistance when working on their résumés or CVs. Family, peers, field supervisors, and faculty members all can provide valuable input on the résumé or CV, as well as on other job application materials. Some universities also have career or writing centers with staff that can provide support.

Work Samples

Even if they are not required as part of application materials, it may be helpful for graduating interns to include exemplar pieces of their work in their portfolio. Work samples demonstrate applied competence and professionalism in particular areas of practice. Work samples should be selected based on (a) product quality; (b) what types of work the employer may want to see (i.e., the applicant may wish to provide different work samples for different positions); and (c) what products best demonstrate the applicant's developing skills and professional identity.

A primary type of work sample often included by school psychology job applicants is psychological evaluations (Crespi et al., 1998). Although a psychological evaluation is one piece of data an applicant may include in their portfolio, consistent with the broadening roles of school psychologists, other materials are also important to include. For example, an applicant may incorporate an individual or group counseling summary; a Functional Behavior Assessment and associated Behavior Intervention Plan; a consultation case write-up and summary; curricula that were written or adapted; or slides from a professional development session presented to staff. It is critical that if work samples are included as part of a portfolio, all identifying information is removed. As with the résumé or CV, applicants will not want to include samples of *everything*; materials should be purposefully selected to (a) be representative of the candidate's interests, strengths, and skills, and (b) demonstrate the skills the hiring site is looking for in applicants.

Summaries

In addition to work samples, summaries of other relevant information may be appropriate to include in the portfolio. Such information may act as a supplement or appendix to the résumé or CV. Summaries also save the applicant valuable space on the résumé or CV, and makes it easier for the hiring committee to see a job applicant's credentials. Examples of information that may be summarized include a list of courses taken during graduate training; professional development presentations attended; evidence-based interventions implemented; tests administered; or a breakdown of internship hours by particular categories. Job applicants can easily bring summaries to a job interview and ask the committee if such materials would be helpful to submit.

Transcripts

Academic transcripts are often required as part of the job application process. Interns should order several copies of official transcripts from their undergraduate and graduate institutions and keep those materials on hand to include as part of the portfolio or job application. Following internship completion, interns will want to reorder official graduate transcripts to document their successful completion of their degree. Since the degree may not automatically post on the transcript, interns should call the university registrar to ask when is best to order copies of a finalized, official transcript.

Portfolio Formats

Traditionally, job applicants compile a folder or binder of printed materials to present to potential employers as part of the job application process. More recently, web or disc portfolio formats have become increasingly common (Hill, Kubick, & York, 2011). Job applicants who use such formats may demonstrate to prospective employers their technological competence and innovation. Web-based portfolios have the potential to reach a wide audience, may include a variety of work samples given their large capacity, and are helpful for long-distance interviews. However, they also may make personal information widely available, can be problematic for maintaining confidentiality, and the audience may be unclear or confused about what information they are accessing (Hill et al.). Disc formats (e.g., a CD or flash drive) are easily portable and left with potential employers following an interview, and also can store a great deal of information. Applicants can ask hiring sites about format preferences prior to submitting a portfolio.

Supplementary Experiences

As the intern is gathering materials, he or she should (a) continue to think about professional interests and goals, (b) identify any gaps in training that are preventing the intern from meeting those goals, and in turn (c) seek out these experiences if possible. Supervisors should also be cognizant of what activities the intern has or has not had the chance to complete during the year and, to the extent that they can, support interns to close these gaps in training. As has been mentioned previously in this book, interns cannot possibly complete every activity that is expected of school psychologists during the internship year. However, if the intern and/or supervisor realize early on in the year that the intern is missing a particular opportunity or skill, the preparation stage is an excellent time to address that concern.

Letters of Recommendation

During the preparation stage, interns should determine who they will ask for letters of recommendation and proceed with making requests. There are numerous considerations interns and supervisors should keep in mind during the letter request and writing process.

Who to Ask for Letters

First and foremost, the intern should be careful to ask for letters from individuals who have seen them work at their best, and that they are fairly certain will write them a positive letter. As expressed by Baird (2008), "just as positive letters can be the key to open doors, negative letters may well lock them shut" (p. 194). The intern should directly talk to the individual they wish to request a letter from, be clear about post-internship goals, and ask if the person feels they could write a supportive letter on their behalf. When asking for a letter, it is essential for the intern to be sensitive to the potential letter writer's reaction to the request. While enthusiasm likely signals that a positive letter should be expected, hesitancy may be a warning sign that the intern should ask someone else for a letter. Such a reaction warrants a discussion initiated by either party. Although discussing letter-writing concerns is a potentially awkward or disconcerting conversation, if approached sensitively it can (a) provide guidance on what the intern can do to improve; (b) prevent the intern from getting a neutral or negative letter and allow the intern to request a letter from an alternative individual; and (c) provide an opportunity to offer the intern alternative options regarding future goals.

It is helpful for interns to have a representative sample of letter writers such as a mix of practitioners and faculty members. Having all letters from one source (e.g., only university faculty or field-based practitioners) may raise a red flag to employers that the intern's performance was lacking in some way. There are a number of individuals who may provide letters of recommendation in addition to field or university internship supervisors and university faculty. For example, interns may request letters from co-workers they have collaborated with or who have seen them in action such as building principals, school counselors, behavior specialists, the school nurse, resource psychologists, teachers, or district-level psychologists to name a few. In addition to formal letters of recommendation, letters received by the intern during the year from students, families, or colleagues may be appropriate to include in a professional portfolio (e.g., a thank you note from a mother for the intern's effort and success in providing an academic intervention to her child). Of course, as with all materials, confidentiality should be protected.

When to Ask for Letters

Writers appreciate advance notice from those who are requesting letters of recommendation. Requesting letters at least a month in advance of when they are needed is a general rule of thumb. Since several individuals may be asking the same person for letters at the same time, even more notice may be appropriate. The month of December may be a good time to ask for letters as supervisors or other writers often have some additional time during the winter holidays. As a university supervisor who often writes letters for interns, I find it helpful to establish a deadline for when the intern needs my letter. I also request that the intern follows up with me in person or via e-mail several days before the agreed-upon deadline if they have not yet heard from me that the letter was sent out. This acts as a reminder to me and prevents the intern from feeling like a burden for proactively following up.

Other Considerations When Asking for Letters

In addition to being thoughtful about who and when to ask for letters, there are several other considerations for interns requesting letters of recommendation as pointed out by Baird (2008). First, if there is advanced preparation needed on application materials (e.g., filling out information such as addresses or phone numbers or addressing envelopes), it is helpful for the applicant to complete this work in advance. Second, if there are specific instructions (e.g., District A only wants a letter, but District B wants a letter and a specific evaluation tool completed), the intern should make what is needed explicitly clear to the writer. Third, it is helpful for interns to provide a copy of their CV or résumé, and a brief summary letter to the writer, including specific characteristics, skills, or activities they wish the writer to include or emphasize. For example, an intern named Patrice requested that I highlight her leadership in our school psychology program's student group as well as a few of the leadership experiences she took on during her internship because she was applying to a newly established charter school seeking candidates with leadership experience. Fourth, interns should keep letter writers posted on job application results. Supervisors or others spend a great deal of time writing letters on behalf of the intern because they are invested in the intern's success; it is courteous for the intern to stay in touch during the process and let the writer know what happened. Related to this, it is also a courtesy to say thank you to the writer either in person, by phone, in an e-mail, or a handwritten note once the process is complete.

Issues for Supervisors and Other Letter Writers

In theory, letters of recommendation written by supervisors are directly informed by processes of evaluation occurring throughout the internship year. In reality, letters often inflate or exaggerate the skills of applicants, and any critical commentary is usually excluded from letters (Kaslow et al., 2007). Stedman, Hatch, and Schoenfeld (2009) found that recommendation letters for pre-doctoral internship applications at medical schools and other settings were not only positively biased but, given their homogeneity, were not contributors to meaningful decision making in the internship selection process. When letter writers *do* include constructive criticism of a candidate, or even weak praise, it may put that individual at a disadvantage when compared to other candidates (Corey et al., 2010). In fact, in a recent study of criteria in psychology internship selection, Ginkel, Davis, and Michael (2010) found that negative letters of recommendation were one of the top variables used to exclude applicants from further consideration for a position.

It is therefore critical for letter writers such as field and university supervisors to be thoughtful about what they put into supervisee letters of recommendation. As stated by Corey et al. (2010), "writing objective letters of reference is an ethical obligation of the supervisor as gatekeeper for the profession" but supervisors must "be aware of the implications and consequences of what [they say] about the supervisee" (p. 233). The authors provided several helpful tips for recommendation writers, including:

- Discuss strengths and deficiencies without overstatement or understatement.
- Pay careful attention to what is written in the first and last paragraphs, as readers may focus in on these summaries.
- Ask the requester when the letter is due, and complete it in a timely manner.
- Keep a copy of the letter, and provide a letter to the supervisee when appropriate.
- Check for accuracy of spelling, grammar, names, and other parts of the letter.
- Be concise.
- Be transparent with the supervisee, if possible, regarding any deficiencies or other negative information that may be included in the letter.
- If describing deficits, do so carefully in an objective way using specific terms. Since negative comments are not common, readers will look carefully at what you wrote.
- If needed, obtain a release to write the letter.

A sample letter of recommendation is presented in Figure 9.3, written for an intern named JoAnne (who was featured in Vignette 6.1 in Chapter 6). The Figure includes callouts highlighting a few features letter writers may want to include in their letters (e.g., the nature of the relationship with the intern; the candidate's knowledge and skills; breadth and depth of experiences; leadership experiences; and unique or distinguishing applicant interests). In the example provided in Figure 9.3, Jack (the supervisor) felt he was ethically obligated to mention the difficulties JoAnne faced during her internship year. He discussed this with JoAnne before composing the letter and included the information in a way that was honest, maintained confidentiality, and demonstrated JoAnne's professionalism and growth.

Initial Action Stage: January and February

During the *initial action* stage, interns actively begin to apply for jobs. They search for openings and decide where to apply, send out applications, and prepare for interviews.

Narrowing the Search

A helpful action early in the job search process is for interns to narrow down what positions they will search for. School-based positions can be narrowed down based on the match between the site and the applicant's specific interests and skills. For instance, during the pre-preparation or preparation stages, an intern may decide they want to work at the high school level, or work with a specific population of children. Pragmatic factors such as geography may also narrow the job search. One intern I supervised who had three young children and had recently purchased a new house determined she would only look for jobs within a 15-minute commute. As previously discussed, some interns may wish to seek alternative types of positions, narrowing the search as well. For example, the doctoral intern named Cordell

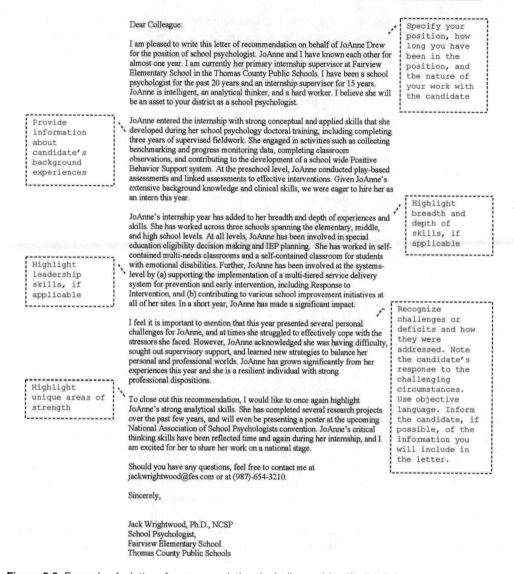

Dear Colleague:

I am pleased to write this letter of recommendation on behalf of JoAnne Drew for the position of school psychologist. JoAnne and I have known each other for almost one year. I am currently her primary internship supervisor at Fairview Elementary School in the Thomas County Public Schools. I have been a school psychologist for the past 20 years and an internship supervisor for 15 years. JoAnne is intelligent, an analytical thinker, and a hard worker. I believe she will be an asset to your district as a school psychologist.

[Specify your position, how long you have been in the position, and the nature of your work with the candidate]

JoAnne entered the internship with strong conceptual and applied skills that she developed during her school psychology doctoral training, including completing three years of supervised fieldwork. She engaged in activities such as collecting benchmarking and progress monitoring data, completing classroom observations, and contributing to the development of a school wide Positive Behavior Support system. At the preschool level, JoAnne conducted play-based assessments and linked assessments to effective interventions. Given JoAnne's extensive background knowledge and clinical skills, we were eager to hire her as an intern this year.

[Provide information about candidate's background experiences]

JoAnne's internship year has added to her breadth and depth of experiences and skills. She has worked across three schools spanning the elementary, middle, and high school levels. At all levels, JoAnne has been involved in special education eligibility decision making and IEP planning. She has worked in self-contained multi-needs classrooms and a self-contained classroom for students with emotional disabilities. Further, JoAnne has been involved at the systems-level by (a) supporting the implementation of a multi-tiered service delivery system for prevention and early intervention, including Response to Intervention, and (b) contributing to various school improvement initiatives at all of her sites. In a short year, JoAnne has made a significant impact.

[Highlight breadth and depth of skills, if applicable]

[Highlight leadership skills, if applicable]

I feel it is important to mention that this year presented several personal challenges for JoAnne, and at times she struggled to effectively cope with the stressors she faced. However, JoAnne acknowledged she was having difficulty, sought out supervisory support, and learned new strategies to balance her personal and professional worlds. JoAnne has grown significantly from her experiences this year and she is a resilient individual with strong professional dispositions.

[Recognize challenges or deficits and how they were addressed. Note the candidate's response to the challenging circumstances. Use objective language. Inform the candidate, if possible, of the information you will include in the letter.]

To close out this recommendation, I would like to once again highlight JoAnne's strong analytical skills. She has completed several research projects over the past few years, and will even be presenting a poster at the upcoming National Association of School Psychologists convention. JoAnne's critical thinking skills have been reflected time and again during her internship, and I am excited for her to share her work on a national stage.

[Highlight unique areas of strength]

Should you have any questions, feel free to contact me at jackwrightwood@fes.com or at (987)-654-3210.

Sincerely,

Jack Wrightwood, Ph.D., NCSP
School Psychologist,
Fairview Elementary School
Thomas County Public Schools

Figure 9.3 *Example of a letter of recommendation, including an identified deficiency*

referenced earlier in this chapter primarily searched for post-doctoral, academic, and research positions rather than also looking for school-based psychologist positions.

How to Search

A primary method to find out about job openings is by using online resources. Although some positions can be identified with vast national job search engines, it may be best for interns to begin with education-, psychology-, or school psychology-specific websites. For interns seeking local positions, a helpful starting point is a state school psychology organization website. For those open to relocating, NASP's Career Center (http://nasponline.org/careers/index.aspx) is an excellent resource for up-to-date school psychology job postings around the country, including a variety of types of positions (e.g., school-based, academic, and clinical settings). School psychology interns may also find it beneficial to explore education-specific job websites such as www.k12jobspot.com. Finally, the website http://PsycCareers.com hosted by the APA provides information about jobs across a variety of psychology disciplines, providing one means for interns to identify alternatives to school-based positions.

Web-based job searching should be supplemented by networking as described in previous chapters. Having an ally that is thinking of you when a position opens up may be the key to finding out about a position, or securing a job interview. In addition, if there is a particular place an intern may wish to work, it is acceptable to make a cold call to the site or to the office of human resources. Cold calling demonstrates the applicant's proactive qualities, and may allow the applicant to access information that is not yet posted elsewhere.

Submitting Applications

Once open positions are identified, the intern should be ready to apply to a few that seem like a good match with his or her interests and skills. Even if an intern is eyeing a particular position, it is advisable to apply for more than one position as most openings will have several applicants. The intern should make sure to pay precise attention to application instructions and deadlines. Violations of either of these put the intern at a disadvantage right out of the starting gate. For electronic submissions, the intern should pay careful attention to issues of formatting and be sure to attach all documents correctly.

Tailoring the Cover Letter, and Other Materials

The intern's professional materials are now created, edited, compiled, and sharpened. Prospective jobs have been identified and targeted. The only application piece that is missing is a cover letter, a brief document submitted with a job application tailored to the specific position. An effective cover letter (a) explains the intern's interest in the position, (b) illustrates the intern's unique qualifications for the position, and (c) supplements and/or underscores information offered in the résumé or CV that is most relevant to the specific job. A sample cover letter is provided in Appendix I. Once a cover letter is developed, it is easy for the intern to use this letter as a template that can be personalized when applying to other positions. If possible, the intern should address the letter to a specific person rather than "To Whom it May Concern".

Materials such as the résumé or CV and work samples should also be tailored to fit with where the intern is applying. For example, the intern may wish to change the order of activities listed on his or her résumé or CV based on what the hiring site is looking for in a candidate, or a new section might be created altogether. Similarly, work samples that may be relevant for one job may be less important to include for another position. Shaping application materials to fit a particular job suggests to the reviewer that the applicant has done his or her homework, and is not casting a ubiquitous net while hoping to land any position.

Following up

Regardless of whether the application was submitted electronically or via "snail mail", the intern should be sure to follow up with a phone call to make sure materials were received (that is, unless the application description specifies that applicants should not call). Following up is important because it is not always clear who collects application materials, or how materials get from the point of submission into the hands of the reviewer(s). It goes without saying that it is to the advantage of the applicant to be polite and considerate during follow-up even if there were any difficulties with the application process. The person reached on the phone may have some influence in making hiring decisions. Finally, following up is made easier if the intern maintains a spreadsheet record of where they have applied including contact information of sites and materials submitted.

Interview Preparation

As stated by Baird (2008), "the key to an effective interview is what you do before the interview, not simply what happens during the interview" (p. 9). Interns can prepare for the interview in terms of *content* and *process*.

Content Preparation

Regarding content, interns should carefully research the site where they are applying and learn about its missions, goals, populations served, challenges, and strengths. In addition, the intern can research the individual(s) who will be conducting the interview to learn about their roles and/or approaches to practice. The intern may have done some of this work in advance when preparing application materials, but prior to the interview the intern can research pertinent information in greater depth. After learning more about the hiring site, the intern should ask himself or herself, "What can I do as a school psychologist to best support positive outcomes at this site?"

Content preparation also includes being able to demonstrate content knowledge verbally during the interview. The intern should be aware of educational jargon that may arise during the interview, some of which may be site-specific. If applying to positions out of state, it will be important for the intern to become familiar with unique qualities of that state. For instance, the structure of school districts may differ from state to state including size, geographical composition, and how school psychologists are assigned. In addition to site-specific information, applicants may be served well by reviewing broad-based materials such as NASP's *Blueprint III* (Ysseldyke, 2006) or chapters from *Best Practices in School Psychology* (Thomas & Grimes, 2008) prior to the interview. This is not to cram in last-minute knowledge, but rather to put pertinent issues in school psychology at the front of one's brain to be able to access with automaticity during the interview.

Process Preparation

Even when an applicant is knowledgeable in relevant content areas, the interview process may make it difficult for the individual to demonstrate all that he or she knows. For example, a supervisor from a hiring school district recently called me for a reference check on a former intern. He was surprised that the applicant appeared nervous and rambling when responding to questions during the interview because this contrasted sharply with how she presented herself in application materials. The supervisor expressed concerns regarding how the intern would present information to parents or school staff. Being nervous is normal when interviewing, and not unexpected by those conducting interviews. However, when nerves drastically affect the applicant's presentation, interviewers may consider it representative of the applicant's dispositions rather than signifying a stressful situation.

Applicants can alleviate interview anxiety by over-preparing and over-rehearsing for the interview. On the companion website for this book, there are three simulated job interview videos that may help applicants prepare for the job interview process. Transcripts of the two mock interviews that allow viewers to practise interviewing skills are featured in Appendix J, with space provided for interns to write out thoughts regarding each question. The transcripts offer some specific questions that might be asked during the interview. In general, interviewees should be prepared to:

- tell the interviewer(s) about themselves including training experiences, interests, and skills;
- state clearly why they are interested in this particular position at this particular site;
- orally work through applied scenarios or case examples using a problem-solving process and/or ethical decision-making model;
- identify personal strengths they will bring to the position;
- identify areas they perceive they will continue to need to develop (Note: This is not a trick question asked by potential employers. Ongoing professional development is essential for school psychologists at all levels of training and practice);
- ask questions about the position and hiring site (Note: The interview process goes both ways; applicants should determine whether the site is a good fit for them).

In addition to practicing interviewing using an online simulation, interns can work with peers to prepare for the interview process, including conducting mock interviews with each another and providing constructive feedback. It may also be helpful for interns to seek out individuals they are not completely familiar with to practice for interviews. For instance, my wife's supervisor (an assistant principal) conducted a mock interview of me prior to me going on job interviews and provided invaluable feedback.

Job Interviews versus Internship Interviews

A final point is for interns to realize that job interviews are different from internship interviews. The internship year is supposed to help the intern grow in numerous ways including content knowledge, ability to apply skills with automaticity, professional identity, and bridging university training with day-to-day practice. Therefore, the answers a prospective intern and a prospective first-year professional give during an interview, even to exactly the same questions, may be qualitatively different. For example, in response to an applied interview question about a crisis response, a few key points for prospective interns would be to maintain client safety and welfare, notify and consult with the supervisor, and not intervene beyond boundaries of competence. For the job applicant, although some facets of the answer would hold true, the ability to respond independently and skillfully during the crisis must be conveyed. Interns should think critically about differences between what is expected of interns versus certified practitioners during the interview and make sure they are able to convey these differences successfully.

Ongoing Action Stage: March, April, May

During the *ongoing action* stage, the job hunt is in full gear. Interns should continue to search for positions as many new openings are posted during the spring months. In addition, interns should continue to follow up on positions previously applied for. In following up with applications it is appropriate to ask the hiring site about their timeline and process. Some sites may be able to provide firm dates of when they are conducting interviews and others might let the applicant know that their position was already filled. Job interviews are likely taking place with greater frequency during the ongoing action stage.

Interviews

Following the initial action stage, interns should feel adequately prepared to be successful interviewees. However, practice interviews are obviously not exactly the same as the real thing. The exact format of the interview (e.g., number of interviewers; number of interviewees; how questions are asked; requirement of an applied activity) varies per hiring site. The level of formality in the interview may also differ from setting to setting. Regardless of precise interview structure, the following are some tips interns can bear in mind:

- Wear professional clothes.
- Leave time for travel. Arriving early may provide an opportunity to meet staff members before beginning the formal interview.
- Remember to bring your portfolio materials and copies of materials to give to each member of the interview committee.
- Answer questions directly, succinctly, and clearly.
- Pay attention to non-verbal behaviors including offering a firm handshake, maintaining eye contact with all interviewers, smiling when appropriate, using a strong voice, and sitting with straight posture.
- Be yourself. Being nervous during an interview is normal, but being too nervous or stiff may prevent the intern from showing his or her knowledge, skills, and personality.

Following the Interview

After the interview, interns should send a thank you note to the head of the interviewing committee. A thank you note may include a comment or two about things the intern enjoyed or learned about the hiring site. In addition, it is appropriate to ask any lingering questions about the position. For some positions, a first interview will be followed by subsequent interviews which also may vary in format. Second- and/or third-round interviews are not uncommon, and might take place with individuals not on the initial interview committee, for instance a school superintendent. Later-round interviews may also be a time when compensation and benefits for the position are discussed.

Learning from Interviews

Each interview can be seen as an opportunity for the intern to practice interviewing. Moreover, when an intern is not hired for a position, some interviewers may provide feedback to the interviewee. Feedback may be unsolicited or may be requested by the interviewee when learning about the decision ("Is there any feedback you have for me based on the interview?"). Interview feedback can greatly aid interns in future interviews. For instance, one intern was told by an interviewer that the interview committee was impressed with her skills, but they hired a candidate who had more experience with crisis prevention and intervention. In fact, the applicant did have such experiences but realized she did not adequately describe her experiences during the interview.

Getting Targeted Experiences

Even though job interviews are taking place and the intern's eyes are moving towards next year, the internship year is not yet complete. During the ongoing action stage, the intern is able to seek out particular experiences that best fit with particular jobs or that fill in any existing training gaps. Further, these are supervised training experiences for learning, opportunities that can make the intern a more complete job candidate and professional school psychologist.

VIGNETTE 9.1 **ILEANA'S TARGETED EXPERIENCES**

An intern named Ileana was informed that a school psychologist position in her district was opening in a school working with students with severe and profound disabilities. She had done some related work in a self-contained classroom during her practicum which she excelled at and enjoyed, but still felt inexperienced in this area. With the support of her internship supervisor, Ileana sought out related experiences in the spring including spending one day a week at the school that would have the opening. During the interview, Ileana was able to talk about (a) her interests, (b) her proactive behaviors to get more experience, and (c) relevant experiences from her practicum and internship. She was offered and accepted the position.

Patience, Persistence, and Payoff Stage: June, July, August

The final stage in the job process, *patience*, *persistence*, and *payoff*, occurs during the tail end of the internship and ends when an intern secures a job. Anecdotally, I have found that as the internship comes to a close, interns get apprehensive if they have not yet secured a position. Naturally, it is scary to close one door when another door is not yet open. However, many excellent positions open up late in the summer due to unplanned situations such as a school psychologist's relocation, retirement, or maternity leave, or changes in a school district's budget. The need for interns to stay patient cannot be overstated. In addition, ongoing persistence is essential including continuing to search for positions and following up as needed on applications already in progress.

Accepting a Position

With patience and persistence, the graduating intern will get offered a position – the payoff of the job hunt. Applicants should remember that just because they have gotten an offer, they are not obligated to accept. Further, if for whatever reason an intern needs to accept a less than ideal position, it does not mean he or she is obligated to stay in that position forever. Just as an employer may determine the employee was not a good fit, the employee may decide after a year that the position did not work out. On the other hand, a position that may not be the intern's top choice may turn out to be a perfect fit.

Choosing Between Multiple Offers

Sometimes dilemmas arise in the process of making decisions about what position to accept or not to accept. Challenging situations may include having to choose from two or three positions; waiting to hear from a preferred district while sitting on an offer from a less-preferred district; or accepting one position and then getting offered a preferred position a few hours later. Ironically, it is frequently the interns who are most anxious about whether they will get any offers that end up having to choose from among a few.

When advising interns on challenging circumstances such as these, I always emphasize the importance of being professional and transparent. Being professional includes not violating any contracts (written or verbal) and not lying to potential employers. Being transparent means letting potential employers know the current circumstances which are being navigated (e.g., "I am very interested in working at your district, but I am also expecting to hear from another district later this week. I would like to make a fully informed decision before accepting your offer. Is there any way I can let you know my final decision by Friday afternoon?"). Potential employers appreciate a candidate's honesty and integrity. Further, the intern may have future interactions with individuals in this district, or even decide they want to work at that district one day down the road. Acting with a lack of transparency or professionalism may inadvertently damage relationships or burn professional bridges.

Summary

Obtaining a job is an ongoing process that commences before the internship begins. The pre-preparation stage (pre-internship to early fall) serves as a time for interns to build foundational materials such as a professional portfolio, to engage in preparatory experiences such as internship interviews, and to begin to focus professional goals. Most interns will pursue school-based psychologist positions, but others may seek out alternative career options. The preparation stage of the job process involves compiling and editing all materials in the professional portfolio including cover letters, the résumé or CV, work samples, work summaries, transcripts, and letters of recommendation. Interns should be thoughtful about who, when, and how to ask for letters of recommendation, and supervisors should also take care in composing letters for students. Interns should also determine if there are additional supervised experiences that would be beneficial to complete in order to bridge any gaps in training.

The initial action stage of the job process includes beginning the job search, applying for positions, and preparing for interviews. To effectively search for positions, interns should narrow their search to the extent possible, and utilize online resources and professional networks. Prior to submitting applications, materials should be tailored to particular positions. Interns should carefully prepare for interviews, and remember that the job interview is not the same thing as the internship interview completed one year earlier. Once initial applications are submitted, interns engage in the ongoing action stage which includes continuing to search and apply for positions, following up on previously submitted applications, and engaging in interviews. Interviews can be intimidating but provide opportunities for learning. During the summer, with adequate patience (e.g., waiting for new positions to open) and persistence (e.g., following up on applications submitted), interns will eventually achieve the payoff of landing a full-time job.

Critical Thinking Questions and Activities

The following are critical thinking questions and activities for interns, site supervisors, and university supervisors to ponder regarding the job application and interview process.

For Interns:

■ Using the simulated interview tool provided on the book's companion website, practice job interviewing with a peer. Request specific feedback on what you did well and what you could do better.

- Thinking back to your internship interview, how would you answer some of the questions differently at this point in time?
- Write a list of at least five questions you have for the site(s) where you will be interviewing.

For Field Supervisors:

- How would you respond if an intern who has not performed well during their internship requested a letter of recommendation?
- What are some ways you might support your intern during the job application and interview process?
- Are there additional experiences that the intern should complete before the end of the year to become a better job candidate and a more well-rounded school psychologist?

For University Supervisors:

- What guidance or support, if any, is offered to students from your training program in the job hunt process? If what is currently provided is not sufficient, how might guidance or support be supplemented?
- An intern named Felix accepted a job offer last week, but received an offer today from a district where he would much prefer to work. He asks your advice on what to do. How would you respond?
- How does formative and summative evaluation of interns connect to letters of recommendation that are written during the job application process?

Chapter 10

Concluding the Internship

Over the past several months the intern has entered the internship site; developed and nurtured relationships with supervisors, staff, children, and parents; expanded professional competencies; and applied and interviewed for jobs. Now the time has come for the intern to close out the internship year. Just as there are numerous tasks involved in effective internship entry, successfully concluding the internship year involves several considerations.

To explore these issues, the chapter is organized according to the three intern identities described in Chapter 4: trainee, professional, and supervisee. First, completion of trainee responsibilities is addressed including program and university requirements and doctoral dissertation work. Second, closing out professional responsibilities such as terminating with students and staff, and applying for certification as a school psychologist are discussed. Third, concluding supervisee responsibilities is explored including summative evaluations, terminating supervisory relationships, the role of final site visits, and how to pursue supervision and professional development beyond the internship year. The chapter concludes with some final thoughts tied to big ideas interwoven throughout the text, as well as critical thinking questions and activities for interns and supervisors.

Closing Out Trainee Responsibilities

Interns are nearing the finish line of their graduate training, an accomplishment that is accompanied by a number of tasks to be completed before the year is through. Although much attention is paid to closing out professional responsibilities at the internship site, requirements for interns to complete their training program may not receive adequate consideration.

Completing Program and University Requirements

Before being eligible to graduate, the intern likely has to complete various degree requirements. If the intern is enrolled in a university-based internship seminar, there may be lingering assignments to finish prior to the official end of the course. It is easy for requirements to be neglected when interns are consumed by so many other year-end activities such as closing out cases, saying goodbye to colleagues, applying for state and national certification, and continuing to apply and interview for jobs. Aside from specific course assignments that remain, some school psychology programs require students to complete a culminating project such as a portfolio. While faculty may view final assignments as critical for numerous reasons (e.g., helping the intern link theory and practice, providing a summative evaluation of the intern, and providing data on training program outcomes), interns may view remaining requirements as time consuming busywork, or final hoops to jump through before moving on to bigger and better things. However, both faculty and interns can contribute to university-based assignments being meaningful learning tools.

Making Assignments Meaningful

Interns and supervisors tend to view program requirements as valuable when they are strategically aligned to meet intern needs such as completing degree and certification requirements and enhancing professional readiness. Some assignments may even alleviate interns' end-of-year stress and prevent frantic last-minute scrambling. For example, in our school psychology program's internship seminar, students are required to submit a monthly log and pie graph of their internship hours. Monthly logs are easily produced using a program such as Microsoft Excel or Time2Track and (a) demonstrate the ongoing breadth and depth of interns' experiences, (b) document interns' progress towards completing hours required for certification, and (c) prevent a desperate push to account for time when the year is done.

To provide another example of how assignments may actually be helpful or stress-reducing, interns are required to complete monthly papers in the internship seminar that help them reflect on the work they are doing at their internship sites. Papers are directly connected to interns' day-to-day work, course big ideas, course readings, and NASP Standards, and are aligned to meet part of the program's end-of-year portfolio requirement. To paraphrase a recent graduating intern from a course evaluation: "At first I thought the papers were going to be annoying, but they actually forced me to stop and think about what I was doing. Actually, I kind of liked them!" Papers also provide a way for supervisors to formatively monitor interns' developmental progress during the year (e.g., case conceptualization, problem-solving skills, and work quality), and to provide ongoing feedback.

Interns share with university faculty the responsibility of making assignments valuable. When given a choice, interns should write about or present on topics that are relevant to their interests and their ongoing internship work. For instance, one intern was asked by her field supervisor to provide professional development to middle school teachers about managing difficult behaviors in the classroom. She practiced her presentation during the internship seminar and received constructive feedback from peers that helped her restructure a few unclear slides. Another intern was assigned by her field supervisor to complete a reevaluation of a student with autism, and reflected on this process in an internship seminar paper. In writing the paper, the intern completed a few self-selected readings to help her think through the recommendations to be included in her evaluation.

To summarize, there are likely at least some university-based requirements to be completed prior to the intern's graduation. When developing assignments, university educators should be thoughtful about how requirements align with interns' professional needs. In turn, interns should treat requirements as meaningful opportunities for learning, and complete work strategically based on their own professional goals.

Doctoral Dissertation

For doctoral interns, one requirement that may be particularly challenging is completing a dissertation. Approximately 80% of doctoral-level interns have a significant amount of dissertation work remaining upon internship entry, and most interns overestimate how much dissertation progress they will make during the year (Krieshok, Lopez, Somberg, & Cantrell, 2000). Not completing the dissertation by the internship's end results in an All but the Dissertation (ABD) status – having completed all doctoral degree requirements and acquiring certification, but not having completed the dissertation. Some students take many years post-internship to complete the dissertation and others do not finish their dissertation work at all, never completing the doctoral degree (Sternberg, 1981).

Perhaps the greatest obstacle to dissertation completion during the internship is finding the time to work on the project in addition to completing full-time internship responsibilities and maintaining some semblance of a personal life. This barrier is particularly problematic given the finding that the number of hours put into dissertation work is the single best predictor of dissertation completion during the internship (Krieshok et al., 2000). Other challenges to dissertation completion include poor self-efficacy regarding the ability to complete the dissertation (Krieshok et al.), as well as perfectionism and procrastination (Green, 1997). In addition, Sternberg (1981) suggested feeling unsupported by faculty; working with unreliable faculty; lacking a supportive graduate student community; and being unprepared to tackle a dissertation are also obstacles to dissertation completion. Given the difficulties of completing a dissertation *at all* (Sternberg, 1981), let alone during the hectic internship year (Krieshok et al., 2000), how can interns successfully finish their dissertation work?

Some recommended actions for interns, internship supervisors, and university educators to promote dissertation progress during the internship are summarized in Table 10.1. Perhaps the most salient point is that interns should begin the internship with some dissertation work already completed. Krieshok et al. (2000) found that interns who had not proposed their dissertations prior to the internship only had a 7% chance of defending by the end of the year. In contrast, 78% of those interns who had a formal proposal meeting prior to beginning the internship made at least some dissertation progress. What is more, nearly 50% of interns who began the year with data collected, and 88% of those who began the internship with complete dissertation drafts, successfully completed and defended their research. The message is clear that the more dissertation progress trainees make prior to the internship, the better. In addition to these recommendations, interns may wish to access any of myriad books written to support students in successfully navigating a doctoral dissertation (e.g., Cone & Foster, 2006; Heppner & Heppner, 2004; Rudestam & Newton, 2007; Single, 2009; Sternberg, 1981).

Table 10.1 *Actions Interns, Internship Supervisors, and University Faculty Can Take to Support Dissertation Completion During the School Psychology Internship*

Who	Actions to take
Intern	Pre-internship: • Choose a school psychology program with a strong research culture, where faculty have a record of supporting trainees' successful dissertation progress and completion • Collaborate with faculty that are actively involved in research • Choose a dissertation chair with a positive track record (i.e., trainees who work with this professor successfully propose and defend), and consider politics in selecting a committee (see Sternberg, 1981, pp. 138–156) • Be a part of a research team, and provide and receive research support • Develop a research project that is doable • If possible, align the dissertation work to other requirements (e.g., study something already being worked on; use pre-existing data; use course requirements/deadlines as deadlines to complete parts of the dissertation work) • Complete as much dissertation work as possible prior to beginning the internship, including proposing the dissertation (or *at least* set a proposal meeting date) During the internship: • Work on the dissertation a bit every day to create and maintain momentum • Set clear goals and deadlines • Maintain communication with training program faculty (especially the dissertation advisor) even if the internship site is geographically far away
Internship field supervisors	• Consider requiring students to propose the dissertation prior to beginning the internship • Provide interns time during the internship to complete research • Offer support and encouragement for dissertation progress • Encourage the student to maintain ties with the university during the internship • Require an end-of-year research project that can be aligned with dissertation work
Training program faculty	• Consider requiring students to propose the dissertation prior to beginning the internship • Be engaged in your own research, model the research process, and encourage trainee involvement/collaboration • Encourage trainees to be involved in research early in their training sequence • Encourage trainees to be a part of a research team before and during the dissertation • Maintain ties with trainees during the internship year • Work with advisees to set goals and deadlines for dissertation work completion

Degree Audits

Interns should not take for granted that all requirements for the degree have been successfully completed, or are in the process of being completed. Instead, degree information should be verified through a degree audit. A degree audit is a computer-generated analysis that allows students and advisors to see a student's academic progress up to that point in time, including courses completed and remaining requirements. Audits are often easily processed through the university registrar's office. Even for individuals that are confident they have completed all requirements, it is useful to get a degree audit because there are sometimes errors in administrative documentation. For example, an advisor may have forgotten to sign or submit a particular form at some point during training. It is recommended that the student gets an audit approximately halfway through the internship year which will provide enough time to decipher and correct any existing errors.

Forms, Deadlines, and Other Details

A final facet of successfully closing out the year from the perspective of trainee involves paying careful attention to deadlines, required forms, and other tasks that if accidentally neglected might be disruptive to graduating. Administrative requirements may be from the training program, a college within the university (e.g., the College of Education), or the university itself. Examples of common administrative requirements are applying for graduation, ordering a diploma, submitting forms regarding the dissertation, and completing evaluations. Students should proactively seek out information, usually available online, on administrative deadlines and requirements early on during their training. In addition, interns should verify with an academic advisor, the training program coordinator, and/or appropriate university personnel that they have completed everything required for graduation. If any snafus do arise, they are typically correctable. Interns should bear in mind that university faculty and administrators want students to graduate and will by and large provide pragmatic support.

Closing Out Professional Roles and Responsibilities

As described in Chapter 4, in addition to being trainees, interns are burgeoning professionals with a variety of responsibilities. The end of the internship year necessitates terminating and transitioning current cases; saying goodbye to students, staff, and families; and completing requirements for state and/or national certification.

Termination

Termination is a term frequently used by mental health professionals to describe the concluding stage of clinical work during which therapeutic relationships with clients come to an end. In my opinion, the word termination inadvertently conveys a haphazard, hasty, or insensitive ending ("Hasta la vista, baby!"). However, when given sufficient planning and preparation from interns and supervisors, and when approached with sensitivity, termination can be a meaningful process of closure that results in growth for clients and interns (Gelman, Fernandez, Hausman, Miller, & Weiner, 2007). An intern's readiness to facilitate the termination process hinges on (a) understanding clients' reactions to termination; (b) understanding one's own reactions to termination; (c) addressing the fact that the internship role is time limited; and (d) acting strategically during termination with the support of supervision.

Student Reactions to Termination

The majority of interns reading this book are likely concluding internships in school-based settings. For termination with students to be successful, it is helpful for interns to be aware of how students might feel about or react to the relationship coming to an end. In therapeutic relationships, common client reactions to termination include anxiety, depression, anger, and reappearance of symptoms (Baird, 2008). Responses vary between individuals, depending on multiple variables such as the age, personality, length and quality of the relationship, and the client's prior experiences with termination or loss (Baird, 2008; Gelman et al., 2007). Although delivering individual or group counseling may only be one part of an intern's role, other direct service activities (e.g., delivering academic or behavioral interventions) may also involve establishing close relationships with students. Therefore interns and supervisors should determine together which students need a termination process, anticipate potential reactions these students may have to termination, and strategize how to most effectively say goodbye.

Intern Reactions to Termination

Like their students, interns may also have reactions to closing out the relationships developed during the internship year, and these reactions may influence the termination process. Some potential intern reactions to termination described by Baird (2008) include feeling guilty about ending a relationship before the work is complete; feeling that no one else sufficiently understands the client(s) to provide the help needed; or worrying that the next individual will be more effective in helping the student than the intern. It is also not uncommon for an intern to feel a sense of relief about terminating with a particular client or clients. Baird additionally pointed out that interns' reactions to termination may be affected by their own pending transitions. For example, if an intern feels relief or excitement about finishing the year and moving on to a full-time job it may make it difficult to understand a student who has difficulty coping with termination. By recognizing and understanding their own emotions, interns may be more effectively prepared to close their work with students as well as others in the school.

Challenges of Forced Termination

Given the time-limited nature of the intern role, termination may feel forced, premature, or artificial. The work is ending due to completion of the intern's placement rather than achievement of a client's goals or consideration of a client's needs (Gelman et al., 2007). Even though the internship placement finishes rapidly, there are several preventive strategies that interns and supervisors can bear in mind regarding termination. First, knowing the intern will only be at the site for one year, supervisors may decide not to assign the intern as primarily responsible for a student with a history of multiple losses (Baird, 2008). Second, especially in the context of therapy, interns should make the time-limited duration of their work transparent to students from early on (Semrud-Clikeman, 1995). As the actual termination date approaches, it is important to provide students with sufficient notice (at least a few weeks in advance) to allow time to appropriately close relationships. Third, there are natural transitions during the school year (e.g., vacations) that may provide a preview of student reactions to termination, and a chance for the intern to discuss such issues with the student. Such transitions also may help the intern prepare and practice termination (Gelman et al., 2007; Semrud-Clikeman, 1995).

Strategies for Saying Goodbye to Students

Given the complex nature of termination, it is important for interns (with guidance from supervisors) to be strategic in how they approach this process. Following are a few strategies identified by Bundy (2010) to help facilitate termination:

- Encourage students to share a self-assessment of their own progress, and share observations regarding student progress. It is helpful to describe behaviors in measurable terms to provide evidence that the student changed.
- Anticipate future challenges students may encounter, and talk through how the student might address such concerns.
- Identify resources a student may access in the future when he or she is having difficulties, and discuss a positive vision of the student's future (i.e., how the student can continue a positive path of progress).
- Write a note to say goodbye, including encouragement for the student's continued growth and learning.

In addition to these strategies, the termination process may be connected to various rituals that recognize an ending and/or transition (Baird, 2008). Semrud-Clikeman (1995) analogized termination as a type of graduation for clients, pointing out that the process should be about success rather than loss. Gelman et al. (2007) suggested that creative activities (e.g., composing a memory book), or having a formal celebration may also be contributors to successful termination. The termination of groups may include similar strategies to those previously discussed such as an ending celebration that includes refreshments; asking group members to assess the progress they made in the group; the intern providing oral feedback to the group as a whole, and individually to each group member; and the intern writing personalized notes to group members (Bundy, 2010).

Strategies for Saying Goodbye to Colleagues

In addition to saying goodbye to students, interns must also terminate relationships with colleagues. Concluding relationships with supervisors is discussed in greater detail later in this chapter; for now, the focus is on the intern saying goodbye to teachers, administrators, and other staff. Similar to when working with students, interns will want to let their colleagues know in advance when they will be finishing the internship. Although the intern or supervisor may assume others know the intern is leaving the school or district, staff may actually not realize the intern is departing. The intern or field supervisor may wish to make a brief public announcement at a staff meeting regarding the intern's status. If appropriate, the announcement may include congratulations regarding a new job the intern will begin the following year. Supervisors may also wish to organize a farewell party (e.g., a breakfast, lunch, happy hour, or ceremony) that gives the intern and staff members a chance to say goodbye in an informal setting.

It is important for interns to note that saying goodbye to colleagues does not mean cutting off relationships. If the intern stays at the school or district following the internship, or works at the site at any point in the future, these will be the intern's professional colleagues. If the intern is at another site, former colleagues are now part of the individual's professional network, and may continue to provide emotional and informational support. Making time for personal goodbyes with administrators such as principals and assistant principals is also critical. Interns should be sure to thank administrators for welcoming them into the site and for providing supporting resources (e.g., office space, time for professional development, the supervisor's time that was devoted to supervision). Administrators may wish to ask interns about the overall internship experience, and debrief on what they could do better as a site in supporting future school psychology interns.

Writing letters may provide one means for interns to say goodbye to colleagues. Just like sending a letter of introduction to staff at the beginning of the year, interns can send out a universal goodbye note via e-mail, as a letter placed in staff mailboxes, or as a posting in the staff lounge. Interns are also encouraged to write personal thank you notes to any staff they developed special relationships with during the year.

How Supervisors Can Support Interns During Termination

As with other professional tasks during the internship, terminating with students may be a new activity for many interns; having adequate supervisory support during this process is essential. Baird (2008) described several ways field and university supervisors can support interns to smoothly close out the internship year:

■ In training programs that require a university seminar, time can be devoted to discussing termination issues in general, and with regard to specific concerns interns are facing. Issues of *content* (i.e., what is involved in termination) and *process* (i.e., how to terminate) should be addressed.
■ Field supervisors can assist interns in understanding reactions to termination (both from students and the intern), and offer strategies to prevent and respond to such reactions.
■ Termination of the supervisor–supervisee relationship can be treated as a model for the termination between the intern and students. Supervisor–supervisee termination discussions may model cognitive

(e.g., assessment of strengths, challenges, progress during training, and future directions) and affective (e.g., feelings about one another, the supervision experience, and termination) components that will also be included in intern–student termination.

- Field supervisors and interns should discuss how cases are finishing, if the student will need to work with another individual (e.g., an incoming intern, the supervisor, another staff member), and how best to make such a transition.

In sum, termination is a complex process that requires a great deal of thought and planning. When executed carefully, the termination process can provide opportunities for the intern to say goodbye to students and colleagues, achieve closure on the work they have done together, and celebrate a successful year.

Certification, Licensure, and Other Credentials

As the year comes to a close, most interns will apply for state certification as a school psychologist in order to be credentialed to practice school psychology in public schools. In addition to state credentials, some school psychologists pursue various national certifications, and some doctoral-level school psychologists may eventually seek clinical licensure (Crespi, 2010). Given the numerous types of state and national credentials, graduating interns may be unclear about their options. It may be helpful to interns as well as supervisors to briefly unpack certification and licensure processes.

State Certification

Each state delineates its own credentialing requirements for school-based practice as a school psychologist. On NASP's (2011b) website is a recently updated list of school psychology credentialing requirements by state including step-by-step credentialing procedures, continuing education requirements to maintain credentials, whether the state accepts the NCSP credential as an alternative route to credentialing, scope of practice in the state, and contact information for the state department of education. This website is a helpful starting point in getting ready to apply for state certification as a school psychologist.

In addition, school psychology program faculty members as well as field supervisors tend to be knowledgeable about certification processes and can provide clarification and support; in fact, most have even gone through these processes themselves. Former students who have recently gone through the certification process are also excellent resources for information regarding certification. Sometimes hiring districts, through an administrative supervisor or human resources staff, may also provide support to newly hired school psychologists to navigate state credentialing. Prior to submitting materials, interns are encouraged to contact the state department of education certification office to make sure they have correctly followed all steps towards certification.

National Certification

The NASP created the National School Psychology Certification System (NSPCS) to credential school psychologists who meet nationally recognized school psychology qualifications. Graduating trainees from NASP-approved and non-approved programs may be eligible for the NCSP, and both NASP members and non-members can apply. Although the NCSP is not required for school psychology practice (i.e., only state certification is needed), according to NASP (2011a) there are several reasons why it may be advantageous to obtain the NCSP degree:

- *Professional recognition.* The NCSP designation signifies the school psychologist has met national standards for training, and may increase the individual's professional recognition, respect, and credibility.
- *Professional accountability.* The NCSP conveys the school psychologist's commitment to professionalism and ethical school psychology practice.

■ *Professional identity and growth.* Continuing professional development is required for maintenance of the NCSP.
■ *Professional benefits.* The NCSP is recognized in 30 states, and is also recognized for reciprocity of credentialing. Therefore, having the NCSP may allow the school psychologist greater ease of mobility if moving to another state. Further, some states and school districts award salary bonuses to NCSPs.

NCSP requirements include (a) completion of 60 graduate semester/90 quarter hours of study in school psychology (at least 54 of which are exclusive of the internship experience) in a school psychology program; (b) successful completion of a 1,200-hour internship in school psychology, with at least 600 hours in a school setting; (c) a passing score (660, as of August, 2010) on the School Psychologist Praxis II Examination administered by the Educational Testing Service (ETS); and (d) actively engaging in ongoing professional development. The NCSP must be renewed every three years. The reader may refer to materials available on NASP's website for a full description of the application process and requirements to obtain the NCSP.

Licensure

Individuals who are completing a doctoral degree in school psychology may wish to pursue licensure as a psychologist through state departments of health services. Licensure is a prerequisite for independent professional practice as a psychologist, and is intended to protect the public and to assure quality service delivery (Crespi, 2010). The Association of State and Provincial Psychology Boards (ASPPB) is an alliance of agencies responsible for the licensure of psychologists in the United States and Canada. According to the ASPPB (2008), typical jurisdictional requirements for licensure as a psychologist include: (a) a doctoral degree from a program acceptable to the licensure board (often including APA accreditation); (b) a specified number of hours of supervised experience (usually at least 3,000, with 1,500 being post-doctoral); (c) passing the Examination for Professional Practice in Psychology (EPPP); (d) administrative requirements including fees; (e) continuing professional development to maintain licensure; and (f) the expectation that the psychologist will practice within the scope of his or her education and training.

Other Credentials

Crespi (2010) identified and described numerous additional credentials school psychology graduates may pursue. Of note, doctoral-level school psychologists may be interested in obtaining the American Board of Professional Psychology (ABPP) credential, considered the highest credentialing standard in professional psychology. The problem is that since there are an incredible number of credentialing options, knowing what is available and pursuing these credentials is a daunting task (Crespi, 2010; Hall, Wexelbaum, & Boucher, 2007). As stated by Crespi (2010), "Sometimes more is not better. Sometimes it is only more" (p. 243). It is advisable for students to research and contemplate options prior to even beginning school psychology training or selecting an internship (Hall et al., 2007). If such pre-planning did not occur, it will be helpful for interns to seek out selected faculty or field mentors to discuss potential professional pursuits, and what the intern needs to do to achieve his or her professional goals.

Closing Out Supervisee Responsibilities

In addition to concluding trainee and professional responsibilities, the intern must close out the year as a supervisee including (a) completing and reviewing summative evaluations; (b) terminating supervisor–supervisee relationships; and (c) thinking about supervision and professional development in the future.

Summative Evaluations

As discussed in previous chapters of this book, evaluation is a critical component of supervision during the school psychology internship. Summative evaluation occurs at the end of a period of time, and is used to make supervisory decisions such as whether or not an intern is ready to enter the field (Harvey & Struzziero, 2008). Summative evaluations may be completed by field supervisors, university supervisors, and interns. Field and university supervisors will want to evaluate knowledge of content, application of skills, and professionalism (see Appendices C and D). Interns can complete self-assessments as well as assessments of their field and university experiences (see Appendices E and F). As described in earlier chapters, interns and supervisors should complete formative evaluations throughout the year, and discuss and address any concerns that arise. Therefore, summative evaluation results should not be surprising for any party.

Nonetheless, providing and accepting critical feedback at the end of the year can be a challenge for interns and supervisors. Interns often hope to hear nothing but praise from supervisors during a final evaluation, and supervisors likely want to provide positive reviews of interns' work (Baird, 2008). Although praise is an important part of evaluations, supervisors should also identify areas in which the intern can continue to progress. After all, the intern's career as a school psychologist is just beginning. To help increase interns' receptiveness to feedback, supervisors may ask interns to share a self-evaluation including strengths and areas for continued growth (Baird). Supervisors can also model receptiveness to feedback by encouraging interns to share evaluations of the internship experience, including internship supervision.

Terminating the Supervisor–Supervisee Relationship

In addition to formally ending relationships with students and colleagues, the intern must conclude relationships developed with supervisors. Depending on the nature of the supervisory relationship, this process may be more or less challenging. As described by Baird (2008):

> The breadth of feelings expressed at termination ranges from bland to profound. I have supervised interns with whom lasting relationships were developed and with whom I still maintain contact. On the other hand, I'm sorry to say that in some cases it seems I have scarcely known interns, and they have known little about me. Talking about these issues at termination helps bring a resolution to the supervision relationship and makes it easier for both intern and supervisor to move on.
>
> (p. 194)

No matter the closeness of the dyad, explicitly discussing and concluding the supervisory relationship is an important part of the supervision process. When relationship issues are not addressed, it may prevent interns or supervisors from feeling closure, and perhaps even obstruct moving onwards to future endeavors (e.g., the supervisor beginning a new supervisory relationship or the intern confidently beginning a new job).

Final Site Visits

At the end of the internship, university supervisors should initiate a final contact with the field supervisor(s) and the intern. The final meeting may occur over the phone, via teleconference, or in person. Topics that may be addressed during a final site visit are consistent with the content of this chapter so far and include (a) termination and closing out or transitioning cases; (b) summative evaluations; and (c) the transition from the internship into professional practice. Relevant questions within each of these areas that can be addressed during the final site visit are listed in Table 10.2. In my own experience, I find the end of the year sneaks up suddenly and interns and supervisors appreciate using site visits as an opportunity to stop, reflect on, and discuss the conclusion of the internship.

Table 10.2 *Topics to be Addressed During Final Site Visits*

Topic	Questions for consideration
Termination and closing/ transitioning cases	• Has the intern begun to terminate relationships with students and staff? • What termination issues have come up, if any? How have they been addressed? • How will cases the intern worked on be transitioned? • Is there any information that the intern needs to transfer to the field supervisor?
Summative evaluations	• What progress has the intern made towards goals developed throughout the internship year? • What areas will require continued support as the intern transitions to his or her first year of professional practice? • What constructive feedback does the intern have for the internship supervisor regarding the field-based experience? • What constructive feedback does the intern have for the university supervisor regarding training program support during the internship?
Transition into professional practice	• Where is the intern in the job process? What supports are needed from supervisors? • What are common issues in the early career that the intern should bear in mind upon his or her transition (e.g., need for ongoing supervision and professional development)? • What are some steps the intern can take immediately prior to or upon beginning a new position? • What resources should the intern access from field supervisors prior to ending the internship? • Does the intern have any questions regarding obtaining state or national certification?

Supervision and Professional Development Throughout the Career

Closing out the supervisee role also means thinking about ongoing supervision and professional development following the move from graduate training to first year of school psychology practice. As expressed by Sullivan and Conoley (2008), "although the internship may represent the final point of the graduate education in school psychology, this is really only the beginning of a lifelong process of professional learning" (p. 1966). Accessing supervision and professional development is a career-long process that may be considered essential for moving beyond competence to levels of proficiency and expertise (Armistead, 2008).

Current research suggests that clinical supervision is not always available or common at the inservice level (Chafouleas et al., 2002; Curtis et al., 2012), even for early career school psychologists. Therefore, it is advisable for graduating interns to inquire about what supervision, mentorship, and professional development will be provided at hiring sites, and to use such information to inform employment decisions. State and national certification, clinical licensure, and other credentialing usually require individuals to complete continuing professional development. Although there may be some requisite topic areas (e.g., NASP requires professional development on ethics as part of NCSP renewal), school psychologists can often select targeted learning opportunities that meet professional goals, interests, and needs. A summary of several ways that school psychologists can access professional development, adapted from the work of Armistead (2008), is provided in Table 10.3. These strategies provide helpful starting points following graduation, and are relevant to school psychologists at all points in the career trajectory.

Final Thoughts: Extending the Book's Big Ideas Beyond the Internship

Two purposes of this book identified in the Preface are (a) to provide interns and supervisors with actions to promote a high quality internship experience, and (b) to demystify what tends to be a mysterious

Table 10.3 *How School Psychologists Can Access Professional Development*

School psychologist actions	
• During job interviews, inquire about access to mentorship, professional development, and supervision • Engage in ongoing self-assessment, and strategically seek professional development to address needs • Be *active participants* in professional development activities • Organize, coordinate, and participate in peer supervision • Plan, develop, and participate in professional development in a psychological service unit	• Participate in online discussion groups or listservs including reading *and* posting conversation topics • Seek out a professional mentor that can help support clinical skill development • Be aware of and address barriers to accessing professional development • Join local, state, and national professional organizations • Seek leadership positions in professional organizations

Note: Adapted from "Best Practices in Continuing Professional Development for School Psychologists," by L. Armistead, 2008, in *Best Practices in School Psychology V* (pp. 1983–1987) by A. Thomas and J. Grimes (Eds.), 2008, Bethesda, MD: National Association of School Psychologists.

and often anxiety-provoking process for school psychology students. I sincerely hope that the book has accomplished its purposes, and is a useful and pragmatic resource to support the internship year. Further, I hope interns reading this text can extend the big ideas described in the Preface of this text beyond the internship into their professional careers.

Let's begin by jointly considering the first two big ideas of this book: (a) *the school psychology internship is a dynamic and formative experience, not a static event,* and (b) *the development of an intern's professional skills should be treated as an integrated process, not a series of isolated activities.* Following the internship, it may be easiest to shape one's professional work solely based on employer expectations (i.e., this is what our last school psychologist did) and crystallized knowledge and skills developed during the internship year. However, just as the internship is dynamic, formative, and integrated, professional practice and professional development are as well.

School psychology is rapidly changing (Neimeyer, Taylor, & Rozensky, 2012). Knowledge attained during graduate training has a half-life, defined by Dubin (1972) as:

> the time after completion of professional training when, because of new developments, practicing professionals have become roughly half as competent as they were upon graduation to meet the demands of their profession.
>
> (p. 487)

The half-life of school psychologists' graduate training is shortened by advances in research and practice, newly developed and changing legislation, shifting characteristics of student populations, and updated legal, ethical, and professional guidelines (Harrison, 2010; Reynolds, 2011).

Clearly, school psychologists must stay in touch with changes in the field and adapt. Like when they were interns, school psychologists can (a) engage in ongoing formative assessment of their own strengths and weaknesses, the needs of clients, and the needs of systems; (b) seek out targeted professional development; and (c) make changes in their own professional practices. Remaining static in knowledge and skills is antithetical to the value of lifelong learning instilled during graduate training. Although maintaining a static level of knowledge, skills, and practice may be experienced as *comfortable*, like when they were interns, school psychologists should seek experiences outside of their comfort zones. When crossing from comfort zones into risk zones, school psychologists enter more fertile spots for professional learning – especially when they have immediate access to supervision.

Which brings us to the third big idea underlying this book: *Supervision is a critical component of the internship year, but supervision processes need increased clarity . . . to be maximally effective.* Supervision is pivotal not only during the internship year, but also throughout school psychologists' careers (Knoff, 1986). The NASP (2011c) *Position Statement on Supervision in School Psychology* advocates that professional supervision should be available to all practitioners, whatever their level of experience or proficiency. In addition to being supervised, school psychologists may also act as supervisors for others, as noted in NASP's (2010b) *Principles for Professional Ethics*. Those who supervise should seek out ongoing professional development on supervision, including metasupervision (see Chapter 6). Harvey and Struzziero's (2008) text *Professional Development and Supervision of School Psychologists: From Intern to Expert* provides an in-depth consideration of supervision throughout the career, and is an excellent resource for school psychology supervisors' ongoing professional development.

Finally, the fourth big idea of this book is that *interns should be active planners, coordinators, and shapers of the internship experience.* Being proactive (as discussed in Chapter 5) is an important behavior during the internship, and remains relevant during the professional career. As interns complete their internships and enter practice, they are presented with a unique opportunity to shape their own work. Of course, having a "new-hire" status can be challenging, and successful site entry is a prerequisite to making significant systems-level changes. Further, districts likely have particular service needs (which have hopefully been made clear during the job interview). However, recent graduates are also optimistic, enthusiastic, and informed with up-to-date knowledge. During the internship they have developed opinions about what it means to be a school psychologist, and what is effective professional practice. The time is ripe to make a difference.

Summary

Concluding the internship year involves the intern closing out responsibilities associated with the roles of trainee, professional, and supervisee. As a trainee, the intern must be sure to complete all school psychology program and university requirements. Faculty can align assignments with other internship requirements, and interns can shape assignments to meet individualized needs. For doctoral students, completing the doctoral dissertation during the internship is a challenge. Getting started on the research prior to beginning the internship is a strong predictor of progress. Interns are advised to seek a degree audit prior to graduation to make sure they are ready to graduate, and should also pay careful attention to required forms and deadlines.

As burgeoning professionals, interns work with numerous students and staff with whom they must say goodbye. Termination is a complex process that results in mixed feelings from the intern as well as those he or she has worked with. The fact that the internship is time limited means that some relationships may end somewhat abruptly. Interns should give advanced notice and be transparent with others about when they are leaving, and plan with supervisors about how to best approach termination. Applying for state and/or national certification, and planning to pursue licensure or other credentialing options are also part of closing out professional responsibilities.

Finally, interns must conclude supervisee responsibilities. Completing and discussing summative evaluations helps serve the gatekeeping function of supervision, and allows interns and supervisors to critically reflect on the intern's professional growth in an observable and measureable way. Supervisors and supervisees must close out the supervisory relationship, which may act as a model for other terminations the intern will facilitate. University supervisors should complete a final site visit where a formal discussion about concluding the internship may take place. Interns should note that supervision and professional development are relevant across the career, not only the internship, and that there are numerous ways to seek out ongoing learning throughout the career.

Critical Thinking Questions and Activities

The following are critical thinking questions for interns, site supervisors, and university supervisors to ponder as the internship year comes to a close.

For Interns:

- How did your internship goals and internship plan change throughout the year?
- What role will professional development and supervision have for you next year as you commence your first year of practice as a school psychologist?
- Write out three lessons you have learned during the year. Lessons may be learned from negative or positive experiences. How will you apply these lessons in the future?

For Field Supervisors:

- How will you terminate the supervisor–supervisee relationship with your intern?
- How will you support the intern to terminate relationships with students and staff?
- Write out three lessons you have learned during the year. Lessons may be learned from negative or positive experiences. How will you apply these lessons in your future supervision of interns?

For University Supervisors:

- What program or university assignments do interns from your training program have to complete? What is the purpose of these requirements?
- What level of scaffolding is appropriate to provide students with regard to completing program and university requirements?
- Write out three lessons you have learned during the year. Lessons may be learned from negative or positive experiences. How will you apply these lessons in your future supervision of interns?

Best Practice Guidelines for School Psychology Internships[1]

By Joseph S. Prus

The NASP Delegate Assembly voted unanimously to endorse a new set of best practice guidelines for school psychology internships at its meeting in Boston on February 28, 2009. The guidelines, which were developed as part of the NASP Standards revision process, are intended to:

- Promote quality preparation of school psychologists and service provision to children, youth, and families
- Foster the internship as an educational experience involving collaboration between university training programs and internship sites
- Encourage greater consistency in opportunities and support across internship sites

The guidelines were developed over several years, beginning with an examination of existing NASP training standards (NASP, 2000a) and the school psychology internship guidelines of some national organizations and states. Drafts were then developed with input from various NASP constituencies, including NASP volunteer leaders, executive officers and staff, student leaders, and members of the Program Approval Board and Standards Writing Committee. They were also posted for comment on various NASP Listservs, and on the Listservs of the Trainers in School Psychology and the Council of Directors of School Psychology Programs.

Although adherence by internship field sites is voluntary, it is hoped that the guidelines will encourage quality experiences, supervision, and support during what is universally recognized as a critical period in professional development. NASP will be exploring ways to make the guidelines relevant and helpful to school psychology graduate programs and field sites.

The guidelines address four general aspects of internships, including: principles, conceptualization, and management of the internship; depth, breadth, and focus of the internship; supervision, mentoring, and collaboration; and intern evaluation, feedback, and support. The specific guidelines are as follows. Note that an asterisk (*) signifies the existence of a corresponding NASP training standard. The 2000 NASP *Standards for Training and Field Placement Programs in School Psychology* served as the initial base. Modifications in the guidelines will be made if/when the corresponding standard is revised.

I. Principles, Conceptualization, and Management of the Internship

1.1 The internship is conceptualized as a culminating training experience* in which the primary focus is on providing breadth and quality of training to the intern.

1.2 The site, preparing university program, and intern adhere to NASP Principles of Professional Practice/Ethics.

1.3 The internship site, university program, and intern have a written agreement* that includes a clear statement of the expectations and responsibilities of each party (including total hours and duties

1 Reprinted with permission of the publisher. www.nasponline.org

to be performed by the intern), benefits and support to be provided by the internship site, and the process by which interns are to be supervised and evaluated.

1.4   If the site solicits direct applications from prospective interns, it provides information about the site and the internship application and selection process. It notifies applicants whether or not they have been selected in a timely manner.

1.5   The site uses a title, such as "school psychology intern", that designates the training status of the intern. Psychological reports or similar professional reports to consumers, other professionals, or other audiences must be signed by the credentialed intern supervisor.

1.6   In states in which provisional certification or an intern certificate is required for internship, the site makes the training program and intern aware of such requirements and assists the preparing program and intern as necessary in applying for or securing such credential.

II. Depth, Breadth, and Focus of the Internship

2.1   The internship for specialist level interns includes at least 1,200 hours, and the internship for doctoral interns includes at least 1,500 hours completed on a full-time basis over 1 academic year or on a half-time basis over 2 years.*

2.2   At least 600 hours of the internship occur in a "school setting" as defined in NASP standards.* Nonschool settings that serve children, youth, and families may serve as appropriate internship sites as long as the intern has already completed or has the opportunity to complete at least 600 hours of supervised experience in a school setting.

2.3   The internship site provides opportunities for a range of school psychological services consistent with NASP Domains of School Psychology Training and Practice,* including varying types of assessment linked to intervention for academic, behavioral, and social/emotional issues; consultation; behavior analysis and intervention; counseling; prevention at varying levels; research and program evaluation; and other activities consistent with NASP standards and deemed appropriate by the field site and university program. In order to ensure breadth of training, activities in no single major function predominates the intern's time.

2.4   Most of the intern's time is spent providing direct and indirect psychological services to children, youth, and/or families.

2.5   The internship site endeavors to provide opportunities to work with children and adolescents of varying ages, ethnicities, socioeconomic backgrounds, and with varying abilities and disabilities, characteristics, and needs.

2.6   In assigning duties to the intern, the internship site recognizes and supports the internship as an educational experience. A student-to-intern ratio that is less than NASP guidelines for credentialed, full-time school psychologists (1:1,000) is expected, with the actual assignments based on such factors as the needs of students to be served, the intern's expertise and prior experience, and the intensity of intern supervision and support.

III. Supervision, Mentoring, and Collaboration

3.1   Professional field supervision of each intern is provided by a credentialed school psychologist or, in a nonschool setting, by a psychologist credentialed for that setting.* Field supervision may be shared with other appropriately credentialed personnel in the unit, but the credentialed school psychologist or psychologist provides the preponderance of direct supervision and assumes full responsibility for the supervision provided.

3.2   The intern field supervisor has at least 3 years of full-time experience as a credentialed school psychologist or psychologist and is employed as a regular employee or consultant by the district or agency.

3.3   Unless supervisors have been assigned a significant portion of their time to devote to supervising interns, each supervisor is assigned to no more than two interns at any one time.* Intern supervision is taken into account when determining supervisor workload.

3.4 The internship includes an average of at least 2 hours of supervision per full-time week. The preponderance of field supervision is provided on at least a weekly, individual, face-to-face basis, with structured mentoring and evaluation that focus on development of the intern's competencies.* Supervision time may be adjusted proportionately for less than a full-time week or schedule.

3.5 The university program assigns to each intern a faculty supervisor* with training in school psychology who maintains regular communication with the intern and field supervisor. Such communication may occur through faculty supervisor visits to the internship site (if geographically feasible), telephone or conference calls, e-mails, and other means.

3.6 Interns have the opportunity to develop an affiliation with colleagues and the field* through regularly scheduled training activities with (a) other interns at the site, (b) interns at other sites in the immediate area, and/or (c) school psychologists at the site and/or in the immediate area.

3.7 The preparing program provides field supervisors with information and support for supervision as well as documentation needed to verify supervision activities for such purposes as continuing professional development.

IV. Intern Evaluation, Feedback, and Support

4.1 The intern field supervisor provides the intern and university program informal and formal evaluations (with associated criteria or rubrics) of the intern's performance* at least once each semester and offers suggestions for improvement as necessary.

4.2 The internship site in collaboration with the university program has a process for addressing possible serious concerns regarding an intern's performance that protects the rights of clients to receive quality services, assures adequate feedback and opportunities for improvement to the intern, and provides due process protection in cases of possible termination of the internship.

4.3 The internship site provides office supplies, materials, travel reimbursement, and other support similar to that provided to school psychologists in the district/agency.* Sites are strongly encouraged to provide interns a stipend that recognizes their graduate level of training and the value of services they provide.

4.4 The internship site affords interns opportunities for continuing professional development comparable to those provided to school psychologists in the district/agency.

4.5 Upon conclusion of the internship, the supervisor verifies both the completion of required internship hours and activities and the quality of intern performance.

Joe Prus, PhD, NCSP, is Director of the School Psychology Program at Winthrop University in SC and a member of the NASP Standards Writing Committee.

Sample School Psychology Internship Agreement[1]

INTERNSHIP AGREEMENT

_____

[Name of School System/Agency]

has agreed to accept

_____

[Name of Intern]

as an intern for the _____ academic year. The internship site and the intern agree to observe the following arrangements in meeting the requirements of the internship:

1. **DURATION:** The internship will begin on _____, and continue through _____. The intern is expected to follow the same daily schedule and yearly calendar as other school psychology staff employed by the local school system/agency. The intern is not required to remain in the employment of the local school system/agency beyond the term of the internship. Furthermore, the intern is not guaranteed employment beyond the term of the internship.

2. **HOURS:** The intern is appointed on a full-time basis for one year. The intern must complete at least _____ hours of supervised experience. As with regularly employed pupil services personnel, the intern demonstrates a commitment to the provision of psychological services not necessarily reflected in hourly schedules.

3. **LOCATION:** The internship will be performed at the following location(s):

   Name of School District: _____

   Address: _____

4. **PLAN:** Internship activities shall be determined by a written plan developed jointly by the intern and school district personnel and approved by the university internship supervisor. It is expected the plan will be consistent with the guidelines and objectives as contained in the Internship Handbook and with the internship training standards promulgated by the National Association of School Psychologists (NASP) internship criteria.

5. **COMPENSATION:** The intern is provided a salary commensurate with his or her level of training, experience and period of appointment. The intern will be paid in the amount of $_____ for

1 Adapted from the _Illinois School Psychology Internship Manual_ (pp. 50–52), by the Illinois Directors of University School Psychology Programs, 2006.

the term of the internship. Any work-related travel necessary to fulfill the requirements of the internship shall be reimbursed in accordance with the policies of the local school system/agency.

6. **CONFERENCES, SEMINARS, AND IN-SERVICE TRAINING:** Ongoing conferences, seminars, and in-service training opportunities available to employed school psychologists should also be available to interns. The intern is encouraged to participate in state, regional, and national level meetings for school psychologists. Expense reimbursement consistent with policies pertaining to agency school psychologists is consistent with policies pertaining to agency school psychologists. Released time for attendance at professional meetings is required. The intern will be expected to attend the following conferences, seminars, and/or in-service training program(s):
   - Intern/intern supervision workshop
   - Illinois School Psychologists Association (ISPA) Annual Conference
   - University Internship Seminars

7. **WORK ENVIRONMENT:** Consistent with the availability of resources to employed staff, the intern is provided adequate supplies and materials to carry out the functions of the internship. An appropriate work environment should include adequate privacy of office facilities and access to administrative assistance, telephone services, office equipment, and copying machines.

8. **SUPERVISION:** The cooperating practitioner must hold a valid credential as a school psychologist. Full-time employment at the internship setting for at least one year prior to assuming supervisory responsibilities for an intern is required. Concurrent full-time employment as a school psychologist is required. Cooperating practitioners shall provide at least two hours per week of direct supervision for each intern and be responsible for no more than two interns at a time. The intern will receive at least two hours of supervision per week directly from:

_____/_____

Name of Cooperating Practitioner/Certification Number and State)

The university supervisor (or designate) shall maintain an ongoing relationship with the cooperating practitioner and the intern. The university supervisor (or designate) will make at least one site visit per semester for each intern.

9. **TRAINING COMMITMENT:** The local school system/agency is primarily committed to the internship as a training experience. Employing interns as a means of acquiring less expensive services is unacceptable. Interns are expected to participate in tasks appropriate to the completion of the internship training plan. The intern will not be asked to serve in any capacity other than that for which she or he was appointed.

Signatures for Approval:

_____   **Date**

Intern

_____   **Date**

Cooperating Practitioner

_____   **Date**

University Supervisor (or Designee)

Field Evaluation of Student's Clinical Competencies[1]

Your performance ratings of the student are important to us. In addition to providing performance-based evaluation of this student, feedback from site supervisors helps us evaluate and improve our Program. Thank you, in advance, for your cooperation on this important task.

The ratings should be based on your observation and reports received from other staff, parents, students, etc. Circle the number of the scale that best describes the student's current performance based on the descriptions below. Rate each category independently.

1. **Poor.** Fails to meet expectations. Consistently performs poorly and needs improvement. A specific plan and period of time should be established to improve performance.
2. **Below Standard.** Performance is below average. Requires improvement to perform effectively in a professional environment.
3. **Standard.** Most students will possess skills and judgment sufficient to meet professional demands in this area, and a large proportion of them will remain in this range. Meets typical expectations.
4. **Above Standard.** Performance and judgment of students in this category is decidedly better than average. Shows sensitivity, judgment, and skill beyond what is normally expected or displayed by peers.
5. **Outstanding.** Performance is recognizably and decidedly better than that of a large proportion of other students.
6. **Not Observed.** Insufficient data to make rating at this time.

1 Adapted from several materials in *Professional Development and Supervision of School Psychologists: From Intern to Expert* (2nd ed.), by V. S. Harvey and J. A. Struzziero, 2008, Thousand Oaks, CA: Corwin Press/National Association of School Psychologists.

Student: _____ **Date:** _____

Supervisor: _____ **School/Agency:** _____

Key: 1 – Poor; 2 – Below Standard; 3 – Standard; 4 – Above Standard; 5 – Outstanding; N/O – Not Observed

Performance Domain	Performance Rating	Comments
1. Data-based Decision Making/Accountability		
a. Understands/uses assessment in a problem solving context	1 2 3 4 5 N/O	
b. Uses appropriate assessment strategies for individual students	1 2 3 4 5 N/O	
c. Uses appropriate assessment strategies for program evaluation and accountability	1 2 3 4 5 N/O	
d. Uses assessment to inform special education eligibility decisions	1 2 3 4 5 N/O	
2. Evidence-based Interventions		
a. Interventions match appropriately with identified problem(s)	1 2 3 4 5 N/O	
b. Knowledge/application of evidence-based social-emotional/behavior interventions	1 2 3 4 5 N/O	
c. Knowledge/application of evidence-based counseling interventions	1 2 3 4 5 N/O	
d. Knowledge/application of evidence-based academic and instructional interventions	1 2 3 4 5 N/O	
e. Intervention fidelity is assessed	1 2 3 4 5 N/O	
f. Follows up to provide necessary support	1 2 3 4 5 N/O	
3. Consultation/Collaboration		
a. Displays knowledge/skill in consultative problem solving	1 2 3 4 5 N/O	
b. Conveys information accurately/effectively	1 2 3 4 5 N/O	
c. Works collaboratively with others	1 2 3 4 5 N/O	
d. Displays appropriate interpersonal communication skills	1 2 3 4 5 N/O	
e. Understands/uses organizational consultation (e.g., consultation with administrators or groups)	1 2 3 4 5 N/O	

4. Multicultural/Diversity		
a. Possesses adequate knowledge base regarding age, race, ethnicity, gender, disability, sexual orientation, and culture	1 2 3 4 5 N/O	
b. Understands how race, ethnicity, and culture may affect client behavior and attitudes	1 2 3 4 5 N/O	
c. Uses culturally appropriate assessment and intervention methods	1 2 3 4 5 N/O	
d. Is aware of how own culture affects her/his work and how it impacts others	1 2 3 4 5 N/O	
e. Works to increase the multicultural/diversity sensitivity of the school/agency	1 2 3 4 5 N/O	
5. Prevention, Crisis Intervention, Mental Health		
a. Knows/recognizes behaviors and risk factors that are precursors to disorders or threats to wellness	1 2 3 4 5 N/O	
b. Is familiar with prevention and risk reduction programs/activities	1 2 3 4 5 N/O	
c. Knows principles for responding to crises (e.g., suicide, death, natural disaster, violence)	1 2 3 4 5 N/O	
6. Home-School-Community Collaboration		
a. Knowledge of family systems	1 2 3 4 5 N/O	
b. Communicates effectively with parents/caregivers	1 2 3 4 5 N/O	
c. Creates/strengthens links with community-based agencies and resources	1 2 3 4 5 N/O	
7. Research and Program Evaluation		
a. Is aware of current literature in the field of school psychology and education	1 2 3 4 5 N/O	
b. Understands measurement practices and outcomes and can explain to others	1 2 3 4 5 N/O	
c. Designs evaluations relevant to own work	1 2 3 4 5 N/O	

8. Professional Issues		
a. Knows/applies laws regarding school policies and practices including special education identification and IEP development	1 2 3 4 5 N/O	
b. Knows/applies legal and ethical standards in professional practice	1 2 3 4 5 N/O	
c. Demonstrates professional behavior in his or her work	1 2 3 4 5 N/O	
d. Participates in professional development activities	1 2 3 4 5 N/O	
9. Information Technology		
a. Demonstrates knowledge of information resources	1 2 3 4 5 N/O	
b. Uses technology to safeguard and enhance quality of services	1 2 3 4 5 N/O	
10. Supervision		
a. Prepares for supervision	1 2 3 4 5 N/O	
b. Exhibits appropriate levels of independence	1 2 3 4 5 N/O	
c. Prioritizes own needs for support	1 2 3 4 5 N/O	
d. Uses supervision time productively	1 2 3 4 5 N/O	
Overall Rating of Student:	1 2 3 4 5 N/O	

Appendix D

Professional Behaviors Evaluation of Student[1]

The Professional Behaviors evaluation is to be completed for students at the end of the Fall, Winter, and Spring quarters. The purpose is to provide feedback on student progress, identify students' strengths and weaknesses, and identify activities or procedures that may be considered with students who are not performing up to program/departmental expectations.

Please rate the student in those areas for which you have information. Circle the number of the scale that best describes the student's current performance based on the descriptions below. Each evaluator is encouraged to provide additional comments at the end of this form. Ratings will be discussed with the student.

1. **Poor.** Fails to meet expectations. Consistently performs poorly and needs improvement. A specific plan and period of time should be established to improve performance.
2. **Below Standard.** Performance is below average. Requires improvement to perform effectively in a professional environment.
3. **Standard.** Meets typical expectations. Most students will possess skills and judgment sufficient to meet professional demands in this area, and a large proportion of them will remain in this range.
4. **Above Standard.** Performance and judgment of students in this category is decidedly better than average. Shows sensitivity, judgment, and skill beyond what is normally expected or displayed by peers.
5. **Outstanding.** Performance is recognizably and decidedly better than that of a large proportion of other students.
6. **Not Observed.** Insufficient data to make rating at this time.

1 Adapted from materials in:
(a) *Professional Development and Supervision of School Psychologists: From Intern to Expert* (2nd ed.), by V. S. Harvey and J. A. Struzziero, 2008, Thousand Oaks, CA: Corwin Press/National Association of School Psychologists.
(b) "Problematic Behaviors: Mediating Differences and Negotiating Change," by T. K. Cruise, and M. E. Swerdlik, 2010, in *Handbook of Education, Training, and Supervision of School Psychologists in School and Community* (Vol. 2, pp. 135–136), by J. Kaufman, T. L. Hughes, and C. A. Riccio (Eds.), 2010, New York: Routledge.

Student: _____   **Rater:** _____

Course: _____   **Quarter:** _____

Key: 1 – Poor; 2 – Below Standard; 3 – Standard; 4 – Above Standard; 5 – Outstanding; N/O – Not Observed

Dispositional Area	Rating	Comments
1. Professionalism and Self-awareness		
a. Exhibits appropriate professional appearance and self-presentation	1 2 3 4 5 N/O	
b. Adapts to the demands of the program/setting	1 2 3 4 5 N/O	
c. Aware of impact of personal values and beliefs	1 2 3 4 5 N/O	
d. Engages in problem solving to address problem situations	1 2 3 4 5 N/O	
2. Ethical Responsibility		
a. Demonstrates knowledge of ethical guidelines	1 2 3 4 5 N/O	
b. Applies ethical guidelines to practice	1 2 3 4 5 N/O	
c. Does not practice beyond areas of competence	1 2 3 4 5 N/O	
d. Seeks out resources when faced with novel problems or situations	1 2 3 4 5 N/O	
3. Initiative and Dependability		
a. Work is organized	1 2 3 4 5 N/O	
b. Meets deadlines	1 2 3 4 5 N/O	
c. Follows through on responsibilities	1 2 3 4 5 N/O	
d. Punctuality	1 2 3 4 5 N/O	
4. Interpersonal Relationships		
a. Understands others' points of view	1 2 3 4 5 N/O	
b. Resolves conflict situations in a professional manner	1 2 3 4 5 N/O	
c. Exhibits positive relationships with faculty, staff, peers, clients, and other professionals	1 2 3 4 5 N/O	

5. Communication Skills		
a. Clearly expresses ideas verbally	1 2 3 4 5 N/O	
b. Clearly expresses ideas in writing	1 2 3 4 5 N/O	
c. Written work is free of errors	1 2 3 4 5 N/O	
d. Demonstrates appropriate non-verbal behaviors	1 2 3 4 5 N/O	
6. Respect for Human Diversity		
a. Sensitive in working with issues of diversity	1 2 3 4 5 N/O	
b. Aware of challenges individual differences pose in the schools	1 2 3 4 5 N/O	
7. Completion of Work		
a. Completes coursework in an appropriate time frame	1 2 3 4 5 N/O	
b. Completes field-based assignments in an appropriate time frame	1 2 3 4 5 N/O	
c. Quality of class assignments	1 2 3 4 5 N/O	
d. Quality of field-based work	1 2 3 4 5 N/O	
8. Processes of Supervision		
a. Prepares for supervision	1 2 3 4 5 N/O	
b. Accepts feedback constructively	1 2 3 4 5 N/O	
c. Seeks to resolve issues raised in supervision	1 2 3 4 5 N/O	
d. Open to professional growth	1 2 3 4 5 N/O	
Overall Rating of Student:	1 2 3 4 5 N/O	
General Comments:		

Evaluation of Field Experience and Field Supervision[1]

Your ratings of your field experience are important to us. Your feedback helps us assess the quality of the opportunities we provide to you and to evaluate and improve our Program. Thank you, in advance, for your efforts to help us on this important task.

Select the number of the scale that best describes your experience based on the descriptions below. Rate each category independently.

1. **Poor.** Failed to meet my expectations.
2. **Below Standard.** Met some, but not most of my expectations.
3. **Standard.** Met my expectations.
4. **Above Standard.** Exceeded my expectations.
5. **Outstanding.** Superior experience based on my expectations.

1 Adapted from several materials in *Professional Development and Supervision of School Psychologists: From Intern to Expert* (2nd ed.), by V. S. Harvey and J. A. Struzziero, 2008, Thousand Oaks, CA: Corwin Press/National Association of School Psychologists.

Intern: _____ **Date:** _____		
Primary Field Supervisor: _____ **School/Agency:** _____		
Key: 1 – Poor; 2 – Below Standard; 3 – Standard; 4 – Above Standard; 5 – Outstanding		

Field Domain	Rating	Comments
1. Support from Host District and School(s)		
a. Initial orientation and welcome	1 2 3 4 5	
b. Explanation of rules, procedures, and policies	1 2 3 4 5	
c. Access to work space and materials	1 2 3 4 5	
d. Access to professional development training	1 2 3 4 5	
e. Coordination between sites (if more than one school)	1 2 3 4 5	
f. Range/diversity of training opportunities	1 2 3 4 5	
2. Assessment of Field Supervision		
a. Clarity of field supervisor's expectations	1 2 3 4 5	
b. Field supervisor's role in developing a practicum or internship plan	1 2 3 4 5	
c. Availability of field supervision	1 2 3 4 5	
d. Constructive written and oral feedback/evaluation	1 2 3 4 5	
e. Level of scaffolding adjusted to meet my needs	1 2 3 4 5	
f. Emotional support	1 2 3 4 5	
g. Range/diversity of training opportunities	1 2 3 4 5	
Overall Rating of Field Experience	1 2 3 4 5	
Overall Rating of Field Supervision	1 2 3 4 5	

Evaluation of University Preparation and Support for Field Experience[1]

Your opinions about university preparation and support for your field experience are important to us. Your feedback helps us assess the quality of opportunities we provide to you and to evaluate and improve our Program. Thank you, in advance, for your efforts to help us on this important task.

Select the number of the scale that best describes your experience based on the descriptions below. Rate each category independently.

1. **Poor.** Failed to meet my expectations.
2. **Below Standard.** Met some, but not most of my expectations.
3. **Standard.** Met my expectations.
4. **Above Standard.** Exceeded my expectations.
5. **Outstanding.** Superior experience based on my expectations.

1 Adapted from several materials in *Professional Development and Supervision of School Psychologists: From Intern to Expert* (2nd ed.), by V. S. Harvey and J. A. Struzziero, 2008, Thousand Oaks, CA: Corwin Press/National Association of School Psychologists.

Intern: _____		**Date:** _____
Primary Field Supervisor: _____		**School/Agency:** _____
Primary University Supervisor: _____		

Key: 1 – Poor; 2 – Below Standard; 3 – Standard; 4 – Above Standard; 5 – Outstanding

Field Domain	Rating	Comments
1. Preparation for Field Experience Through Coursework		
a. Understanding of contemporary roles and responsibilities of school psychologists and school service delivery systems	1 2 3 4 5	
b. Data-based decision making and accountability	1 2 3 4 5	
c. Understanding of legal and ethical issues in practice	1 2 3 4 5	
d. Evidence-based academic/instructional interventions	1 2 3 4 5	
e. Evidence-based social/behavioral support and mental health interventions	1 2 3 4 5	
f. Consultation, coaching, and staff development	1 2 3 4 5	
g. Work in diverse communities and with diverse students, families, and staff	1 2 3 4 5	
h. Communicating with educators and parents through oral presentations, meetings, and presentations	1 2 3 4 5	
i. Crisis intervention	1 2 3 4 5	
j. Producing answers to important school or community questions through data use, including research and program evaluation	1 2 3 4 5	
2. Assessment of University Supervision		
a. Relevance of practicum or internship seminar content (goals, big ideas, readings, discussion)	1 2 3 4 5	
b. Clarity of university supervisor's expectations	1 2 3 4 5	
c. University supervisor's role in developing a practicum or internship plan	1 2 3 4 5	
d. Availability of university supervision with faculty	1 2 3 4 5	

e. Constructive written and oral feedback/evaluation from university supervisor	1 2 3 4 5	
f. Emotional support from university supervisor	1 2 3 4 5	
g. Availability of peer group supervision	1 2 3 4 5	
h. Constructive feedback/evaluation from group	1 2 3 4 5	
i. Communication between university supervisor and field supervisor	1 2 3 4 5	
Overall Rating of Preparation for Field Experience Through Coursework	1 2 3 4 5	
Overall Rating of University Supervision	1 2 3 4 5	

Appendix G

Sample Remediation Plan, Including Use of Personal Therapy and Due Process Rights[1]

DATE:

Dear Elizabeth:

As you know, you have missed another deadline (i.e., the end of summer 2007) regarding the completion of your master's thesis or doctoral Research Apprenticeship project. Consequently, you are now officially prevented from sitting for the fall semester administration of the doctoral comprehensive examination. The School Psychology Coordinating Committee (SPCC) has met to discuss your failure to meet this deadline. The SPCC, consistent with our Graduate Student Evaluation and Remediation Policies and Procedures, has identified your pattern of behavior as indicative of problematic professional competence in the areas of time management, decision making, and self-evaluation/appraisal.

Our concerns about these problematic behaviors have been shared with you in your annual feedback sessions. Regrettably, the problems have not been ameliorated. Indeed, your performance regarding the research requirement in the PhD program creates the impression you are unresponsive to feedback from faculty in School Psychology. As of this date, the SPCC is no longer willing to accept your unfinished master's thesis as potential credit in lieu of the doctoral Research Apprenticeship.

Even though you have many assets considered important for one entering a helping profession, including strong interpersonal skills and intelligence, the SPCC believes your problematic behaviors have high potential to negatively impact your future professional functioning as a doctoral-level school psychologist. Based upon our identification of competency concerns in the areas specified above, the SPCC has determined that your status in the doctoral program is Probationary, and remediation is necessary. As such, the SPCC has developed a remedial plan for you.

The plan has the following requirements:

1. You must immediately begin to meet weekly with Dr. Competent, Chair of your doctoral advisory committee, to set goals related to the completion of your Research Apprenticeship project. These weekly meetings must continue until you have officially selected a research mentor to direct your Apprenticeship. This selection must occur no later than October 1, 2007. Once your research mentor is selected, you are required to meet weekly with him/her until the *completion* of your research project, or until your research mentor has determined these weekly meetings are unnecessary. Failure to make and/or keep these weekly appointments will lead the SPCC to conclude that your remediation plan is unsuccessful.

1 From "Problematic Behaviors: Mediating Differences and Negotiating Change," by T. K. Cruise, and M. E. Swerdlik, 2010, in *Handbook of Education, Training, and Supervision of School Psychologists in School and Community* (Vol. 2, pp. 143–144), by J. Kaufman, T. L. Hughes, and C. A. Riccio (Eds.), New York: Routledge. Copyright 2010 by Taylor & Francis. Reprinted with permission.

2. You must immediately seek personal therapy (available at no cost from the University Student Counseling Center or at an agency of your choice). Treatment goals must include improved time management, more realistic self-evaluation/assessment of your current functioning and future goals, and improved decision making. You must inform the SPCC of the date of your first therapeutic session. Although the details of your work with the therapist will be confidential, you must provide documentation to the SPCC that you are regularly attending these counseling sessions. Failure to *immediately* seek professional therapy, and failure to document your regular attendance at these therapeutic sessions, will lead the SPCC to conclude that your remediation plan is unsuccessful.

3. You must have an officially approved Institutional Review Board (IRB) proposal for the Research Apprenticeship project no later January 1, 2008. This deadline requires that you submit your proposal to the IRB in time for its December meeting. Once submitted and approved, you will be required to provide the SPCC the official IRB approval number. If you fail to meet this IRB proposal submission deadline, you will be summarily dismissed from the doctoral program. Most importantly, you must complete *all* requirements for the Research Apprenticeship no later December 15, 2008. These requirements include, but are not limited to, a colloquium presentation of your project to the Department of Psychology during the fall semester of 2008. If you fail to complete all requirements of the Research Apprenticeship by the stipulated deadline, you will be summarily dismissed from the doctoral program.

If you satisfy *all* requirements specified in the three paragraphs above, you will be restored of Full status in the PhD program (i.e, no longer on Probation). Once you are restored to Full status, the SPCC will determine when it is appropriate for you to take the doctoral comprehensive examination. If, however, one or more of the above requirements is not satisfied, you will be summarily dismissed from the doctoral program.

If you accept all terms of this remedial plan, please indicate such in writing addressed to the SPCC no later than August 22, 2007. If the Committee does not receive such notice by that date, you will be summarily dismissed from the doctoral program. Consistent with program policies, you may appeal this action by contacting Dr. Merit, Department Chair, within 14 days of receipt of this letter or to the Office of Student Dispute Resolution Services www.linktowebsite.edu/

Elizabeth, we feel you have numerous strengths. As such, the faculty in School Psychology stands ready to assist you in completing this remedial plan, including your Research Apprenticeship, so you may continue in the doctoral program.

For the School Psychology Coordinating Committee:
Jared Competent, PhD

Coordinator, Graduate Programs in School Psychology
Professor of Psychology

Sample Curriculum Vitae[1]

Name

123 ABC Street
City, State, Zip
name@address.com
(###) 123 - 4567 (home)
(###) 123 - 4567 (fax)

PhD School Psychology
University of ABC, City, State
NASP-approved, APA-accredited program
Dissertation: Title
Research Advisor: John Smith, PhD
Expected August 20XX

EdS School Psychology
ABC State University, City, State
NASP-approved, NCATE-accredited program
May 20XX

BA Psychology
Minor in Elementary Education
ABC College, City, State
Cum Laude
August 20XX

CREDENTIALS AND CERTIFICATES

Nationally Certified School Psychologist (NCSP)
Certification # 12345
7/20XX – 7/20XX

SPECIALIZED TRAINING IN SCHOOL PSYCHOLOGY

Traineeship, Applied Behavioral Analysis (ABA), 20XX-20XX
Completed the requirements of a USDE grant that trained school psychology graduate students
to work with children with autism spectrum and behavioral disorders within urban school
systems. Requirements included three courses (nine semester credits) of related coursework, and
a year-long practicum at a school site that serves children with autism and behavioral disorders.

1 Reprinted with permission of the publisher. www.nasponline.org

FIELD EXPERIENCES IN SCHOOL PSYCHOLOGY

School Psychology Intern, ABC School District, 20XX-20XX
Sally Smith, NCSP, Supervising School Psychologist
Completed a 1500-hour doctoral internship where I provided a range of psychological services to children in grades K–9.

- Consulted and collaborated with teachers, administrators, and parents
- Participated on School Consultation Teams
- Developed, implemented, and evaluated behavior intervention plans
- Conducted comprehensive evaluations, including ecological, curriculum based measurement, dynamic assessment, and standardized testing
- Contributed to IEP development for children with learning, language, and emotional disabilities
- Maintained an individual counseling caseload
- Provided group counseling that focused on issues related to self-esteem and social skills development

GRADUATE ASSISTANTSHIP

Program Assistant, XYZ University, School Psychology Program, 20XX-20XX
Joe Johnson, PhD, NCSP, Supervising Faculty Member
A 9-Month assistantship consisting of 20-hours per week

- Supported faculty with undergraduate study skills courses
  - Tasks include grading, occasional lecturing, meeting with students, lab set ups, and other duties as assigned
- Assisted with specific tasks and assignments associated with NCATE accreditation preparation (i.e., electronic documents, web interface, data retrieval and entry into databases, consultant/review team arrangements, correspondence, etc.)
- Developed electronic brochures, student survey and generation of program reports as needed by department faculty

RELATED EXPERIENCE

Support Staff, ABC Mental Health Agency, 20XX-20XX
City, State
Jane Doe, PsyD, Supervising Clinical Psychologist
Purpose: A part-time position providing group therapy as an outpatient service for children with emotional disabilities. Completed 1000 hours.

- Consulted and collaborated with staff and parents regarding treatment plans and services
- Developed intervention plans and goals
- Maintained an individual counseling caseload and provided group counseling that focused on a wide range of issues including divorce, drug abuse, and social skills development

PUBLICATIONS

Doe, J. (In press). Culturally competent practice: Training and supervision. *School Psychology Review, XX*, xxx-xxx.

Smith, J., & **Doe, J.** (2008). Working together: The value of supervision. *School Psychology Quarterly, XX*, xxx-xxx.

CONFERENCE PRESENTATIONS

Smith, J., **Doe, J.,** & Brown, R. (2008, March). *Experimental evaluation of a prevention program developing socioemotional competencies.* Symposium presented at the annual meeting of the National Association of School Psychologists, New Orleans, LA.

WORKSHOPS PROVIDED

Doe, J. (2008, August, 18). *All the necessary tools for implementing RTI.* In-service presented to teachers across grades 6–8 at ABC Middle School. Information presented included strategies for data collection and monitoring as well as a review of the problem-solving process used by school-based teams.

PROFESSIONAL DEVELOPMENT

PREPaRE: Prevention and Preparedness–The Comprehensive School Crisis Team
December 20XX
Presenter: Sam Johnson
Received *certificate of continuing professional development* for 8 hours of training

Recent Legal Developments in Special Education
November 20XX
Presenter: ABC Law Offices
Some State Association of School Psychologists Conference 20XX
Received *certificate of continuing professional development* for 3 hours of training

Improving Advocacy Skills Within Your School: A Focus on School-Wide Collaboration
May 20XX
Presenter: Sally Smith
XYZ County School System

PROFESSIONAL ASSOCIATIONS: LEADERSHIP

Student Leader, 20XX–20XX, National Association of School Psychologists
The role of a NASP Student Leader is to serve as a liaison between NASP and the graduate students in a university school psychology program.

- Distributed information to fellow students regarding NASP resources and upcoming events;
- Developed and participated in a School Psychology Awareness Week outreach activity in the fall that included the sale of school psychology t-shirts;
- Developed and participated in an advocacy activity in the spring;
- Gave feedback to NASP as requested on various student initiatives;
- Collected information from colleagues to help with student resource development; and
- Posted regularly on the student and Student Leader Online Communities.

CLD Recruitment Ambassador, 20XX – 20XX, National Association of School Psychologists
The role of a CLD Ambassador is to serve as a spokesperson for the profession and NASP by delivering school psychology recruitment presentations to undergraduate students from culturally and linguistically diverse backgrounds.

- Presented NASP Career PowerPoint presentation to undergraduate classes (psychology & ethnic studies courses) in institutions with large numbers of students from diverse backgrounds
- Provided NASP resources to students, and answered questions
- Distributed surveys at presentations to evaluate the presentation and collect data on the program
- Conducted two school psychology career presentations per year

PROFESSIONAL ASSOCIATIONS: MEMBERSHIPS

National Association of School Psychologists
State Association of School Psychologists
American Psychological Association: Division 16
Local Association of School Psychologists
Student Affiliates of School Psychology: APA
Psi Chi Honor Society

REFERENCES

Anna M. Peña, NCSP
School Psychologist
ABC County School System
Apena@abc.edu
xxx-xxx-xxxx

This fact sheet was developed by Anna M. Peña, NCSP, School Psychologist, and member of the NASP Student Development Workgroup, and reviewed by NASP staff and school psychology faculty members.

Sample Cover Letter

February 15th, 2012

Dear Dr. Chang,

Please accept my application for a school psychologist position in the Appleton County Schools for the 2012–2013 school year. Enclosed you will find my curriculum vitae, three letters of recommendation, my official graduate transcript, and two work samples completed during my internship year. I believe my interests and skills match well with the district's mission and the description of the open position.

I am currently a school psychology intern working in Morris County Schools. I will complete my internship and obtain my state and national certification as a school psychologist in the summer of 2012. As you will see from my CV, I have gotten a breadth of relevant experiences over the past three years, including working at the preschool, elementary, middle, and high school levels with ethnically, linguistically, and economically diverse children and families. In addition to numerous other activities, a main area of focus during my internship has been data-based decision making and problem solving. I have helped structure a multi-tiered system of service delivery including Response to Intervention (RTI) at the elementary school level, and have provided professional development about RtI to all district psychologists. In addition, I have been responsible for collecting assessment data, implementing academic and behavioral interventions, and monitoring student outcomes throughout the year.

A particular area of interest for me is multicultural issues, including social advocacy for underserved or marginalized students and families. For example, my school psychology internship supervisor and I have collaborated extensively to change the special education referral process at the elementary level due to an overrepresentation of minority students in special education. In addition, at the high school level, I have worked with the school counselor to co-facilitate a group to support gay, lesbian, bisexual, transgender, and questioning (GLBTQ) students.

I am eager to begin my career as a school psychologist, and I believe my school psychology training and field experiences have provided me with the ability to hit the ground running next year.

Thank you for your time and for considering this application. Should you have any questions, please contact me at (987)-654-3210.

Sincerely,
Fatima Ali, M.Ed.

Job Interview Transcripts from Videos Featured on Companion Website

Version One: Interview with Dr. Laura Williams

To begin, tell me about yourself.

Why did you decide to be a school psychologist?

Tell me about one of your strengths as a school psychologist.

In what areas do you feel you need more professional development as you begin your early career?

Tell me about a time during practicum or internship when you faced a difficult challenge. How did you approach this challenge? Were you successful in resolving the problem?

Given the multifaceted nature of the school psychologist role . . . what do you view to be the most important aspects of the job?

This position would require you to work in three different school buildings. How would you navigate your position across several schools?

If you were hired, you would be asked to work on various teams within the district. Tell me about a time you were a member of a successful team and describe your role in the team's success.

What experiences have you had working with diverse populations? How should multicultural competencies be incorporated into the school psychologist role?

How do you suppose working full-time as a school psychologist will differ from your work as an intern?

Why are you interested in working at our school district?

Is there anything else you did not get the chance to mention that you feel is important for us to know about you as a candidate?

Do you have any questions for me about the position or the district?

Version Two: Interview with Dr. Allan Turner

Before I begin with my questions, tell me a little about your background and why you decided to become a school psychologist.

Please describe what qualities you believe an effective school psychologist must possess.

What particular areas of interest have you developed during your school psychology training?

Everyone has unique strengths as well as areas that could use improvement. What are your greatest strengths? Also, what areas are more difficult for you?

Now, please tell me about your biggest accomplishment during your internship year.

School psychologists take on many different roles. What role does consultation have in school psychology service delivery?

How do you view counseling fitting into the school psychologist role?

What is your understanding of Response to Intervention? Have you been involved with the implementation of RTI during your practicum or internship?

Now describe a time you had too many things on your plate. How did you prioritize your responsibilities?

What experiences have you had with crisis prevention or intervention?

Describe a time you showed initiative or leadership during your internship.

Tell me what you would do if a parent insisted you test their child when you felt it was either inappropriate or unnecessary.

Now describe your understanding of the special education eligibility decision-making process from start to finish.

We are beginning to implement Positive Behavior Interventions and Supports in several schools in our district. What is your experience with PBIS? Would that be something you could see yourself being involved with?

As you may know, we have many applicants who would love to join our staff. Is there anything else we should know about you that makes you a unique candidate for this position?

Do you have any questions for me about the position or the district?

References

Alessi, G.J., Lascurettes-Alessi, K.J., & Leys, W.L. (1981). Internships in school psychology: Supervision issues. *School Psychology Review, 10,* 461–469.

American Institute of Stress (2011). *What is stress?* Retrieved August 6, 2012 from www.stress.org/what-is-stress/

American Psychological Association (2003). Guidelines on multicultural education, training, research, practice, and organizational change for psychologists. *American Psychologist, 58,* 377–402.

American Psychological Association (2006). *Advancing colleague assistance in professional psychology.* Retrieved November 17, 2011 from www.apa.org/practice/resources/assistance/index.aspx

American Psychological Association (2009). *Guidelines and principles for accreditation of programs in professional psychology.* Washington, DC: Author.

American Psychological Association (2010). *Ethical principles of psychologists and code of conduct.* Washington, DC: Author.

American Psychological Association Advisory Committee on Colleague Assistance (2009). *Who cares? Barriers, benefits, and resources in colleague assistance and self-care.* Retrieved November 17, 2011 from www.apa.org/practice/leadership/colleague-assistance.aspx

Argyris, C. (1990). *Overcoming organizational defenses: Facilitating organizational learning.* Boston: Allyn & Bacon.

Armistead, L. (2008). Best practices in continuing professional development for school psychologists. In A. Thomas & J. Grimes (Eds.), *Best practices in school psychology V* (pp. 1975–1989). Bethesda, MD: National Association of School Psychologists.

Armistead, L., Williams, B.B., & Jacob, S. (2011). *Professional ethics for school psychologists: A problem-solving model casebook* (2nd ed.). Bethesda, MD: National Association of School Psychologists.

Association of State and Provincial Psychology Boards (2008). *ASPPB's guide for students and faculty.* Retrieved November 17, 2011 from www.asppb.net/i4a/pages/index.cfm?pageid=3290

Aten, J.D., Strain, J.D., & Gillespie, R.E. (2008). A transtheoretical model of clinical supervision. *Training and Education in Professional Psychology, 2,* 1–9.

Baird, B.N. (2008). *Internship, practicum, and field placement handbook: A guide for the helping professions* (5th ed.). Upper Saddle River, NJ: Pearson.

Barnett, J.E. (2008). Impaired professionals: Distress, professional impairment, self-care, and psychological wellness. In M. Hersen & A.M. Gross (Eds.), *Handbook of clinical psychology* (Vol. 1, pp. 857–884). Hoboken, NJ: Wiley and Sons.

Barnett, J.E., & Cooper, N. (2009). Creating a culture of self-care. *Clinical Psychology: Science and Practice, 16,* 16–20.

Barnett, J.E., Cornish, J.A.E., Goodyear, R.K., & Lichtenberg, J.W. (2007). Commentaries on the ethical and effective practice of clinical supervision. *Professional Psychology: Research and Practice, 38,* 268–275.

Bateman, T.S., & Crant, J.M. (1993). The proactive component of organizational behavior: A measure and correlates. *Journal of Organizational Behavior, 14,* 103–118.

Bateman, T.S., & Crant, J.M. (1999). Proactive behavior: Meaning, impact, recommendations. *Business Horizons, 42,* 63–70.

Belar, C.D. (2009). Advancing the culture of competence. *Training and Education in Professional Psychology, 3,* S63–S65.

Benner, P. (1984). *From novice to expert: Excellence and power in clinical nursing practice.* Menlo Park, CA: Addison-Wesley.

Bernard, J.M., & Goodyear, R.K. (2009). *Fundamentals of clinical supervision* (4th ed.). Upper Saddle River, NJ: Pearson.

Bindl, U.K., & Parker, S.K. (2011). Proactive work behavior: Forward-thinking and change oriented action in organizations. In S. Zedeck (Ed.), *APA handbook of industrial and organizational psychology* (Vol. 2, pp. 567–598). Washington, DC: American Psychological Association.

Boylan, J.C., & Scott, J. (Eds.). (2009). *Practicum and internship: Textbook and resource guide for counseling and psychotherapy* (4th ed.). New York: Routledge.

Brock, S.E., Nickerson, A.B., Reeves, M.A., Jimerson, S.R., Lieberman, R.A., & Feinberg, T.A. (2009). *School crisis prevention and intervention: The PREPaRE model*. Bethesda, MD: National Association of School Psychologists.

Bundy, M.L. (2010). Transitioning forward. In J.R. Studer & J.F. Diambra (Eds.), *A guide to practicum and internship for school counselors-in-training* (pp. 205–224). New York: Routledge.

Butler, S.K. (2003). Multicultural sensitivity and competence in the clinical supervision of school counselors and school psychologists: A context for providing competent services in a multicultural society. *The Clinical Supervisor, 22*, 125–141.

Canady, B. E., Rivera, M., Gerdes, J., Ford, A., Johnson, K., & Nayak, N. (2011). Cultural roadmap: Developing cultural learning strategies during internship. *Training and Education in Professional Psychology, 5*, 30–37.

Caplan, G. (1970). *The theory and practice of mental health consultation*. New York: Basic Books.

Chafouleas, S.M., Clonan, S.M., & Vanauken, T.L. (2002). A national survey of current supervision and evaluation practices of school psychologists. *Psychology in the Schools, 39*, 317–325.

Chin, E. (2009). Using externships, internships, and post-doctoral placements to your advantage. In S.F. Davis, P.J. Giordano, & C.A. Licht (Eds.), *Your career in psychology: Putting your graduate degree to work* (pp. 135–150). Malden, MA: Wiley-Blackwell.

Cochrane, W.S., Salyers, K., & Ding, Y. (2010). An examination of the preparation, supervisor's theoretical model, and university support for supervisors of school psychology interns. *Trainers' Forum: Journal of the Trainer's of School Psychologists, 29*(1), 6–23.

Collins, J. (2001). *Good to great: Why some companies make the leap . . . and others don't*. New York: Harper Collins.

Cone, J.D., & Foster, S.L. (2006). *Dissertations and theses from start to finish* (2nd ed.). Washington, DC: American Psychological Association.

Corey, G., Haynes, R., Moulton, P., & Muratori, M. (2010). *Clinical supervision in the helping professions: A practical guide* (2nd ed.). Alexandria, VA: American Counseling Association.

Council of Directors of School Psychology Programs (1998). *Council of directors of school psychology doctoral level internship guidelines*. Retrieved April 30, 2010 from: http://sites.google.com/site/cdspphome/cdspp-internship-guidelines.

Counselman, E.F., & Weber, R.L. (2004). Organizing and maintaining peer supervision groups. *International Journal of Group Psychotherapy, 54*, 125–143.

Crespi, T.D. (2010). Certification and licensure for school psychologists: Considerations and implications for education, training, and practice. In J. Kaufman, T.L. Hughes, & C.A. Riccio (Eds.), *Handbook of education, training, and supervision of school psychologists in school and community* (Vol. 2, pp. 229–244). New York: Routledge.

Crespi, T.D., & Dube, J.M.B. (2005). Clinical supervision in school psychology: Challenges, considerations, and ethical and legal issues for clinical supervisors. *The Clinical Supervisor, 24*, 115–135.

Crespi, T.D., Fischetti, B.A., & Lopez, P.G. (1998). Supervision and mentoring for professional employment: Resumes and interviewing for prospective school psychologists. *School Psychology International, 19*, 239–250.

Crespi, T.D., & Kaufman, J. (Eds.). (2003). Clinical supervision in the schools: Challenges, opportunities, and lost horizons [Special section]. *The Clinical Supervisor, 22*, 59–210.

Cruise, T.K., & Swerdlik, M.E. (2010). Problematic behaviors: Mediating differences and negotiating change. In J. Kaufman, T.L. Hughes, & C. Riccio (Eds.), *Handbook of education, training, and supervision of school psychologists in school and community* (Vol. 2, pp. 129–152). New York: Routledge.

Csikszentmihalyi, M. (1990). *Flow: The psychology of optimal experience*. New York: Harper Collins.

Curtis, M.J., Hunley, S.A., & Grier, J.E.C. (2002). Relationships among the professional practices and demographic characteristics of school psychologists. *School Psychology Review, 31*, 30–42.

Curtis, M. J., Lopez, A. D., Castillo, J. M., Batsche, G. M., Minch, D., & Smith, J. C. (2008). The status of school psychology: Demographic characteristics, professional practices, and continuing professional development. *National Association of School Psychologists Communiqué, 36*(5), 27–29.

Curtis, M.J., Castillo, J.M., & Gelley, C. (2012). School psychology 2010: Demographics, employment, and the context for professional practices – part 1. *National Association of School Psychologists Communiqué, 40*(7), 1; 28–30.

Daly, E.J. III, Doll, B., Schulte, A.C., & Fenning, P. (2011). The competencies initiative in American professional psychology: Implications for school psychology preparation. *Psychology in the Schools, 48*, 872–886.

Deal, T.E., & Peterson, K.D. (2009). *Shaping school culture: Pitfalls, paradoxes, and promises* (2nd ed.). San Francisco: Jossey-Bass.

Deketelaere, A., Kelchtermans, G., Struyf, E., & De Leyn, P. (2006). Disentangling clinical learning experiences: An exploratory study on the dynamic tensions in internship. *Medical Education, 40*, 908–915.

Denicola, J.A., & Furze, C.T. (2001). The internship year: The transition from student to new professional. In S. Walfish & A.K. Hess (Eds.), *Succeeding in graduate school: The career guide for psychology students*. Mahwah, NJ: Erlbaum.

Dubin, S.S. (1972). Obsolescence or lifelong education: A choice for the professional. *American Psychologist, 27*, 486–498.

Elizalde-Utnick, G. (2007). Young selectively mute English language learners: School-based intervention strategies. *Journal of Early Childhood and Infant Psychology, 3*, 143–163.

Ellis, M., Ladany, N., Krengel, M., & Schult, D. (1996). Clinical supervision research from 1981 to 1993: A methodological critique. *Journal of Counseling Psychology, 43*, 35–50.

Elman, N.S., & Forrest, L. (2007). From trainee impairment to professional competence problems: Seeking new terminology that facilitates effective action. *Professional Psychology: Research and Practice, 338*, 501–509.

Erdogan, B., & Bauer, T.N. (2005). Enhancing career benefits of employee proactive personality: The role of fit with jobs and organizations. *Personnel Psychology, 58*, 859–891.

Fagan, T.K. (2010). Putting school psychology training into historical perspective. What's new? What's old? In E. García-Vázquez, T.D. Crespi, & C.A. Riccio (Eds.), *Handbook of education training, and supervision of school psychologists in school and community* (Vol. 1, pp. 13–31). New York: Routledge.

Fagan, T.K., & Wise, P.S. (2007). *School psychology past, present, and future* (3rd ed.). Bethesda, MD: National Association of School Psychologists.

Falender, C.A., Erickson Cornish, J.A., Goodyear, R., Hatcher, R., Kaslow, N.J., Leventhal, G., et al. (2004). Defining competencies in psychology supervision: A consensus statement. *Journal of Clinical Psychology, 60*, 771–785.

Fouad, N.A., Grus, C.L., Hatcher, R.L., Kaslow, N.J., Hutchings, P.S., Madson, M, Crossman, R.E. (2009). Competency benchmarks: A model for the understanding and measuring of competence in professional psychology across training levels. *Training and Education in Professional Psychology, 3*, S5–S26.

Fukuyama, M.A. (1994). Critical incidents in multicultural counseling supervision: A phenomenological approach to supervision. *Counselor Education and Supervision, 34*, 142–151.

Fullan, M.G., & Hargreaves, A. (1996). *What's worth fighting for in your school?* New York: Teacher's College Press.

Gambrill, E. (2012). *Critical thinking in clinical practice: Improving the quality of judgments and decisions* (3rd ed.). Hoboken, NJ: John Wiley and Sons.

Gelman, C.R., Fernandez, P., Hausman, N., Miller, S., & Weiner, M. (2007). Challenging endings: First year MSW interns' experiences with forced termination and discussion points for supervisory guidance. *Clinical Social Work Journal, 35*, 79–90.

Gibson, D.M., Dollarhide, C.T., & Moss, J.M. (2010). Professional identity development: A grounded theory of transformational tasks of new counselors. *Counselor Education and Supervision, 50*, 21–38.

Ginkel, R.W., Davis, S.E., & Michael, P.G. (2010). An examination of inclusion and exclusion criteria in the predoctoral internship selection process. *Training and Education in Professional Psychology, 4*, 213–218.

Goddard, Y., Goddard, R.D., & Tschannen-Moran, M. (2007). A theoretical and empirical investigation of teacher collaboration for school improvement and student achievement in public elementary schools, *Teachers College Record, 109*, 877–896.

Goodyear, R.K., & Bernard, J.M. (1998). Clinical supervision: Lessons from the literature. *Counselor Education and Supervision, 38*, 6–22.

Green, K.E. (1997). Psychosocial factors affecting dissertation completion. *New Directions for Higher Education, 99*, 57–64.

Gresham, F., Reschly, D., & Shinn, M.R. (2010). RTI as a driving force in educational improvement: Research, legal, and practice perspectives. In M.R. Shinn, H.M. Walker, & G. Stoner (Eds.), *Interventions for achievement and behavior problems in a three-tier model including RTI* (pp. 47–77). Bethesda, MD: National Association of School Psychologists.

Griffin, M.L., & Scherr, T.G. (2010). Using critical incident reporting to promote objectivity and self-knowledge in pre-service school psychologists. *School Psychology International, 31*, 3–20.

Haboush, K.L. (2003). Group supervision of school psychologists in training. *School Psychology International, 24*, 232–255.

Hall, G.E., & Hord, S.M. (2010). *Implementing change: Patterns, principles, and potholes* (3rd ed.). Boston: Allyn & Bacon.

Hall, J.E., Wexelbaum, S.F., & Boucher, A.P. (2007). Doctoral student awareness of licensure, credentialing, and professional organizations in psychology: The 2005 national register international survey. *Training and Education in Professional Psychology, 1*, 38–48.

Hammer, E.D., & Hammer, E.Y. (2009). Maximizing your graduate training: Issues to think about from the start. In S.F. Davis, P.J. Giordano, & C.A. Licht (Eds.), *Your career in psychology: Putting your graduate degree to work* (pp. 3–12). Malden, MA: Wiley-Blackwell.

Harris, K. (1996). Collaboration within a multicultural society. *Remedial and Special Education, 17*, 355–362.

Harrison, P.L. (2010). Continuing professional development: A foundation for the future of school psychology, *National Association of School Psychologists Communiqué, 38*(5). Retrieved from www.nasponline.org/publications/cq/38/5/presgreet.aspx

Harrison, P.L., & Prus, J.S. (2008). Best practices in integrating *Best Practices V* content with NASP standards. In A. Thomas & J. Grimes (Eds.), *Best practices in school psychology V* (pp. 71–100). Bethesda, MD: National Association of School Psychologists.

Harvey, V.S., Amador, A., Finer, D., Gotthelf, D., Hintze, J., Kruger, L., Wandle, C. (2010). Improving field supervision through collaborative supervision institutes. *National Association of School Psychologists Communiqué Online, 38*. Retrieved August 13, 2010 from www.nasponline.org/publications/cq/mocq387FieldSupervision.aspx

Harvey, V.S., Monahan, K., & Lineman, J.M. (2011). *Ethical and supervision issues in school psychology internships*. Special session presented at the annual convention of the National Association of School Psychologists, San Francisco, CA.

Harvey, V.S., & Pearrow, M. (2010). Identifying challenges in supervising school psychologists. *Psychology in the Schools, 47*, 567–581.

Harvey, V.S., & Struzziero, J.A. (2008). *Professional development and supervision of school psychologists: From intern to expert* (2nd ed.). Thousand Oaks, CA: Corwin Press and National Association of School Psychologists.

Hatcher, R.L. (2011). The internship supply as a common-pool resource: A pathway to managing the imbalance problem. *Training and Education in Professional Psychology, 5*, 126–140.

Haworth, C.E., & Brantley, J.C. (1981). Bilevel training in school psychology: Interlocking degrees for program accreditation. *Professional Psychology, 12*, 279–287.

Hebert, G.W., & Patterson, C. (2010). Collaborative supervision of internship experiences. In J. Kaufman, T.L. Hughes, & C.A. Riccio (Eds.), *Handbook of education, training, and supervision of school psychologists in school and community* (Vol. 2, pp. 55–70). New York: Routledge.

Heppner, P.P., & Heppner, M.J. (2004). *Writing and publishing your thesis, dissertation, and research: A guide for students in the helping professions*. Pacific, CA: Brooks/Cole.

Hess, R.S., & Copeland, E.P. (2006). Stress. In G.G. Bear & K.M. Minke (Eds.), *Children's needs III: Development, prevention, and intervention* (pp. 255–265). Bethesda, MD: National Association of School Psychologists.

Hill, B., Kubick, R., & York, J. (2011). *Getting and keeping your first job as a school psychologist*. Special Event presented at the annual convention of the National Association of School Psychologists, San Francisco, CA.

Hoff, S. (2006). Internship – a rite of passage. *National Association of School Psychologists Communiqué Online, 35*. Retrieved July 17, 2010 from www.nasponline.org/publications/cq/mocq351internship.aspx

Holloway, E.L. (1995). *Clinical supervision: A systems approach*. Thousand Oaks, CA: Sage.

Holloway, E.L., & Neufeldt, S.A. (1995). Supervision: Its contributions to treatment efficacy. *Journal of Consulting and Clinical Psychology, 63*, 207–213.

Hosp, J.L., & Reschly, D.J. (2002). Regional differences in school psychology practice. *School Psychology Review, 31*, 11–29.

Howard, E.E., Inman, A.G., & Altman, A.N. (2006). Critical incidents among novice counselor trainees. *Counselor Education and Supervision, 46*, 88–102.

Huebner, E.S. (1993). Burnout among school psychologists in the USA: Further data related to its prevalence and correlates, *School Psychology International, 14*, 99–109.

Huebner, E.S., Gilligan, T.D., & Cobb, H. (2002). Best practices in managing stress and burnout. In A. Thomas & J. Grimes (Eds.), *Best practices in school psychology IV* (pp. 173–182). Bethesda, MD: National Association of School Psychologists.

Hughes, T.L., Kaufman, J., Crespi, T.D., Riccio, C.A., & García-Vázquez (2010). Envisioning the future: Looking into the crystal ball. In J. Kaufman, T.L. Hughes, & C.A. Riccio (Eds.), *Handbook of education, training, and supervision of school psychologists in school and community* (Vol. 2, pp. 321–327). New York: Routledge.

Hughes, T.L., Kaufman, J., & Hoover, S.A. (2010). Creating congruent change: Linking research to practice. In J. Kaufman, T.L. Hughes, & C.A. Riccio (Eds.), *Handbook of education, training, and supervision of school psychologists in school and community* (Vol. 2, pp. 309–319). New York: Routledge.

Hunley, S., Harvey, V.S., Curtis, M., Portnoy, L.A., Grier, E.C., & Helssrich, D. (2000). School psychology supervisors: A national study of demographics and professional practices. *National Association of School Psychologists Communiqué*, *28*(8), 32–33.

Illinois School Psychology Internship Manual (2006). Retrieved April 30, 2010 from www.ilispa.org/modules/smartsection/item.php?itemid=15

Illinois State Board of Education. (2007). *23 Illinois administrative code 226*. Springfield, IL.

Jacobs, S.C., Huprich, S.K., Cage, E.A., Elman, N.S., Forrest, L., Grus, C.L., Kaslow, N. (2011). Trainees with professional competency problems: Preparing trainers for difficult but necessary conversations. *Training and Education in Professional Psychology*, *5*, 175–184.

Jones, J.M. (2009). *The psychology of multiculturalism in the schools: A primer for practice, training, and research*. Bethesda, MD: National Association of School Psychologists.

Joyce, B., & Showers, B. (1980). Improving inservice training: The messages of research. *Educational Leadership*, *37*, 379–385.

Joyce, B., & Showers, B. (2002). *Student achievement through staff development* (3rd ed.). Alexandria, VA: Association for Supervision and Curriculum Development.

Kaslow, N.J. (2004). Competencies in professional psychology. *American Psychologist*, *59*, 774–781.

Kaslow, N.J., Grus, C.L., Campbell, L., Fouad, N.A., Hatcher, R.L., & Rodolfa, E.R. (2009). Competency assessment toolkit for professional psychology. *Training and Education in Professional Psychology*, *3*, S27–S45.

Kaslow, N.J., & Rice, D.G. (1985). Developmental stresses of psychology internship training: What training staff can do to help. *Professional Psychology: Research and Practice*, *16*, 253–261.

Kaslow, N.J., Rubin, N.J., Forrest, L., Elman, N.S., Van Horne, B.A., Jacobs, S.C., Thorne, B.E. (2007). Recognizing, assessing, and intervening with problems of professional competence. *Professional Psychology: Research and Practice*, *38*, 479–492.

Kaufman, J. (2010a). Contemporary issues in supervision. In J. Kaufman, T.L. Hughes, & C.A. Riccio (Eds.), *Handbook of education, training, and supervision of school psychologists in school and community* (Vol. 2, pp. 19–35). New York: Routledge.

Kaufman, J. (2010b). Creating a school psychology training program: The horse that became a camel, or what tail wags the dog? In E. García-Vázquez, T.D. Crespi, & C.A. Riccio (Eds.), Handbook of education training, and supervision of school psychologists in *school and community* (Vol. 1, pp. 33–47). New York: Routledge.

Kaufman, J. & Schwartz, T. (2003). Models of supervision: Shaping professional identity. *The Clinical Supervisor*, *22*, 143–158.

Kelly, R.M., Cruise, T.K., Swerdlik, M., Newman, D., & Simon, D. (2012). School psychology intern supervisor training: A state-wide universal system – the Illinois model. Poster presented at the annual convention of the Trainers of School Psychologists, Philadelphia, PA.

Klose, L.M., Plotts, C., & Lasser, J. (2010). Qualitative evaluation of school psychology consultation experiences. *Trainers' Forum: Journal of the Trainer's of School Psychologists*, *29*, 24–37.

Knoff, H.M. (1986). Supervision in school psychology: The forgotten or future path to effective services? *School Psychology Review*, *15*, 529–545.

Krieshok, T.S., Lopez, S.J., Somberg, D.R., & Cantrell, P.J. (2000). Dissertation while on internship: Obstacles and predictors of progress. *Professional Psychology: Research and Practice*, *31*, 327–331.

Ladany, N., & Friedlander, M.L. (1995). The relationship between the supervisory working alliance and trainees' experience of role conflict and role ambiguity. *Counselor Education and Supervision*, *34*, 220–231.

Ladany, N., Friedlander, M.L., & Nelson, M.L. (2005). *Critical events in psychotherapy supervision: An interpersonal approach*. Washington, DC: American Psychological Association.

Lamb, D.H., & Swerdlik, M.E. (2003). Identifying and responding to problematic school psychology supervisees: The evaluation process and issues of impairment. *Clinical Supervisor*, *22*, 87–110.

Levitov, J.E., & Fall, K.A. (2009). *Translating theory into practice: A student guide to counseling practicum and internship*. Long Grove, IL: Waveland Press.

Little, S.G., & Akin-Little, K.A. (2004). Academic school psychologists: Addressing the shortage. *Psychology in the Schools*, *41*, 451–459.

Loganbill, C., Hardy, E., & Delworth, U. (1982). Supervision: A conceptual model. *The Counseling Psychologist*, *10*, 3–42.

Lopez, E.C., & Rogers, M.R. (2010). Multicultural competence and diversity: University and field collaboration. In J. Kaufman, T.L. Hughes, & C. Riccio (Eds.), *Handbook of education, training, and supervision of school psychologists in school and community* (Vol. 2, pp. 111–128). New York: Routledge.

Magyar-Moe, J.L., Pedrotti, J.T., Edwards, L.M., Ford, A., Petersen, S.E., Rasmussen, H.N., & Ryder, J.A. (2005). Perceptions of multicultural training in predoctoral internship programs: A survey of interns and training directors. *Professional Psychology: Research and Practice*, *36*, 446–450.

Marks, E.S. (1995). *Entry strategies for school consultation.* New York: Guilford.

Maslach, C. (2003). Job burnout: New directions in research and intervention. *Current Directions in Psychological Science, 12,* 189–192.

Mastoras, S.M., & Andrews, J.J.W. (2011). The supervisee experience of group supervision: Implications for research and practice. *Training and Education in Professional Psychology, 5,* 102–111.

McCutcheon, S.R. (2009). Competency benchmarks: Implications for internship training. *Training and Education in Professional Psychology, 3,* S50–S53.

McIntosh, D.E., & Phelps, L. (2000). Supervision in school psychology: Where will the future take us? *Psychology in the Schools, 37,* 33–38.

Merrell, K.W. (2008). Foreward. In V.S. Harvey & J.A. Struzziero, *Professional development and supervision of school psychologists: From intern to expert* (2nd ed.) (pp. vi–viii). Thousand Oaks, CA: Corwin Press.

Merrell, K.W., Ervin, R.A., & Gimpel, G.A. (2006). *School psychology for the 21st century: Foundations and practices.* New York: Guilford.

Miller, D.C., DeOrnellas, K., & Maricle, D. (2010). What is so special about the specialist degree? In E. García-Vázquez, T. Crespi, & C. Riccio (Eds.). *Handbook of education, training and supervision of school psychologists in school and community* (Vol. 1, pp. 49–61).

Morrison, E.W. (1993a). Longitudinal study of the effects of information seeking on newcomer socialization. *Journal of Applied Psychology, 78,* 173–183.

Morrison, E.W. (1993b). Newcomer information seeking: Exploring types, modes, sources, and outcomes. *Academy of Management Journal, 36,* 557–589.

Morrison, E.W. (1995). Information usefulness and acquisition during organizational encounter. *Management Communication Quarterly, 9,* 131–155.

Munsey, C. (2006). Helping colleagues to help themselves. *Monitor on Psychology, 37*(7), 35.

National Association of School Psychologists (2000a). *Standards for training and field placement programs in school psychology.* Bethesda, MD: Author.

National Association of School Psychologists (2000b). *Standards for the credentialing of school psychologists.* Bethesda, MD: Author.

National Association of School Psychologists (2010a). *Model for comprehensive and integrated school psychological services.* Bethesda, MD: Author.

National Association of School Psychologists (2010b). *Principles for professional ethics.* Bethesda, MD: Author.

National Association of School Psychologists (2010c). *Standards for the graduate preparation of school psychologists.* Bethesda, MD: Author.

National Association of School Psychologists (2011a). *National school psychology certification system.* Retrieved November 17, 2011 from www.nasponline.org/certification/ncsp_system.aspx

National Association of School Psychologists (2011b). *State school psychology credentialing requirements.* Retrieved November 17, 2011 from www.nasponline.org/certification/state_info_list.aspx

National Association of School Psychologists (2011c). *Position Statement on Supervision in School Psychology.* Bethesda, MD: Author.

National School Reform Faculty (n.d.). *National school reform faculty resource book.* Bloomington, IN: Author.

Nebbergall, A. (2011). Alternative careers in school psychology: My experience in the field of education research. *National Association of School Psychologists Communiqué, 39*(8), 10.

Neimeyer, G.J., Taylor, J.M., & Rozensky, R.H. (2012). The diminishing durability of knowledge in professional psychology: A delphi poll of specialties and proficiencies. *Professional Psychology: Research and Practice, 43,* 364–371.

Neufeldt, S.A., Karno, M.P., & Nelson, M.L. (1996). A qualitative study of experts' conceptualizations of supervisee reflectivity. *Journal of Counseling Psychology, 43,* 3–9.

Newman, D.S. (2012). Supervision of school-based consultation training: Addressing the concerns of novice consultants. In S.A. Rosenfield (Ed.). *Becoming a school consultant: Lessons learned* (pp. 49–70). New York: Routledge.

Newman, D., Cocol, P., & Coffin, T. (2010). A differential approach to consultation training on internship. *National Association of School Psychologists Communiqué, 39*(3), 8–10.

Newman, D.S. & the NASP Early Career Workgroup (2010). Essential tools for prospective and early career school psychology faculty. *National Association of School Psychologists Communiqué, 39*(4), 24.

Oberman, A.H., (2010). The accountability component and the school counselor-in-training. In J.R. Studer & J. F. Diambra (Eds.), *A guide to practicum and internship for school counselors-in-training* (pp. 133–145). New York: Routledge.

Olk, M.E., & Friedlander, M.L. (1992). Trainees' experiences of role conflict and role ambiguity in supervisory relationships. *Journal of Counseling Psychology, 39,* 389–397.

Ortiz, S.O., Flanagan, D.P., & Dynda, A.M. (2008). Best practices in working with culturally and linguistically diverse children and families. In A. Thomas & J. Grimes (Eds.), *Best practices in school psychology V* (pp. 1721–1738). Bethesda, MD: National Association of School Psychologists.

Peña, A. (n.d.). *Bringing your vita to life: Preparing for internship and early career positions.* Retrieved July 26, 2011 from the National Association of School Psychologists Website: www.nasponline.org/earlycareer/earlycareer_resources.aspx

Phelps, L., & Swerdlik, M.E. (2011). Evolving internship issues in school psychology preparation. *Psychology in the Schools, 48*, 911–921.

Plante, T.G. (1998). How to find a first job in professional psychology: Ten principles for finding employment for psychology interns and postdoctoral fellows. *Professional Psychology: Research and Practice, 29*, 508–511.

Pritchard, R.J., Morrow, D., & Marshall, J.C. (2005). School and district culture as reflected in student voices and student achievement. *School Effectiveness and School Improvement, 16*, 153–177.

Proctor, B. (1986). Supervision: A co-operative exercise in accountability. In A. Marken and M. Payne (Eds.), *Enabling and ensuring: Supervision in practice* (pp. 21–23). Leicester National Youth Bureau/Council for Education and Training in Youth and Community Work.

Prus, J.S. (2009). Best practice guidelines for school psychology internships. *National Association of School Psychologists Communiqué, 37*(8). Retrieved from www.nasponline.org/publications/cq/mocq378 internship.aspx

Reschly, D. (2008). School psychology paradigm shift and beyond. In A. Thomas & J. Grimes (Eds.), *Best practices in school psychology V* (pp. 3–15). Bethesda, MD: NASP Publications.

Reynolds, C.R. (2011). Perspectives on specialization in school psychology training and practice. *Psychology in the Schools, 48*, 922–930.

Romans, J.S.C, Boswell, D.L., Carlozzi, A.F., & Ferguson, D.B. (1995). Training and supervision practices in clinical, counseling, and school psychology programs. *Professional Psychology: Research and Practice, 26*, 407–412.

Rønnestad, M.H., & Skovholt, T.M. (1993). Supervision of beginning and advanced graduate students of counseling and psychotherapy. *Journal of Counseling and Development, 71*, 396–405.

Rønnestad, M.H., & Skovholt, T.M. (2003). The journey of the counselor and therapist: Research findings and perspectives on professional development. *Journal of Career Development, 30*, 5–44.

Rosenfield, S. (1987). *Instructional consultation.* Hillsdale, NJ: Lawrence Erlbaum.

Rosenfield, S. (2004). Consultation as dialogue: The right words at the right time. In N.M. Lambert, I. Hylander, & J.H. Sandoval (Eds.), *Consultee-centered consultation* (pp. 337–347). Mahwah, NJ: Lawrence Erlbaum.

Rosenfield, S., Levinsohn-Klyap, M., & Cramer, K. (2010). Educating consultants for practice in the schools. In E. García Vázquez, T. Crespi, & C. Riccio (Eds.), *Handbook of education, training, and supervision of school psychologists in school and community* (Vol. 1, pp. 259–278). New York: Routledge.

Rudestam, K.E., & Newton, R.R. (2007). *Surviving your dissertation: A comprehensive guide to content and process* (3rd ed.). Thousand Oaks, CA: Sage.

Sarason, S. (1996). *Revisiting "The culture of the school and the problem of change".* New York: Teachers College Press.

Sarason, S. (2003). The school culture and processes of change. In R.L. Fried (Ed.), *The skeptical visionary* (pp. 79–91). Philadelphia, PA: Temple University Press. (Original work published in 1969.)

Seibert, S.E., Crant, J.M., & Kraimer, M.L. (1999). Proactive personality and career success. *Journal of Applied Psychology, 84*, 416–427.

Semrud-Clikeman, M. (1995). *Child and adolescent therapy.* Boston: Allyn & Bacon.

Senge, P.M., Kleiner, A., Roberts, C., Ross, R.B., & Smith, B.J. (1994). *The fifth discipline fieldbook.* New York: Currency-Doubleday.

Sheridan, S.M., & Gutkin, T.B. (2000). The ecology of school psychology: Examining and changing our paradigm for the 21st century. *School Psychology Review, 29*, 485–502.

Shinn, M.R., & Walker, H.M. (Eds.). (2010). *Interventions for achievement and behavior problems in a three-tier model including RTI.* Bethesda, MD: National Association of School Psychologists.

Single, P.B. (2009). *Demystifying dissertation writing: A streamlined process from choice of topic to final text.* Sterling, VA: Stylus.

Smith, P.L., & Moss, S.B. (2009). Psychologist impairment: What is it, how can it be prevented, and what can be done to address it? *Clinical Psychology: Science and Practice, 16*, 1–15.

Solway, K.S. (1985). Transition from graduate school to internship: A potential crisis. *Professional Psychology: Research and Practice, 16*, 50–54.

Stedman, J.M., Hatch, J.P., & Schoenfeld, L.S. (2009). Letters of recommendation for the predoctoral internship in medical schools and other settings: Do they enhance decision making in the selection process? *Journal of Clinical Psychology in Medical Settings, 16*, 339–345.

Sternberg, D. (1981). *How to complete and survive a doctoral dissertation.* New York: St. Martin's Press.

Stevanovic, P., & Rupert, P.A. (2004). Career-sustaining behaviors, satisfactions, and stresses of professional psychologists. *Psychotherapy: Theory, Research, Practice, Training, 41,* 301–309.

Stoltenberg, C.D. (2005). Enhancing professional competence through developmental approaches to supervision. *American Psychologist, 60,* 857–864.

Stoltenberg, C.D., & Delworth, U. (1987). *Supervising counselors and therapists: A developmental approach.* San Francisco, CA: Jossey-Bass.

Stoltenberg, C.D., McNeill, B.W., & Delworth, U. (1998). *IDM supervision: An integrated developmental model for supervising counselors and therapists.* San Francisco: Jossey-Bass.

Strein, W. (1996). Professional supervision. In T.K. Fagan & P.G. Warden (Eds.), *Historical encyclopedia of school psychology* (pp. 297–298). Westport, CT: Greenwood Press.

Sugai, G., Horner, R.H., & Gresham, F. (2002). Behaviorally effective school environments. In M.R. Shinn, H.M. Walker, & G. Stoner (Eds.), *Interventions for academic and behavior problems II: Preventive and remedial approaches* (pp. 315–350). Bethesda, MD: National Association of School Psychologists.

Sullivan, J.R., & Conoley, J.C. (2008). Best practices in the supervision of interns. In A. Thomas & J. Grimes (Eds.), *Best practices in school psychology V* (pp. 1957–1974). Bethesda, MD: National Association of School Psychologists.

Tamura, L.J., Vincent, W.L., Bridgeman, D.L., & Hanbury, R.F. (2008). *Psychologists' pursuit of wellness across the life span: Benefits and barriers to self-care practices.* Retrieved November 17, 2011 from www.apa.org/practice/leadership/colleague-assistance.aspx

Tarquin, K. & Truscott, S. (2006). School psychology students' perceptions of their practicum experiences. *Psychology in the Schools, 43,* 727–736.

Thomas, A., & Grimes, J. (Eds.). (2008) *Best practices in school psychology V.* Bethesda, MD: NASP Publications.

Torki, R.N., & Nese, J.F. (2010). Acronyms in education. *National Association of School Psychologists Communiqué, 38*(6), 34.

Turner, J.A., Edwards, L.M., Eicken, I.M., Yokoyama, K., Castro, J.R., Tran, A.N-T., & Haggins, K.L. (2005). Intern self-care: An exploratory study into strategy use and effectiveness. *Professional Psychology: Research and Practice, 36,* 674–680.

Walker, H.M., & Shinn, M.R. (2010). Systemic, evidence-based approaches for promoting positive student outcomes within a multitier framework: Moving from efficacy to effectiveness. In M.R. Shinn, H.M. Walker, & G. Stoner (Eds.), *Interventions for achievement and behavior problems in a three-tier model including RTI* (pp. 1–26). Bethesda, MD: National Association of School Psychologists.

Ward, S.B. (2001). Intern supervision in school psychology: Practice and process of field-based and university supervisors. *School Psychology International, 22,* 269–284.

Wasik, B.H., Song, S., & Knotek, S. (2009). Preparing for careers in school psychology. In S.F. Davis, P.J. Giordano, & C.A. Licht (Eds.), *Your career in psychology: Putting your graduate degree to work* (pp. 231–244). Malden, MA: Wiley-Blackwell.

Webb, A. (2000). What makes it difficult for the supervisee to speak? In B. Lawton & C. Feltham (Eds.), *Taking supervision forward: Enquiries and trends in counseling and psychotherapy* (pp. 60–73). London: Sage.

Wei, R.C., Darling-Hammond, L., Andree, A., Richardson, N., & Orphanos, S. (2009). *Professional learning in the learning profession: A status report on teacher development in the United States and abroad.* Dallas, TX: National Staff Development Council.

Wheeler, S., & Richards, K. (2007). The impact of clinical supervision on counsellors and therapists, their practice and their clients. A systematic review of the literature. *Counselling and Psychotherapy Research, 7,* 54–65.

Wilbur, M.P., Roberts-Wilbur, J., Hart, G.M., & Morris, J.R. (1994). Structured group supervision (SGS): A pilot study. *Counselor Education and Supervision, 33,* 262–279.

Ysseldyke, J.E., Burns, M.K., Dawson, M., Kelly, B., Morrison, D., Ortiz, S., Telzrow, C. (2006). *School psychology: A blueprint for training and practice III.* Bethesda, MD: National Association of School Psychologists.

Ysseldyke, J., Burns, M.K., & Rosenfield, S. (2009). Blueprints on the future of training and practice in school psychology: What do they say about educational and psychological consultation? *Journal of Educational and Psychological Consultation, 19,* 177–196.

Ysseldyke, J.E., Dawson, P., Lehr, C., Reschly, D., Reynolds, M., & Telzrow, C. (1997). *School psychology: A blueprint for training and practice II.* Bethesda, MD: National Association of School Psychologists.

Ysseldyke, J.E., Reynolds, M., & Weinberg, R.A. (1984). *School psychology: A blueprint for training and practice.* Minneapolis, MN: University of Minnesota National School Psychology Inservice Training Network.

Index